THE GARDENING WHICH? GUIDE TO

SUCCESSFUL
PERENNIALS

THE GARDENING WHICH? GUIDE TO
SUCCESSFUL PERENNIALS

LIZ DOBBS

CONSUMERS' ASSOCIATION

Which? Books are commissioned and researched by
Consumers' Association and published by
Which? Ltd, 2 Marylebone Road, London NW1 4DF
Email address: books@which.net

Distributed by The Penguin Group:
Penguin Books Ltd, 27 Wrights Lane, London W8 5TZ

First edition 1997

British Library Cataloguing-in-Publication Data
A catalogue record for this book is available from the British Library

ISBN 0 85202 657 9

Credits
Designed and typeset by Romanesque Ltd
Edited by Jonathan Edwards with assistance from Kate Hawkins, Hetty Burdon and Rose Ward

Perennials on trial
Gardening Which? has been carrying out trials of popular hardy perennials for a number of years. We have used eight test sites
spread throughout Britain to find out how each variety fared in a wide range of soils and climates. We have kept detailed records
of their flowering performance, noted their tolerance to different growing conditions and checked for any pests and diseases.
Using this unique research we can say with authority which are the best.

***Gardening Which?* magazine**

You can find up-to-date information on all the latest plants, gardening products and techniques in *Gardening Which?* magazine.
It regularly carries out tests and trials of plant varieties and suppliers, as well as gardening equipment and sundries such as
composts and fertilisers. Each issue is packed with ideas, practical advice and results of the magazine's independent evaluations.

Plus
- Free expert advice by letter, fax, email or telephone.
- OnHand telephone information service which gives instant access to the most up-to-date gardening advice, 24 hours a day.
- Border Design Service for a full planting plan and plant list, while our 'Ten tips for a tenner' service offers professional design
  ideas for gardeners on a really tight budget.
- Soil Analysis Service.
- Open Days and Garden Shows

Gardening Which? is available by subscription only. To try it free for 3 months
write to *Gardening Which?*, Consumers' Association, Freepost
Hertford X, SG14 1YB or Freephone 0800 252100

Colour reproduction by FMT Colour, London SE1

Printed and bound in Spain by Bookprint, Barcelona (The Hanway Press Ltd)

Contents

How to use this book

What is a successful perennial?

A successful perennial is one that is thriving and showing off its most attractive features in a way that complements the rest of the garden.

The plants in this book are hardy perennials that you will find in garden centres and nurseries. They will come up year after year, filling your garden with flowers or foliage. In the autumn, most will become dormant and new growth will emerge the following spring. A few are evergreen so will contribute foliage throughout most seasons.

There are perennials to suit every situation, even dry shade. By combining varieties carefully you can achieve a succession of colour to last throughout the year. Use the following sections to help you make your selection.

Finding the right plant

The plants are arranged in alphabetical order by their Latin name, with a separate section on grasses and bamboos – which is how most perennials are offered for sale. If a plant has a widely used common name this is given in the coloured panel at the edge of the page.

For each genus we have chosen a specific example to look out for. Each one is illustrated and its size, shape, features and requirements are given in the coloured panels on the left of each page.

If you do not have a specific plant in mind, use the features calendar for ideas or consult the plant lists at the back of the book. Alternatively, take the book around garden centres and shows and check out the plants that catch your eye.

Perennials

Grasses and bamboos

Shape and size

Perennials lined up in small pots on sale can all look similar in size, but once they are growing they start to look very different. You can get an idea of the size and shape by looking at the silhouette for each one – sizes are also given in the text. We have grouped all the featured examples into three sizes:

- small – up to 50cm tall
- medium – 50 to 100cm tall
- large – over 100cm tall.

Remember to check the scale alongside the silhouette when comparing different plants.

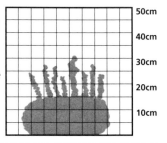

Position

Most perennials prefer sunny or partially shaded spots, but if these are at a premium in your garden, it is useful to know which plants actually require such places. Some plants have evolved to tolerate or even thrive at low light levels and it is worth looking out for these if you have a shaded garden. A few plants really need a sheltered site either because their stems, flowers or leaves are prone to wind damage or because they cannot tolerate cold.

Sun

Partial or light shade

Shade

Needs shelter

Hardiness

We have concentrated on perennials that are hardy; these are the easiest to grow because you do not need to lift plants and move them under cover or to take cuttings. Plants described as very hardy should survive the winter in most parts of Britain. Moderately hardy plants can withstand sub-zero temperatures, but may die if in a waterlogged soil or if they are exposed to strong winds. Plants needing winter protection can cope with temperatures of at least -5°C (20°F) but are best insulated. The plant can be left in the ground provided it is protected with a 15cm (6in) layer of chipped bark, bracken or dry leaves put over the top and held in place with twigs or a piece of netting. Remove insulation in spring.

Moderately hardy

Hardy

Very hardy

Good companions

It is always worth jotting down pleasing plant combinations that you come across. Here you will find our suggestions for successful plant partnerships.

Soil

Most perennials like a well-drained but moisture-retentive loam. This sounds like a contradiction but it is a soil that does not get waterlogged in winter and does not bake dry in summer. Whether you start off with a free-draining sandy or chalky soil or a sticky, heavy clay, you can improve it by adding well-rotted organic matter each autumn and spring. Organic matter needs to be added regularly every year.

Alkaline *Any* *Moist* *Well-drained*

Uses

If you are looking for a perennial for a particular spot – perhaps you have a gap in a border to fill, flick through the book to find plants with the relevant symbol and make a shortlist of the ones that appeal to you.

Front of border *Middle of border* *Back of border*

Filler *Specimen* *Groundcover*

Container *Cut flowers* *Cut and dried*

Features calendar

Use the features calendar to help you plan for seasonal highlights.

		Attractive foliage	Scent		Flowers
Jan	Feb	Mar	Apr	May	June
July	Aug	Sept	Oct	Nov	Dec
		Seedhead	Berries		

Growing guide

The growing guide explains what conditions your chosen plants like. There are also details on propagation, which can save you money, and any major problems such as susceptibility to particular pests and diseases are highlighted.

Which variety?

One of the exciting aspects of perennials is how varied the different species and varieties are. For each genus we give you a potted guide to the alternatives and make recommendations.

Buying tips *Tracking down the perennial you want is not always easy. Some are hidden away in garden centres and nurseries with alpines, pond plants or in bulb catalogues or only stocked at certain times of the year. You also need to be wary of the cheaper seed-raised plants. We help to point you in the right direction. General advice on choosing plants is given on pages 18 and 19, but individual tips, such as when not to buy but to beg a cutting from a friend, are given with each entry. For an up-to-date list of perennial specialist nurseries write to Gardening Which?, PO Box 44, Hertford X, SG14 1SH and ask for factsheet GWF413.*

WARNING

Some perennials are poisonous or are known to cause severe skin irritation if touched. We have highlighted all those plants where cases have been recorded of plants causing problems to people. Others thought to be poisonous are indicated in the text.

Using perennials

Variegated iris combine with winter-flowering pansies and hellebores to provide winter colour

Perennials are an ideal way of boosting the colour in garden displays. You can either combine varieties that flower at different times for a succession of interest, or concentrate your efforts to create an eye-catching blitz in one or two seasons of the year. On pages 10–13 we offer ideas for creating a herbaceous border from scratch. First we look at using perennials to improve existing borders.

Renovating existing borders

Popping in one or two new perennials is unlikely to improve a border that has been neglected or lacks interest. To make a long-term difference you must first tackle any underlying problems. To start with, remove any plants that no longer perform. Some shrubs will throw up new strong growth in response to pruning, while old perennials can be reinvigorated by lifting and dividing (see page 15) – put back only healthy young divisions. Dig over any vacant ground and improve the soil by incorporating well-rotted organic matter and a general fertiliser such as growmore 35–70g per sq metre (1–2oz per sq yd). After planting, mulch well to retain moisture in the soil and suppress weed growth.

If you have a border stocked wholly with herbaceous plants it is probably easiest to lift the entire border of plants to start with, then improve the soil with organic matter and fertiliser before replanting. Again, select healthy sections of the best plants to replant.

Agapanthus add a touch of drama to a late summer border

Island beds

When planting an island bed, remember that it will be viewed from all sides. In such beds the taller plants should be planted in the centre with filler plants and edging plants encircling them. Island beds are a good way of growing perennials because more air and light reaches each plant. This makes them sturdier and healthier, so they are less likely to need staking or to succumb to mildew. However, island beds are best viewed from a distance, across a lawn, say. They also need to be at least 3x3m (10x10ft) to work well.

Containers

You do not need a border to grow perennials, many can be grown successfully in containers and enjoyed as patio plants. While they will not flower for as long as bedding plants, choose those with worthwhile foliage as well as flowers for a long season of interest.

Three sorts of perennials are worth growing in containers:
● Specimen plants that offer an interesting shape or attractive foliage as well as flowers. Grow as single subjects for maximum impact.
● Invasive plants that you do not want running riot in the rest of the garden.
● Foliage fillers, these are plants you may already have in the garden but small sections can be used in containers to set off other plants such as bulbs or bedding. This saves having to buy tender foliage plants for containers each year.

For lists of suitable plants see page 223.

Smaller perennials need a container at least 25cm (10in) in diameter and at least 23cm (9in) deep. Most specimen and invasive plants will need containers with a diameter of 30–40cm (12–16in). Permanent plants, such as hostas and agapanthus, that will be left for many years to develop impressive clumps will require 45cm (18in) diameter tubs.

Most perennials are not that fussy about the type of compost, but for permanent plantings left outside for several years consider a John Innes compost. This will keep its physical structure for longer, but you will still need to add extra nutrients either via a liquid feed or by replacing the top 5cm (2in) of compost with fresh each spring.

Feed plants with a liquid feed like you would other container plants. The exceptions are grasses which are easy to overfeed – use a slow-release fertiliser for these. Regular deadheading will prolong flowering. Tidy up and cut back after

Plant in a bucket with the bottom cut out to keep invasive perennials, such as golden rod (Solidago), michaelmas daisies and variegated ground elder under control.

Disguise the edges of the pot with soil or a mulch

Keep new plants well-watered until established

Try planted pots in the border to create an extra tier of interest

Hostas are ideal for containers

flowering to prevent mildew. Water regularly while they are growing.

Natural plantings

Perennials do not have to be grown in regimented borders and garden designers are coming up with many exciting ways of using them. Natural plantings are a cross between wild gardens and border schemes. For example, flowering perennials grown alongside ornamental grasses. The plants are chosen carefully, the aim is to combine plants from the same habitat and plant them according to ecological principles rather than artistic design considerations. The end result should be a low-maintenance display. See list on page 222.

Primulas add instant colour in early spring

9

Using perennials

Heuchera 'Palace Purple', Sisyrinchium striatum and the lavender 'Hidcote' make good companions

New borders

Planting herbaceous perennials in long, deep beds usually between a garden boundary such as a wall, fence or hedge and the lawn is the traditional way of using them. When such plantings are done well they can look stunning in summer – but do not offer much year-round interest for small and medium-sized gardens. They are also labour-intensive, unless you choose plants which do not need staking, spraying or regular lifting and dividing. Where year-round interest and lower maintenance are important, consider a mixed border. Here shrubs, trees, bulbs and

Design guidelines

- *Borders are often designed to have a minimum of three layers. Backdrop plants provide height, structure and screen eyesores. Plants in the middle contribute seasonal interest and anchor the other two layers. Frontal plantings mark the transition from border to lawn or path – they can be neat and formal or floppy and informal, depending on the style of the garden.*
- *Larger clumps of fewer plants will create more impact from a distance than lots of different varieties. Plant in groups of three or five rather than single plants.*
- *Consider foliage attributes when choosing plants – evergreen perennials or those with interesting leaf colour, shape or texture will add more to a border for longer periods than those chosen simply for flowers.*
- *Make your garden appear longer by planting small-leaved or feathery plants in blues, purples and greys at the far end of the border. Conversely, large leaves and bright colours, such as golden-yellow and white, at the far end of the border will make the garden look shorter.*

SHADY BORDERS

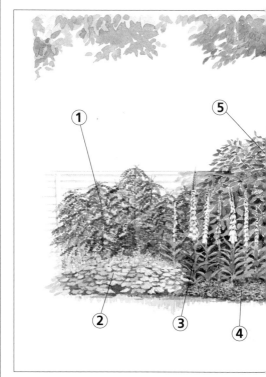

bedding are used along with perennials. A permanent framework of evergreen and deciduous shrubs provides year-round interest, leaving the perennials free to add seasonal highlights. Bulbs and bedding plants can be included too.

Planning a border

A rough sketch of your border drawn to scale on squared paper will help get you started. Mark in any sunny or shady areas, any frost pockets or places where the ground is very wet or very dry. Put in existing features such as the boundary fence or overhanging trees. You can use a computer program but it can over-complicate things, especially if you use plant lists written for other countries.

Choose plants you like that will be happy in the situation you are going to plant them – do not feel constrained too much about 'rules' or 'good taste'. After all, the idea is to have fun and experiment rather than worry about mistakes. Remember, you can move most of the perennials around in the dormant season (autumn to spring) if your ideas need fine-tuning.

The border here illustrates many of the design guidelines for a mixed border. All the plants can cope with shady or semi-shady conditions and a backbone of shrubs adds presence and year-round interest. There are bold drifts of the same perennial which will make the border look impressive from a distance.

Pale yellow and white flowers help to lighten a shaded area as does golden-leaved or variegated foliage. When planting in shaded areas, it is useful to know if the soil is moist or dry. While there are many woodland plants for moist, shady sites, dry shade is more tricky.

Key
1. Mahonia aquifolium
2. Alchemilla mollis
3. Digitalis albiflora
4. Vinca minor
5. Sambucus nigra 'Aureo-Marginata'
6. Tiarella cordifolia
7. Cotoneaster 'Coral Beauty'
8. Campanula poscharskyana
9. Daphne odora 'Aureomarginata'
10. Nicotiana sylvestris
11. Euphorbia robbiae

A combination of foliage perennials

Start at the back of the border. Do you need to disguise a fence? Climbers, wall shrubs or free-standing shrubs are obvious candidates, especially if they are evergreen, but include some perennial backdrops too.

The middle row and frontal plants will add seasonal highlights. Do not stick to the 'three layers' too rigidly – a distinctive plant, such as a phormium or upright conifer, would add interest to the eye. Plants that are tall but are 'see through' add a light, airy texture to borders.

Planting ideas

Most perennials are not too fussy when it comes to soil – and given enough time and digging most soils can be improved so that they retain moisture in summer yet do not become waterlogged over winter. If you have an extreme soil, like a wet clay or well-drained chalk, consult the lists at the back of the book and use the icons.

Plants differ markedly in their response to sun or shade. Here and overleaf are plant combinations for either shady or sunny situations. Each grouping could be used on its own in a small bed or incorporated into a larger border as a middle layer.

Achillea 'Cerise Queen' with Echinops

Using perennials

EARLY SUMMER COLOUR IN SUN

The flowering peak will be in June, with the geranium and verbascum lasting throughout July. To add extra interest in late summer, cut back spent flowers and drop in pots of dahlias or cannas. The poppy will die back after flowering, the verbascum will produce a second flush of flowers on side shoots. Both live only two or three years but will freely self-seed.

Key
1. Geranium psilostemon
2. Papaver orientale 'Beauty of Livermere'
3. Verbascum 'Gainsborough'

Oriental poppies make a bright splash

MID-SUMMER COLOUR IN SUN

Just these three plants will produce a brilliant display for June and July. There is a contrast of flower shape as well as colour. If you were prepared to lift them after flowering they could be moved to a reserve plot until the autumn and their place taken by late bedding. In autumn, the original plants could be returned.

Key

1. White phlox such as 'Fujiyama', 'Mother of Pearl', or 'White Admiral'
2. Lychnis chalcedonica
3. Salvia nemorosa 'East Friesland'

LATE SUMMER COLOU IN SUN

Campanula and Alchemilla mollis in early summer

Blazing mixed herbaceous border in late summer

Lychnis chalcedonica

Phlox paniculata 'Mother of Pearl'

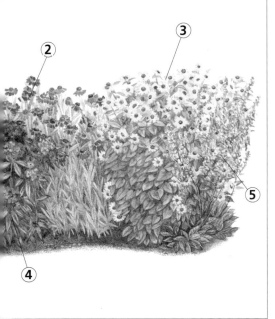

Helenium 'Moerheim Beauty'

The first to flower will be the aconitum and helenium, producing a contrast of blue and orange. From mid-July the phlox will add more colour. As the aconitum starts to fade, the bright yellow perennial sunflower and the tall delicate salvia produce a later burst of colour.

Key
1. Aconitum 'Spark's Variety'
2. Helenium 'Moerheim Beauty'
3. Helianthus 'Capenoch Star'
4. Phlox paniculata – a mauve variety like 'Amethyst'
5. Salvia uliginosa

Caring for perennials

An annual mulch will help keep the soil moist and weeds down

Plants with rooted rhizomes, like this bergenia, can be lifted and cut up with a pair of secateurs or a sharp knife

Preparation and planting

When planting up a new border it is worth preparing the soil well at the outset as it will be harder to get it into condition once the plants are in. The first step is to get rid of persistent weeds. Once this has been done, spread over plenty of well-rotted organic matter in autumn and fork in lightly to improve both drainage over winter and moisture-retention in dry spells. Well-rotted garden compost, or farmyard manure, spent potting compost and leafmould are all suitable. Planting can then be done the following spring or autumn.

Spring and autumn are the usual periods for planting perennials and it is best to stick to these times when dealing with bare-rooted plants (plants that have been grown in the ground and lifted and sold, usually by mail-order). Almost all perennial plants sold in garden centres are now container-grown and these can be planted at any convenient time. However, it makes sense to avoid planting in dry spells or you will have a lot of watering to do. Also be guided by your soil – plant when it is easy to work, when the soil is not wet and sticky. Anything that is prone to winter wet or is of doubtful hardiness is best planted in spring or early summer; grasses seem to establish better from spring planting, too.

When planting up a whole bed, lay out the plants (while still in their pots) in their final positions so you can check planting distances. Groups or drifts of filler and groundcover plants are more effective than single plantings. Water the plants well while still in their pots, then dig a hole large enough to take the whole rootball. Knock the plant out of its pot and position in the hole, then fill and firm the soil. Water thoroughly after planting. Planting is similar for bare-rooted plants but their roots are more prone to drying out, so cover the roots with damp compost if you cannot plant straight away.

Mulching

To keep down weeds and help prevent water evaporating from the surface of the soil, apply a generous mulch to weed-free beds in spring. A 5cm (2in) layer of well-rotted manure, chipped bark, gravel or cocoa shells is effective and attractive. To save money you can put down layers of newspaper or polythene and cover with a thinner layer of bark, gravel or soil. An alternative is to lay down woven polypropylene, cut slits in it and plant through. Cover with gravel. This material works well, but is expensive for large areas and is not suitable for densely planted schemes.

Watering

Newly planted perennials will need to be watered during dry spells until they are established, which usually takes one or two years. A thorough soaking of 2.5–5 litres (½–1 gallon) around each plant once a week will do more good than a daily sprinkling. A length of leaky hose (seep hose) along a border is easier than using a watering can. Established perennials should not need regular watering if they have been well-mulched in spring.

Feeding

Feeding is not essential on most well-cultivated soils. But it can help where plants are densely planted or where you notice poor growth. A general fertiliser, such as growmore, applied in spring at a rate of 35–70g per square metre (1–2oz per square yard) will suffice.

Staking

It is perfectly possible to grow a wide range of flowering perennials and never have to stake them. But if you favour the larger flowers, have an exposed garden or have a border shaded on one side so the plants become thin and tall, staking might be necessary.

Many staking systems are available but they are expensive and unless fitted at the right time they

Carefully lift clumps of fibrous rooted plants with a fork

can be unsightly. A cheaper and more natural alternative is to make your own supports using twiggy sticks or bamboo canes and string. Twiggy sticks or pea sticks are cuttings from hazel, chestnut or oak; they need to be at least as tall as the mature plant. Push half a dozen sticks through the clump and into the ground in spring. Bend the tops over, so the sticks are just below the eventual height of the flowers. Mesh the tops together.

Borders containing only herbaceous plants can have a length of green or black plastic mesh suspended over the border 30–60cm (12–24in) above the ground and held in position by wooden stakes or canes. The plants grow through the mesh and it saves having to support plants individually.

Stakes need to be in place by May. Ensure any pointed canes or wires are covered with cane tops or similar to protect people against eye injuries.

Pests and diseases

Perennial plants sometimes fall victim to a pest or disease – specific problems are mentioned under each entry. The most common problems are slug and snail damage, especially in wet years, so it is worth putting down slug pellets. Even if you do not usually use chemical slug pellets they are

worth considering for newly planted perennials and each spring when new foliage first emerges above ground.

Cutting back

Border plants that become unsightly after flowering can be cut back in late autumn, and the dead top growth composted. Cut back early-flowering perennials sooner if you want mounds of fresh green foliage.

Once the top growth has been cleared, any plants requiring winter protection can be sorted out – a 15cm (6in) layer of chipped bark, dead leaves or straw held in place is adequate. All insulating coverings must be removed in spring or the plants can grow soft and rot.

Some people do not hold with cutting back in autumn, they like the seedheads and the flowering grasses to remain, providing food for the birds and perhaps some protection from frost for the plants.

Lifting and dividing

Over several years you might find the vigour or flowering of a perennial will begin to deteriorate. The most likely cause is that the roots have become congested and have exhausted the soil. By lifting the plant out of the ground and dividing it up and replanting younger, healthy sections into enriched soil you can rejuvenate your plants.

Lifting and dividing mature perennials can be hard work, but most plants can last three to five years before it is needed. As far as the plant is concerned the best time to lift and divide is after flowering (or after it should have flowered). In practice, it is often easier to divide most plants in spring or autumn when the plants are dormant. Choose a time when the soil is easy to work.

The tools you need depend on the size of plant, the type of root it has and personal preference. A pair of border forks back-to-back is the traditional method and this works well for large clumps with fibrous roots. But where the crown of the plant is dense or woody, a sharp spade or knife is easier.

Start by loosening the soil around the plant and lift it out of the ground with its rootball. Insert two border forks back-to-back into the side of the rootball. Gently prise the forks apart using a push-and-pull action to split the plant. Further divisions can be made by hand. Discard the older central sections, replant the young, healthy sections. Firm in and water well. Plants with rhizomes such as bergenias and bearded irises can be cut with a knife.

Use two border forks back-to-back to prise apart the roots

Some perennials, such as this sedum, can be divided into many sections. Each division should have at least two healthy buds

Propagating perennials

In the Gardening Which? *trial many perennials flowered in their first year after sowing*

Perennials with fine seed are worth sowing in pots of multipurpose compost indoors

Most herbaceous perennials need to be lifted and divided every three to five years or so to keep them growing well. This can be a useful way of getting more plants. You can also propagate herbaceous plants by cuttings and from seed.

Division

The lifting and division of plants has been covered on page 15. Usually plenty of extra divisions can be replanted straight away or potted up and grown on.

Seed

The main benefits of growing from seed are lots of plants for very little outlay and the satisfaction of raising plants from seed. What is not so obvious is how quickly you get plants to flowering size. *Gardening Which?* trials on 39 perennial species over two years found that half the species flowered in the first year. So it is worth considering raising from seed even if you are in a hurry for your plants.

Most seeds can be sown outdoors in a seedbed or in a coldframe between March and July, but smaller seeds are best sown in pots under cover. For outdoor sowings, choose a piece of well-cultivated, weed-free ground such as a section of

the vegetable patch. Make a shallow drill and sow the seed thinly and cover with a thin layer of soil. The alternative is to sow in pots of multipurpose compost. Keep these in a cool greenhouse or coldframe until the seedlings emerge. Prick out into 7.5cm (3in) pots.

When the young plants are 7.5cm (3in) high, transplant them to their final planting positions if they are likely to flower in their first year. Those that do not flower until their second year, or if you want to check the colours or height before putting into a border can be lined out in a nursery bed.

Stem cuttings

Basal cuttings are taken in spring from the new shoots that can be seen growing up from the base of the old stems. Remove them when they are 5–7.5cm (2–3in) long and grow on in pots of multipurpose compost. Place in a propagator if you have one, otherwise put on a window-sill and cover with a clear polythene bag.

Soft cuttings can be taken in summer. Remove tips of side shoots with about three pairs of leaves attached. Non-flowering shoots are best, but flowering shoots can be used too if you remove any flower buds. Trim the cutting to below a leaf

Stem tip and stem cuttings from Penstemon

A simple runner tip cutting from Ajuga

joint and remove the lower leaves. Insert into pots of multipurpose compost and cover with a clear polythene bag. Keep lightly shaded until cuttings have rooted.

A 'heel' cutting is one where the side shoot also has a strip from the main stem attached.

Root cuttings

Some plants do not respond well to lifting and dividing and will not root from stem cuttings. Such plants can often be raised from sections of root. The following method is based on *Gardening Which?* trials.

Cut 5cm (2in) sections from strong, healthy young roots (pencil thickness). Use a sharp knife and make an angled cut furthest from the crown and a straight cut nearest to it. Dust the root sections in a fungicide powder. Insert into a free-draining compost (up to 80% grit) so that the straight cut is just proud of the compost. Lay thin roots horizontally on the compost surface. Add a layer of fine grit until it just covers the fine root cuttings, or is flush with the tops of the roots inserted vertically. Place in an unheated greenhouse or a coldframe. A heated propagator is not essential, but it will speed up rooting. Shade the plants to prevent scorching and water if necessary.

Fresh seed

With most herbaceous plants you can remove the seed stalk up to a week before the seeds disperse naturally and keep them in a dry, airy room to finish ripening. Put the seedheads in open paper bags. Some plants, such as hardy geraniums, eject their seed, so tie a paper bag over the seedheads before they ripen. Some seeds must be sown fresh, but most can be stored in a cool, dry place until required. Seed from named varieties will not produce plants identical to the parents.

Collect selected seedheads and label carefully

Hang up the paper bags in a warm, dry room or cupboard until the seedheads have ripened fully

Take 5cm (2in) sections of pencil-thick root with an angled cut furthest from the crown

Dip each section in fungicide powder before inserting in compost

17

Buying perennials

GARDEN CENTRES

If you are new to growing perennials or are not searching for specific varieties, a trip to your local garden centre is a good starting point. The selection should not be too daunting there, labelling should be reasonable and you can see the plants. Most garden centres will have the plants arranged in A–Z beds by their Latin name, but there may also be areas where 'ornamental grasses' or 'plants for shade' are displayed.

From early spring onwards there should be a selection of perennials in 9cm (3½in) or 13cm (5in) pots. These small pots are a cheap way to buy lots of different plants. If the small pots have been in the garden centre for a couple of months the plants do become stressed and you may see signs of premature flowering or red tinges to the foliage. So, when buying in late spring to summer you will probably be better off with larger pots. Large pots of perennials are often reduced in price at the end of the summer – these can be worth buying and splitting before planting.

Autumn is an excellent time to plant hardy perennials but it is depressing that so many outlets do not restock, relying instead on neglected spring stock. A *Gardening Which?* survey published in 1996 found that almost a third of garden centres and DIY stores visited in the autumn had poor plants.

Small pots

In spring, garden centres should be well-stocked with perennials in 9cm (3½in) pots. Expect to pay

around £1 to £2 each. These can often catch up with the larger, more expensive sizes if you get them in the ground in April to early May. We have found small sizes of *Geranium* 'Johnson's Blue', *Euphorbia polychroma* and *Sedum* 'Autumn Joy' particularly quick to catch up with larger-sized plants. They are garden-worthy plants too. You need to buy small plants while they are in top condition (see checklist left) as they soon deteriorate in such small pots.

Larger pots

The larger-sized pots, at about £4 to £6, can come into their own if you want several plants of the same variety. One large, established clump could be split up into many pieces prior to planting. A word of warning though, some retailers pot up unsold small plants into larger pots in late spring – make sure you look at the size of the plant's crown and roots not the pot!

Larger specimens often cope better with stress from erratic watering and hot spells while on sale, so are worth buying later in the season. Plants like Japanese anemones, peonies and lily-of-the-valley are best bought in larger pots as their roots do not like to be pot-bound.

Impulse buys

Beware the hyped-up 'new' perennial on full display near the entrance to the garden centre along with glossy labels and gimmicks. It may not be that new or significantly different to other varieties displayed more modestly elsewhere.

Plant quality checklist

It is important to check over plants before you buy as they can vary greatly in quality. The best-quality plants are those that have been recently delivered to the garden centre. However, early in the season beware of really fresh-looking plants with lots of young growth as these will have been forced into growth and will need to be hardened-off.

- ***Shoots and leaves** Avoid plants with weak growth, unnatural yellowing (many perennials yellow naturally in late summer and autumn), speckling, or signs of pests or diseases.*
- ***Roots** Inspect roots by tipping the plant out of its pot. If there are masses of roots encircling the pot the plant is pot-bound and best avoided. Also avoid plants where the compost falls away because the plant has probably only just been potted up.*
- ***Signs of neglect** Weeds in the compost and faded labels are a sure sign that the plant has been hanging around at the garden centre for a long time. Also avoid leggy plants as well as those with liverworts on the compost (tell-tale sign of overwatering) and where compost has shrunk away from the pot (sign of underwatering).*

Discount plants

In late summer perennials can be half the usual price in garden centres. Real bargains are large pots with lots of healthy shoots and buds at the base of the plant. Look carefully, these may be hidden by tatty foliage. Very pot-bound plants or those with unwelcome visitors such as weeds, pests or diseases are best avoided. Also avoid unnamed plants.

SPECIALIST NURSERIES

If you have set your heart on a particular variety or you want to start a collection of, say hellebores or hostas, you will need a specialist nursery. Some sell a wide range of perennials, others concentrate on a particular plant or feature such as variegated foliage. For an up-to-date list of herbaceous specialists, write to *Gardening Which?*, PO Box 44, Hertford X, SG14 1SH and ask for factsheet GWF413.

Many specialist nurseries are run by just one or two people from home and opening times and plant availability can vary greatly. To avoid disappointment, telephone first. If you want to buy a few plants from a number of specialists, you may save time by going to garden shows. Many specialists have stalls at garden shows where you can pick up one or two unusual plants without having to pay the carriage charges. However, check that the plants are well-rooted in the pots – some are sold very young and may need growing on before planting.

BUYING BY MAIL ORDER

Buying plants by mail order seems an attractive alternative to driving around, particularly if you want to plant in the autumn. The important point to bear in mind is there is no requirement for the seller to state the size of plant on offer – they could be decent-sized plants equivalent to those on sale in garden centres or they may be little more than rooted cuttings which will need potting up and growing on before planting out. Regardless of when you place your order, plants tend to be despatched during the dormant season so this is not instant shopping.

There are a few cautionary points to keep in mind when ordering plants:

- Postage and packing charges and minimum orders can push up the price if you only want a few plants.
- The plants may be delivered at an inconvenient time. Most plants are despatched between September and mid-November or

Large plants can be split before planting

March to April but you probably will not know the date in advance. If you know you are going to be away, specify the dates you cannot accept the plants on the order form.
- You may order from a nursery because they have unusual varieties – only to find several months later you have been sent substitute plants. So specify when you order if you will accept substitutes or not.

Your rights

If you are not satisfied with a recent plant purchase, send or take it back and you should get a replacement or your money back. The law says that goods must be 'as described', of 'merchantable quality' and 'fit for the purpose'. So plants not true to name, that are too small or poor quality or have major drawbacks that were not made clear at the time are covered. Many garden centres offer 'no-quibble' two-year guarantees on hardy plants.

Mail-order checklist

Mail-order plants could be container-grown or could have been grown in a field then lifted – these are bare-rooted plants which are more prone to drying out. Once the plants arrive, make the following checks:
- *Compare the plant labels against the delivery note.*
- *Make sure the plants are the size you were expecting.*
- *Although the plants will be dormant, check that the roots have not suffered from drying out or mechanical damage in transit.*
- *Inspect the stems or crowns to make sure they are undamaged and bear no sign of pests or disease.*
- *Plants packed too wet and stored too warm can shoot into leggy growth which could make them hard to establish – you would have cause for complaint if you had stored them correctly and unpacked them straight away.*
- *Contact the nursery at once if you find a problem.*

Acanthus
Acanthus spinosus

Shape and size

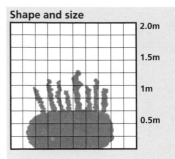

2.0m
1.5m
1m
0.5m

Position

Hardiness   Soil

WELL-DRAINED

Uses

Features calendar

Jan	Feb	Mar	Apr	May	June
July	Aug	Sept	Oct	Nov	Dec

Buying tips *Older plants resent having their roots disturbed. Buy young plants in small pots from garden centres from spring onwards.*

Acanthus mollis foliage

Acanthus spinosus with Brachyglottis compacta 'Sunshine'

Growing guide

These superb, imposing plants offer handsome, jagged foliage and spikes of attractive flowers that make them ideal for the larger border.

They tolerate shade, but they flower much better in sunny spots. Any reasonable soil will do; they tolerate drought well once they are established but dislike waterlogged soil. Acanthus has quite a spread and the leaves have spiny points, so think carefully before planting it near paths. They are best situated where they can be left to grow into sizeable clumps. Plant either in the spring or in autumn. If the latter, protect the crown during the first winter with a layer of chipped bark or bracken.

The flower spikes with their white and mauve blooms are particularly valued for dried winter floral arrangements, but beware of their prickles.

Good companions

Acanthus have bold foliage and a striking habit, so are eye-catching enough to be grown on their own in a gravel bed or in a large container. At the back of the border they could be combined with fine-textured plants such as sea lavender (*Limonium latifolium*) or *Gypsophila paniculata*. They can also add interest to low-growing carpeting plants such as hardy geraniums or bergenias.

Propagation

Root cuttings or seed.

Troubleshooting

They can crowd out other plants with their invasive roots.

Which variety?

A. spinosus has clumps of dark, deeply cut leaves up to 60cm (24in) long above which rise tall stems of mauve and white flowers. *A. mollis* is similar but with less distinctive foliage and taller spikes 1.5m (5ft).

Achillea

Achillea 'Moonshine'

Shape and size

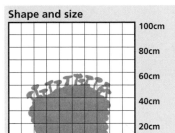

	100cm
	80cm
	60cm
	40cm
	20cm

Position   Hardiness   Soil

WELL-DRAINED

Uses

Features calendar

Jan	Feb	Mar	Apr	May	June
			🌿	✿	✿

July	Aug	Sept	Oct	Nov	Dec
✿	🌿	🌿	🌿	🌿	🌿

Buying tips *Buy young plants in 9cm (3½in) pots in early spring – they will soon produce a substantial display.*

Achillea 'The Beacon' (also known as 'Fanal')

Achillea 'Moonshine', A. ageratum 'W.B. Childs' with Geranium nodosum

Growing guide

Most achilleas have distinctive feathery, green or silvery-green, aromatic leaves which make an attractive foil for other border plants. The flat plate-like flower clusters come in a range of colours including white, cream, yellow, pink and crimson but the best colours are to be found among the yellows. The flowers last well and can be cut and dried for winter arrangements.

Most border achilleas are drought-tolerant and like a sunny spot. They are not too fussy about soil, but they can get killed off by heavy, wet soils in winter. Cut back the tatty foliage in March to encourage new shoots and divide every three years in early spring. Some varieties need staking and can be invasive. If your soil is heavy, divide plants every other year to encourage fibrous roots.

Good companions

Yellow achilleas combine well with blue flowers like those of delphiniums or *Salvia* x *superba*.

Propagation

Lift and divide in autumn or spring.

Troubleshooting

Apart from slugs and snails, the only pests are birds, which like to gather the grey-leaved achilleas to line their nests.

Which variety?

We've picked the variety **'Moonshine'** as one of the best border achilleas for its sulphur-yellow flowers from May to July with grey-green foliage. It does not need staking and is widely available.

The following achilleas flower later from June or July to August and have green foliage unless otherwise stated. **A. ageratum 'W.B. Childs'** (was *A. decolorans* 'W.B. Childs') has white flowers from May to August. A reliable choice for heavy soils. **'Coronation Gold'** with mustard-yellow flowers and grey-green foliage is 90cm (36in) tall, but only needs staking in exposed borders. **A. filipendulina 'Cloth of Gold'** and **'Gold Plate'** are similar, but 30cm (12in) taller.

A. millefolium is better known as the lawn weed yarrow, however, there are some named varieties such as **'Cerise Queen'** with cerise-pink flowers. But, as the flower colour may revert to a paler colour and the plants usually need staking, they are not ideal border plants. You may also come across a range of German-bred achilleas, the best of which are: **'Appleblossom'** (syn. 'Apfelblüte'); **'The Beacon'** (syn. 'Fanal'), **'Salmon Beauty'** (syn. 'Lachsschönheit') all shades of pink or red; and **'Great Expectations'** (syn. 'Hoffnung') which is cream.

A. 'Taygetea' is a useful border plant with pale yellow flowers and grey-green foliage 60x60cm (24x24in).

A. tomentosa has yellow flowers on neat 10x25cm (4x10in) mounds. Ideal for the front of the border.

Aconitum
Aconitum 'Spark's Variety'

Shape and size

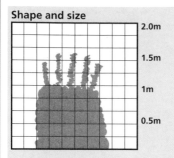

2.0m
1.5m
1m
0.5m

Position

Hardiness **Soil**

MOIST

Uses

Features calendar

Jan	Feb	Mar	Apr	May	June
✿	✿				
July	Aug	Sept	Oct	Nov	Dec

Buying tips *Worth buying and planting in the autumn as they start into growth in early spring.*

WARNING
All parts of this plant are poisonous.

Aconitum 'Spark's Variety'

Growing guide

Aconitums have interesting helmet-shaped flowers arranged on upright or branched spikes. Growing to around 1.5m (5ft) tall, these plants are an easy alternative to delphiniums as they generally do not need staking and are easier to grow.

Most of the garden-worthy varieties are blue or purple, but there are pinky-purple and white ones too. You can sometimes get a second flush of flowers in the autumn, although the foliage by this time is a little tatty.

A major drawback is that all parts of this plant are poisonous, so wear gloves as a precaution when handling it. Even if children do not visit your garden you still need to be on your guard. For example, there have been documented accounts of pets becoming sick after eating the roots and cases of florists falling ill after handling the flowers.

All aconitums need a substantial rooting depth, so prepare a hole at least 45cm (18in) deep and dig in some well-rotted organic matter if the soil is free-draining. They will grow in sun or shade, but it is vital they do not dry out in summer.

Most aconitums have tuberous roots and individual plants may need lifting, thinning and replanting every three years to produce strong stems.

Good companions
The blue-flowered varieties can be contrasted with yellow daisy-shaped flowers like rudbeckia. For autumn colour, use the ruby-red flowers of *Persicaria amplexicaulis* as a contrast to later-flowering blue varieties.

Propagation
Division or seed.

Troubleshooting
Generally trouble-free.

Which variety?

There are a lot of garden-worthy varieties, varying in colour and flowering time. We've chosen **'Spark's Variety'** for its deep blue-purple flowers on branching stems. Other summer-flowering ones include: **'Bressingham Spire'**, violet-blue with erect spikes; **A. x cammarum 'Bicolor'**, violet-blue and white with branching stems.

The native **A. napellus** flowers in late summer, but for even later flowering in early autumn look for **A. carmichaelii** and its varieties. For example, the mid-blue **'Arendsii'** or **'Barker's Variety'** or the richer violet-blue of **'Kelmscott'**.

Agapanthus

Agapanthus 'Headbourne Hybrids'

Shape and size

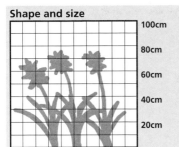

100cm
80cm
60cm
40cm
20cm

Position   Hardiness   Soil

WELL-DRAINED

Uses

Features calendar

Jan	Feb	Mar	Apr	May	June
❀	❀	❀	🌿	🌿	
July	Aug	Sept	Oct	Nov	Dec

Buying tips *Named varieties are hard to track down as they are slow to propagate – try herbaceous or bulb specialists.*

The seedheads make an interesting winter feature

Agapanthus 'Headbourne Hybrids'

Growing guide

During late summer, stiff, upright stems topped with loose globes of blue or white flowers appear above the fountain of strap-shaped foliage. By autumn, the seedheads look attractive and can be left on the plant as a winter feature or cut and dried for indoor decoration.

Although agapanthus have a reputation for being tender, the deciduous *A. campanulatus* varieties can withstand frost, as can the 'Headbourne Hybrids' which were raised in Britain in the late 1940s.

In mild gardens, these hardier types are long-lived perennials that require very little maintenance. In colder areas they need either a winter mulch of bracken or, safer still, to be grown permanently in a large container which can be moved under cover in winter or insulated with bubble polythene.

Agapanthus need a position where they get full sun; if not, their stems tend to lean towards the light. The soil or compost needs to be well-drained but not dry.

Good companions

They make excellent single subjects in containers. When growing them in borders, combine with soft yellow, apricot, silver or grey.

Propagation

Division every 3 to 4 years, or from seed.

Troubleshooting

Hardy varieties are generally trouble-free. Plants can be left for many years, but if their roots become congested fewer flower heads will be produced. Tender types need winter protection.

Which variety?

We would recommend the **'Headbourne Hybrids'** as they are among the hardiest, but they can vary in height and colour as they are generally raised from seed. Named varieties can be difficult to obtain. A recent *Gardening Which?* trial found that **'Bressingham White'** flowered the longest. Of the blue varieties the following were recommended: **'Bressingham Blue'** is a deep blue; *A. campanulatus* is hardy in most areas and has soft blue flowers, it grows from 60–120cm (24–48in) high; the variety **'Isis'** has clear lavender blue flowers and is 80cm (32in) high.

Variegated agapanthus are becoming more available, for example, the new **'Tinkerbell'** has narrow silver stripes on the leaves, and grows to 45cm (18in) high with mid-blue flowers.

23

Agastache
Agastache mexicana

Shape and size

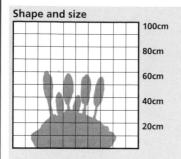

100cm
80cm
60cm
40cm
20cm

Position

Hardiness

Soil

WELL-DRAINED

Uses

Features calendar

Jan	Feb	Mar	Apr	May	June
July	Aug	Sept	Oct	Nov	Dec

Aug, Sept, Oct marked with flower symbols

Buying tips *Not widely sold in garden centres; you may need to order from a herbaceous specialist or try growing from seed.*

Agastache mexicana

In Gardening Which? seed trials, Agastache 'Fragrant Mixed' flowered in its first year

Growing guide

Flowering from August to October, these sun-lovers are ideal for a sunny, well-drained bank or border. They are easy to grow and their flowers are a favourite with bees. Some, such as *A. mexicana*, are short-lived and so need raising from seed each year – though self-sown seedlings can often be found.

Good companions

Agastache are suitable for growing among herbs or in a small, sunny border with grey or silver foliage plants. They also combine well with Japanese anemones.

Propagation

Seed. In *Gardening Which?* trials, 'Fragrant Mixed' flowered in its first year. Divide in spring or autumn.

Troubleshooting

Generally trouble-free.

Which variety?

A. foeniculum (syn. *A. anethiodora*, *A. anisata*) is available from many specialist nurseries. It is hardy, 90cm (36in) tall with lots of spikes of violet flowers from well-branched plants. The foliage smells of aniseed. *A. foeniculum* 'Alabaster' is a white variety. **A. mexicana** (syn. *Cedronella mexicana*) is smaller at 60x30cm (24x12in) with pink flowers.

New ones to look out for include: **'Blue Fortune'** with blue flowers on spikes reaching 70cm (40in); **'Firebird'** 60x30cm (24x12in) with coral pink flowers.

'Fragrant Mixed' available as seed has blue, lilac and white flowers. **'Liquorice Blue'**, a newish variety that should flower in its first year, has blue flowers with leaves that smell of liquorice.

Ajuga
Ajuga reptans 'Multicolor'

Shape and size

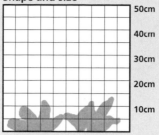

50cm
40cm
30cm
20cm
10cm

Position

Hardiness Soil

MOIST

Uses

Features calendar

Jan	Feb	Mar	Apr	May	June
July	Aug	Sept	Oct	Nov	Dec

Buying tips *Either buy in small (7.5cm/3in) pots from garden centres in the spring or buy larger plants later in the year and divide up before planting.*

Ajuga reptans 'Multicolor'

Growing guide

Bugles, or ajugas, are carpeting plants grown for their decorative foliage. Many of the colourful evergreen forms make ideal year-round groundcover. They also produce attractive pink or blue flower spikes during April, May or June – depending on the variety.

Ajugas are very easy to please, growing in sun or shade and any type of soil as long as it retains some moisture. The variegated forms can sometimes die back over winter. To encourage new leaves with their brighter colours, apply a top-dressing of a balanced slow-release fertiliser in spring and water the plants during dry spells.

For groundcover, use about eight plants per square metre (*A. reptans* 'Catlin's Giant' is so vigorous you could get away with just one large plant per square metre).

Good companions

Ajugas, underplanted with snowdrops, are an ideal way of brightening up the ground beneath and between shrubs. They can also be used in containers as cheap foliage fillers for spring, summer or autumn displays.

Propagation

Division – every two years.

Troubleshooting

Mildew can be a problem in dry shade. Clumps can die out with age in the centre, so lift and divide to revitalise them.

Which variety?

We've chosen the widely available ***A. reptans* 'Multicolor'** (syn. 'Rainbow' or 'Tricolor') for its striking foliage colours of bronze, red, green and creamy yellow. Other useful variegated varieties are: **'Burgundy Glow'**, crimson and pink foliage edged with cream, flowers April to May; the best variegated variety for shade is **'Variegata'** (syn. 'Argentea'), the grey-green leaves with cream edges keep their colour well.

Of the purple-leaved varieties of *A. reptans*, there is the reddish-purple **'Atropurpurea'** (syn. 'Purpurea') also **'Braunherz'** with dark purple-bronze foliage. Both flower from April to June. A vigorous one is **'Catlin's Giant'** with purple-bronze foliage and a flowering height of 23–30cm (9–12in) in May.

Several attractive pink forms of *A. reptans* flower in April: **'Pink Elf'** has lilac-pink flowers above green foliage; **'Pink Surprise'** has magenta-pink blooms above beetroot-coloured foliage.

Alcea (Althaea)

Alcea rosea

Shape and size

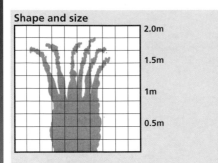

- 2.0m
- 1.5m
- 1m
- 0.5m

Position

Hardiness

Soil

MOIST

Uses

Features calendar

Jan	Feb	Mar	Apr	May	June
✿	✿	✿			
July	Aug	Sept	Oct	Nov	Dec

Buying tips *Check seed catalogues for garden varieties – they often have more choice than nurseries and seed is cheaper than plants. Opt for single colours where possible.*

Alcea rugosa is said to be less prone to rust disease

Alcea rosea 'Nigra'

Growing guide

This once-popular cottage garden plant was almost wiped out during the nineteenth century by rust disease. Today, only a few hollyhocks are available, named either *Alcea* or *Althaea* in books and catalogues. All are short-lived perennials producing tall spires of flowers from July to September.

For best results, plant in a sheltered position in a moisture-retentive soil. They will grow in sun or partial shade.

Self-sown seedlings will appear in future years, these seldom come true and doubles will revert to singles. But you may get some beautifully coloured singles.

Good companions

Hollyhocks tend to be associated with cottage gardens – towering above lavender, catmint, perfumed stocks and mignonette. But they can also add summer interest to spring-flowering and evergreen shrub borders, or be grown in front of wall-trained shrubs or climbers to extend the period of flowering interest.

Propagation

Seed – either sow in autumn to grow as a biennial or, to get them to flower the same year, sow in early spring. Look for self-sown seedlings.

Troubleshooting

Rust is the main problem. Look for raised buff, orange or brown spots, usually on the undersides of leaves, from April onwards. Spray with Murphy Tumbleblite every 10 to 14 days to slow down the disease. Keep the plants well-watered during dry spells. Dig up and burn badly affected plants and clear away leaf debris.

Which variety?

The varieties of **A. rosea** are available in a range of colours either as single flowers or as doubles. **'Nigra'** is burgundy/near black and single. All the following are doubles. **'Chater's Double Group'** is one of the tallest at 1.8–3m (6–10ft). It has peony-type flowers in pink, apricot, red, crimson, salmon, pale yellow and white. Look out for single-coloured varieties. **'Majorette'** is a mixture of pastel colours that will reach only 60–75cm (24–30in) and flower in its first year from seed.

Other species are: **Althaea cannabina**, pink, 2.1m (7ft), but does not need staking. **Alcea rugosa** (syn. *Althaea rugosostellulata*) is said to be less prone to rust, pale yellow, 1.2–1.8m (4–6ft). **Alcea ficifolia** (Antwerp hollyhock), yellow flower, 1.2m (4ft) or more tall.

Alchemilla
Alchemilla mollis

Shape and size

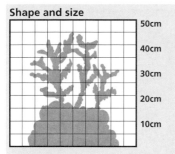

Position

Hardiness   Soil

WELL-DRAINED

Uses

Features calendar

Jan	Feb	Mar	Apr	May	June
July	Aug	Sept	Oct	Nov	Dec

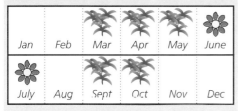

Buying tips *Buy as small plants in spring rather than grow from bought seed because germination can be poor.*

The foliage of lady's mantle is covered in fine hairs which trap water droplets

Alchemilla mollis in June, when its billowing clouds of flowers are at their best

Growing guide

A well-known, versatile perennial that is easy to grow in sun or partial shade. The leaves are a soft green and are covered in fine hairs which trap water droplets on the leaves. The flowers are a greeny-yellow and appear like a froth above the foliage.

It will grow in any fertile soil, including heavy clay and, once established, can tolerate drought. It is an ideal plant to use at the front of a border, or as a filler in containers. It is a reliable flowering groundcover if planted 45cm (18in) apart, but only during the summer as it is not evergreen.

The flowers and some of the foliage can look a bit tatty by August, so cut the lot off – use a trimmer or shears for large plantings. Feed and water if the soil is dry. New fresh foliage will soon appear.

Good companions

The hazy outline of alchemilla makes an effective contrast to plants with upright or spiky flowers or foliage. Try it in front of upright campanulas, kniphofias, hemerocallis or agapanthus, for example. It is also a useful edging for softening raised beds or paving.

Propagation

Division or seed if fresh.

Troubleshooting

Alchemillas can self-seed too much unless the seedheads are removed after flowering.

Which variety?

Alchemilla mollis is widely available and an excellent garden plant. You may also come across the smaller **A. alpina** (syn. *A. conjuncta*) or **A. erythropoda**. These are only 15x25cm (6x10in).

Alstroemeria

Alstroemeria 'Ligtu Hybrids'

Shape and size

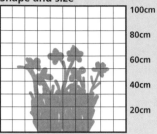

	100cm
	80cm
	60cm
	40cm
	20cm

Position Hardiness Soil

WELL-DRAINED

Uses

Features calendar

Jan	Feb	Mar	Apr	May	June
					✱
July	Aug	Sept	Oct	Nov	Dec
✱					

Buying tips *The 'Ligtu Hybrids' can be bought as young, seed-raised pot plants in spring or can be obtained from specialist nurseries as dormant roots in late summer. The latter are easier to plant deeply.*

Alstroemeria and helenium in summer border

Alstroemeria 'Ligtu Hybrids'

Growing guide

Alstroemerias have sumptuous pink and orange flowers reminiscent of azalea blooms, but with the addition of attractive flecks and spots. They flower early in the summer and are usually grown in the border. When the flowering display is over, usually by mid- to late July, pull the stems up leaving the tuberous roots underground. The space left can be filled with a late-flowering perennial or bedding.

Alstroemerias can be difficult to establish, but given the right conditions will thrive. They need a warm, sunny bed and a well-drained soil. Plant 23cm (9in) deep. Young plants benefit from an insulating mulch of bracken or chipped bark over winter. The stems may need supporting with twiggy sticks.

They make impressive cut flowers, but take care when handling them as they can cause skin irritation.

Good companions

Their rich shades of pink and orange in mid-summer make them ideal mid-border plants for bridging the gap between the early perennials, such as foxgloves, lupins and peonies, and the late summer asters. Alternatively, try growing *Verbena bonariensis* through alstroemerias – it will provide flower interest after the alstroemerias have finished.

Propagation

By seed, in spring.

Troubleshooting

If the plant likes the conditions it can become invasive.

Which variety?

We've chosen ***Alstroemeria* 'Ligtu Hybrids'** as they are the hardiest and come in a wide range of colours in shades of red, pink, yellow and beige. About a dozen are named after princesses, many of these are excellent and there is a new white one called **'Princess Alexandra'**.

A. aurea (syn. *A. aurantiaca*) is easier to establish but can be invasive. The varieties **'Dover Orange'** and **'Orange King'** are often seen.

A. psittacina (syn. *A. pulchella*) has reddish brown flowers that last into the autumn, but it is hardy only in sheltered spots in mild areas.

Anaphalis

Anaphalis triplinervis

Shape and size

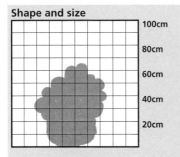

Position

Hardiness

Soil

MOIST

Uses

Features calendar

Jan	Feb	Mar	Apr	May	June
✱	✱	✱			
July	Aug	Sept	Oct	Nov	Dec

Buying tips *Buy young plants as they will quickly establish decent-sized clumps. They can also be raised from seed.*

Anaphalis triplinervis is an easy filler for a border

Anaphalis triplinervis 'Summer Snow'

Growing guide

This useful grey-leaved plant is unobtrusive until late summer when it is highlighted by a display of small, white, papery flowers. It will spread to form large clumps and requires little maintenance, making it an ideal filler. Unlike most grey-leaved plants, it thrives in moist conditions in sun or shade. It cannot tolerate drought, however.

As the common name suggests, the flowers are everlasting and can be cut and dried for flower arrangements.

Good companions

Combine with late-flowering plants such as Japanese anemones and fuchsias.

Propagation

Division, seed or basal cuttings.

Troubleshooting

This plant has a tendency to wilt and flop if it runs short of moisture at the roots.

Anaphalis margaritacea

Which variety?

Anaphalis triplinervis is the main species. However, **'Summer Snow'** (syn. 'Sommerschnee') has a neater habit.

A. margaritacea and its varieties **'Cinnamomea'** (syn. A. cinnamomea) and **'Yedoensis'** are about 25cm (10in) taller than A. triplinervis. They all have green leaves with white undersides, the flowers are held on erect stems.

29

Anchusa

Anchusa azurea 'Loddon Royalist'

Shape and size

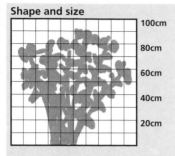

	100cm
	80cm
	60cm
	40cm
	20cm

Position Hardiness Soil

WELL-DRAINED

Uses

Features calendar

Jan	Feb	Mar	Apr	May	June
					✿
✿	✿				
July	Aug	Sept	Oct	Nov	Dec

Buying tips *Buy young, healthy plants that are well-branched. Tip plant out of its pot and check it is well rooted.*

Anchusa with aquilegia and myosotis

Anchusa azurea 'Loddon Royalist'

Growing guide

This charming upright perennial will colour a border with rich shades of blue all summer. The flowers resemble giant forget-me-not blooms on loosely branched stems and are very attractive to bees.

Anchusas will do well in any reasonable border soil if given a sunny spot.

Good companions

The foliage is rather coarse and is best disguised by an attractive edging plant such as *Achillea* 'Moonshine', *Lamium maculatum* 'White Nancy' or a white hardy geranium. Anchusas look particularly effective when planted with bearded irises or lupins.

Propagation

Root cuttings. Also self-seeds freely.

Troubleshooting

Generally trouble-free apart from the need to stake.

Which variety?

Anchusa azurea '**Loddon Royalist**' is an impressive named variety in deep blue. Other deep blues are '**Dropmore**', '**Morning Glory**', '**Royal Blue**' and '**Little John**', the latter is a dwarf one at 45cm (18in). For a lighter blue, go for '**Opal**'.

Anemone

Anemone x hybrida 'Honorine Jobert'

Shape and size

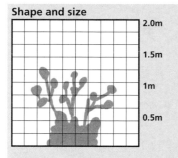

Position

Hardiness   Soil

  ANY

Uses

Features calendar

Jan	Feb	Mar	Apr	May	June
July	Aug	Sept	Oct	Nov	Dec

(flowers shown in Aug, Sept, Oct)

Buying tips *Buy in flower if you want a specific variety as plant labelling is not reliable. Inspect foliage carefully for signs of rust.*

Anemone japonica hupehensis 'Prince Henry'

Anemone x hybrida 'Honorine Jobert'

Growing guide

The *Anemone* x *hybrida* varieties (which may also be listed under *A. japonica* or *A. hupehensis*) are a welcome addition to the border as they flower in late summer to early autumn. As well as beautiful flowers, they have a good habit, tall flowering stems rise up from mounds of dark green, vine-shaped leaves. In time, they make impressive clumps in a border.

They thrive in sun or partial shade and are not fussy about soil, in fact they do well on chalky soil and in heavy ground. The important thing is to choose the planting site carefully as they don't like being moved.

Good companions

Japanese anemones are an essential ingredient of an autumn border alongside chrysanthemums and asters. They can be used in front of shrub roses, large spring-flowering or evergreen shrubs. In a small garden, they make reliable back-of-the-border plants behind summer bedding, which can be removed as the anemones are ready to flower.

Propagation

Rather than lifting and dividing the tough roots, try to remove soil from alongside an established clump, detach a root with a bud and pot up. Alternatively, take root cuttings.

Troubleshooting

They can take up to two years to become established, but after that they spread rapidly.

Yellow spots on the upper surface of leaves is a sign of rust disease. Dig up and burn badly affected plants.

Which variety?

We've chosen **A. x hybrida 'Honorine Jobert'** for its clear white, single flowers and dark green leaves, but the following varieties did well in recent *Gardening Which?* trials: **A. hupehensis 'Hadspen Abundance'**, rich, deep pink single flowers; **A. japonica hupehensis 'Bressingham Glow'**, rosy-red, semi-double flowers, only 45cm (18in) high; **'Prince Henry'** (syn. 'Prinz Heinrich') deep pink, long flowering; **'September Charm'** soft pink, single, long flowering.

A. x hybrida 'Queen Charlotte' (syn. 'Königin Charlotte'), a large-flowered, almost semi-double, pale pink variety. **'Margarete'** (syn. 'Lady Gilmour') deep pink, almost double, 45cm (18in) tall. **'Richard Ahrens'**, deep pink, semi-double flowers, 90cm (36in) tall, lasts into November. **'Whirlwind'** (syn. 'Wirbelwind'), white, semi-double, 75cm (30in) tall.

Anthemis

Anthemis tinctoria 'E.C. Buxton'

Shape and size

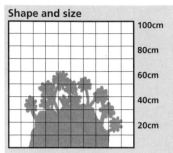

100cm
80cm
60cm
40cm
20cm

Position   Hardiness   Soil

WELL-DRAINED

Uses

Features calendar

Jan	Feb	Mar	Apr	May	June
					❋
❋	❋	❋	Oct	Nov	Dec
July	Aug	Sept			

Buying tips *Buy young, well-branched plants in spring. If buying older plants in flower, check there are plenty of buds.*

Anthemis punctata 'Cupaniana'

Anthemis tinctoria 'E.C. Buxton'

Growing guide

A hardy, clump-forming perennial with daisy-like flowers. Worth a place in a sunny, well-drained border for the masses of lemon-yellow blooms that are produced all summer. The foliage is green, neat and aromatic, but plants may need support for the best effect.

Good companions

The pale yellow flowers combine well with any blue or purple flowers, such as catmint or blue campanulas. The darker yellows can be teamed with red *Monardas*.

Propagation

Take basal cuttings and root in a coldframe. Plant out in spring.

Troubleshooting

Plants sometimes flower to exhaustion, so cut down the stems after flowering to encourage new growth from the base.

Which variety?

***A. tinctoria* 'E.C. Buxton'** has been chosen for its pale lemon flowers. You may also come across **'Grallach Gold'**, bright yellow, **'Sauce Hollandaise'** pale yellow flowers on plants 45x60cm (18x24in), and **'Wargrave'** with creamy-yellow flowers. *A. tinctoria* is the ox-eye daisy, often used for naturalising on poor, dry soils.

***A. punctata* 'Cupaniana'** is a mound-like plant about 30x45cm (12x18in) with aromatic, grey foliage and white daisy-like flowers in May and intermittently until the autumn. Useful as an edging or groundcover, although it can die back in winter.

A. sancti-johannis or St John's chamomile is a bushy, semi-evergreen with grey foliage and bright orange flowers.

Anthericum

Anthericum liliago 'Major'

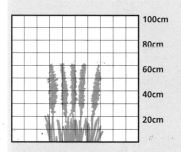

Position   **Hardiness**   **Soil**

WELL-DRAINED

Uses

Features calendar

Jan	Feb	Mar	Apr	May	June
				✿	✿
July	Aug	Sept	Oct	Nov	Dec
✲	✲				

Buying tips *Rarely found in garden centres, try a herbaceous specialist or order dormant roots from a bulb specialist.*

Anthericum liliago 'Major'

Anthericum liliago

St Bernard's lily

Growing guide

This is an easy perennial to grow in a sunny border with a reasonably fertile soil. It produces clumps of grey-green grassy foliage. The white starry flowers are borne profusely on wiry stems in early summer, followed by good seed spikes.

The fleshy roots need a moisture-retentive soil in summer but which is not cold, wet or boggy in winter. Although hardy in a well-drained soil, in cold, wet areas it is best to lift the root over winter. Plant dormant roots 10cm (4in) deep.

Good companions

The large blooms of early peonies contrast well with the delicate, starry flowers.

Propagation

By division, in spring.

Troubleshooting

Generally trouble-free. *A. liliago* seeds readily.

Which variety?

A. liliago and its variety **'Major'** (syn. *A. liliago* 'Algeriense') are similar but the latter is 30cm (12in) taller and less prone to setting seed.

33

Aquilegia

Aquilegia 'McKana Hybrids'

Shape and size

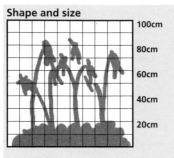

100cm
80cm
60cm
40cm
20cm

Position

Hardiness Soil

ANY

Uses

Features calendar

Jan	Feb	Mar	Apr	May	June
July	Aug	Sept	Oct	Nov	Dec

Buying tips *The variety 'Nora Barlow' can be raised from seed with reliable results – other aquilegias, although cheap and easy, may be more variable so buy these as plants.*

Aquilegia 'McKana Hybrids'

Aquilegia vulgaris 'Nora Barlow'

Growing guide

Once a cottage garden plant, these delightful early summer flowers are becoming popular again. The main feature of interest is their dainty flowers, some of which have elegant, long spurs. There is a wide colour range too, from pastels to more vibrant shades. The flowers are held above mounds of neat foliage.

Aquilegias thrive in any reasonable soil, in sun or partial shade. They are generally short-lived perennials but they do self-seed. Varieties also cross-breed freely so if you have several different types in your garden, you may eventually end up with a mixture of seedlings.

Good companions

Grow them with other early summer flowering plants such as poppies, lupins or bearded irises.

Alternatively, grow them in front of bold foliage plants so the flowers can be highlighted.

Propagation

Seed. Sow in the autumn, stand pots out in a sheltered, shaded spot and plant out young plants in spring.

Troubleshooting

Plants may get powdery mildew or leaf spotting after flowering. Cut back affected leaves, water and feed to encourage new foliage. White wiggly lines on leaves are a tell-tale sign of leaf miner. Pick off and destroy affected leaves.

Which variety?

There are many species and hybrids, the taller ones are most useful in the middle of the border. The **'McKana Hybrids'** grow up to 90cm (36in) and have large flowers

Long, elegant spurred flowers resemble an old-fashioned linen bonnet

Aquilegia canadensis showing its long spurs

Aquilegias are ideal centre-of-the-border plants; here 'Nora Barlow' is set off by the green-yellow bracts of Euphorbia

in a vibrant mixture of white, blue, purple, yellow and shades of red. New varieties are available including the compact mixture **'Biedermeier'** at 20–30cm (8–12in) as well as **'Blue Star'** and **'Red Star'** at 90cm (36in).

Long spurs

Species with long spurs and heights of 40–80cm (16–32in) include:
A. caerulea, blue and white flowers with very long spurs;
A. canadensis, red and yellow, dart-like flowers (**A. formosa** is similar); **A. longissima** has yellow flowers with very long spurs.

Short spurs or no spurs

Aquilegias with short spurs or no spurs include the variable
A. vulgaris. There are named forms too, most of which are 30–60cm (12–24in) tall and flower from May to July. Varieties to look out for

include: **'Nivea'** (syn. 'Munstead White'); **'Vervaeneana Group'** has gold-variegated leaves and flowers in mixed colours; **'Nora Barlow'** has unusual fluffy-headed, double flowers in dark pink and white. New selections with more unusual colours include: **'Mellow Yellow'** with golden foliage in spring, which turns lime-green by summer, when there are white or pale blue flowers. For an unusual flower colour, look out for the burgundy-black and white **'Magpie'** or **'William Guiness'**.

Smaller species

Smaller species about 15cm (6in) in height are also available. They are ideal for growing in rock gardens and raised beds. These include:
A. bertolonii (deep blue),
A. flabellata (white or blue), or the fragrant **A. fragrans** (pale cream).

Aquilegia vulgaris 'Vervaeneana Group'

35

Armeria

Armeria maritima

Shape and size

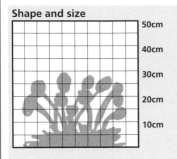

50cm
40cm
30cm
20cm
10cm

Position

Hardiness

Soil

WELL-DRAINED

Uses

Features calendar

Jan	Feb	Mar	Apr	May ✿	June ✿
July ✿	Aug	Sept	Oct	Nov	Dec

Buying tips *You may find them on sale in the alpine section of garden centres and catalogues rather than with herbaceous perennials.*

Armeria juniperifolia 'Bevan's Variety'

Armeria maritima 'Düsseldorf Pride'

Growing guide

As their common name suggests, sea pinks are a natural choice for coastal gardens, but they have plenty to offer other gardens too. The plants are easy to grow if given a sunny, well-drained soil. They have a compact habit with globular heads of pink flowers held above grassy, mat-like foliage. This, together with their long-flowering and evergreen foliage, makes them an ideal edging plant.

The only aftercare they need is deadheading of the faded flowers to enhance the remaining foliage.

Good companions

Thrifts make a neat edging to small borders, and the blue flowers of *Linum narbonense* would be a contrasting backdrop. Alternatively, use thrifts with aubrieta or dwarf phloxes on a sunny rockery.

Propagation

Division or seed.

Troubleshooting

Rust causes brown pustules on the foliage. Lift and destroy any affected plants.

Which variety?

A. maritima (syn. *A. vulgaris*) has many named varieties, one of the best is **'Vindictive',** which is smaller and has deep rose-pink flowers. You may also come across the white-flowered variety **'Alba'** or the deep pink **'Düsseldorf Pride'** (syn. 'Düsseldorfer Stolz').

A. alliacea (syn. *A. plantaginea*) tends to be taller at 45x30cm (18x12in) with larger flowers.

A. **'Bee's Ruby'** is difficult to find but worth seeking out for its bright colour – a deep, shocking pink.

A. juniperifolia (syn. *A. caespitosa*) is widely available, it is smaller than *A. maritima* at 8x15–25cm (3x6–10in). **'Bevan's Variety'** has deeper pink flowers.

Artemisia

Artemisia 'Powis Castle'

Shape and size

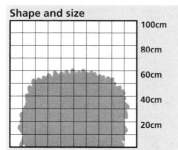

100cm
80cm
60cm
40cm
20cm

Position   Hardiness   Soil

WELL-DRAINED

Uses

Features calendar

Jan	Feb	Mar	Apr	May	June
July	Aug	Sept	Oct	Nov	Dec

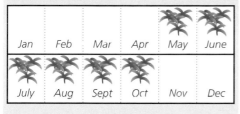

Buying tips *Buy young bushy plants in small pots. Look for the shrubby artemisias like* A. abrotanum *in the shrub section.*

'Silver Queen' grows to 90cm (36in)

Artemisia 'Powis Castle'

Growing guide

Artemisias provide soft, feathery texture to border plantings and they are one of the best silver foliage plants. The leaves are often aromatic. Most are evergreen, 'Powis Castle' is one of the hardiest.

All artemisias, apart from *A. lactiflora*, need full sun and a well-drained soil. They are drought tolerant once established.

Good companions

Artemisias are particularly useful if you want to create a white border. However, their silver foliage can be combined with almost any colour. *Sedum spectabile* or blue hardy geraniums, for example, are effective partners in a dry border. Where the soil has more moisture, use artemisias to cool down bright phloxes or as an underplanting to red or pink roses. Their feathery texture makes the perfect foil for bold flowers or foliage.

Propagation

Division or cuttings ('Powis Castle' is best propagated from cuttings).

Troubleshooting

Use a well-aimed jet of water from a hose to dislodge any 'cuckoo spit'. If the plants wilt suddenly, dig up and inspect the roots for white root aphids. Remove and destroy affected plants including the roots and surrounding soil. The herbaceous types can be cut down to the ground in late autumn.

Which variety?

The widely available **'Powis Castle'** (syn. *A. arborescens* 'Brass Band') has particularly fine silvery, fern-like leaves and tends to be hardier than some others. The following are also admirable foliage plants: **A. abrotanum** (Southernwood, syn. *A. procera*) a shrubby plant 90–20x45cm (36–48x18in) with very aromatic foliage, prune every spring to keep compact; **A. pontica** is similar but only 60x45cm (24x18in); **A. absinthium 'Lambrook Silver'** a silvery form of the native wormwood. It measures 60x60cm (24x24in); **A. alba 'Canescens'** (syn. *A. canescens*) very finely divided grey foliage forming low dome 45x30cm (18x12in); **A. ludoviciana** (syn. *A. gnaphalodes*) is tall at 120x60cm (48x24in) with light silver-grey leaves. Can be invasive. There are also some good named varieties: **'Latiloba'** is shorter at 60cm (24in), **'Silver Queen'** is 90cm (36in). **A. lactiflora** (white mugwort) is a bit different. It likes a moisture-retentive soil and can cope with partial shade. The leaves are dark green and from August to September there are tiny, greenish cream flowers. It reaches 1.5m (5ft) high but does not need staking. The variety **'Guizhou Group'** (syn. 'Purpurea') has dark stems.

Arum

Arum italicum 'Marmoratum'

Shape and size

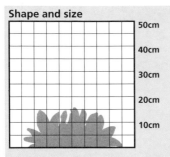

	50cm
	40cm
	30cm
	20cm
	10cm

Position   **Hardiness**   **Soil**

MOIST

Uses

Features calendar

Jan	Feb	Mar	Apr	May	June
July	Aug	Sept	Oct	Nov	Dec

Buying tips *You may find unusual arums listed in bulb catalogues but not all are as hardy as 'Marmoratum'.*

WARNING
The berries of this plant are poisonous.

Arum italicum 'Marmoratum' foliage

Gleaming berries of Arum italicum 'Marmoratum'

Growing guide

One of the few perennials for adding interest in early winter, when new foliage unfurls revealing handsome, arrow-shaped dark green leaves veined with cream. The leaves are also useful for winter flower arrangements.

The leaves may droop in severe cold, but soon revive during mild spells and will last until spring. In spring, the greenish white flowers – the 'lords and ladies' – appear briefly. The leaves disappear by late summer, but spikes of bright orange-red, gleaming berries continue the display – these are poisonous.

The plant is hardy, but a sheltered spot with a fertile soil will produce the best leaves. Plant the dormant tubers 10cm (4in) deep in mid-summer to early autumn, or buy a container-grown plant and plant at any time.

Good companions
Plant with snowdrops to provide autumn and winter interest in a shrub border.

Propagation
Detach offsets from tubers.

Troubleshooting
Generally trouble-free but slugs and snails may eat the young leaves.

Which variety?

A. italicum is variable so it is best to go for a named variety such as **'Marmoratum'** (syn. *A. i.* 'Pictum') which is widely available. You may come across **A. creticum**, which is a striking plant. It is fairly hardy if given a sunny spot and has spear-shaped, green leaves and butter-yellow flowers in spring.

Aruncus

Aruncus dioicus

Shape and size

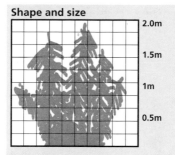

2.0m
1.5m
1m
0.5m

Position

Hardiness

Soil

MOIST

Uses

Features calendar

Jan	Feb	Mar	Apr	May	June
					✿
✿	✿	✿			
July	Aug	Sept	Oct	Nov	Dec

Buying tips *Male plants have better plumes and cannot self-seed. Female plants have seedheads which are excellent for drying.*

Aruncus dioicus 'Glasnevin'

Aruncus dioicus is a good choice for brightening up a semi-shaded area

Growing guide

The elegant, fern-like foliage reaching up to 1.2m (4ft) and the same across makes a superb feature for a large border. Masses of creamy plumes are formed in summer, at which point the height touches 2.1m (7ft). The seedheads (poisonous) of a female plant still look attractive late on in the summer.

A large border with a soil that does not dry out in summer is the ideal spot for aruncus – it is happy in sun or semi-shade. Useful specimen for hiding fences.

Good companions

Use as a background plant for drifts of *Alchemilla mollis*, astilbes, primulas or hostas – either in a moist border or beside a pool. In a mixed border, plant it in front of a dark green or purple shrub. Aruncus flowers at the same time as shrub roses and the two flower types would make a good contrast.

Propagation

Divide every 3 to 5 years.

Troubleshooting

Sawfly larvae may shred the leaves. Remove larvae by hand or spray with contact insecticide.

Which variety?

A. dioicus (syn. *A. plumosus*, *A. sylvestris*) makes the most impressive large clumps. The variety **'Glasnevin'** grows to 1.2m (4ft) but **'Kneiffii'** at 90x45cm (36x18in) is a better choice for smaller gardens.

Asarum

Asarum europaeum

Shape and size

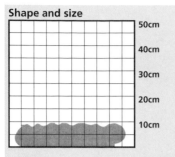

50cm
40cm
30cm
20cm
10cm

Position

Hardiness

Soil

MOIST

Uses

Features calendar

Jan	Feb	Mar	Apr	May	June
July	Aug	Sept	Oct	Nov	Dec

Buying tips *These plants are not widely available, try nurseries specialising in shade or foliage plants.*

Flowers are often hidden under the foliage

Asarum europaeum forms a useful groundcover for a shady spot

Growing guide

Wild ginger was prized by early settlers to North America for its spicy root and aromatic leaves. Today, it is valued for its all-year-round foliage. Another bonus is its ability to cope well with shady positions so long as the soil is cool and moist. Dry soils can be improved by annual additions of garden compost or leafmould.

The leaves are kidney-shaped and a glossy green colour. Bronze flowers appear in late winter to early spring, but these are not striking and are often hidden by the foliage.

Use the plants as an evergreen groundcover – spacing half a dozen plants per square metre.

Good companions

You can create a tapestry effect with wild ginger and other evergreen perennials such as bergenias, euphorbias and epimediums. This could extend the period of interest in shady areas such as mature shrub borders or woodland. In smaller areas, combine asarums with clumps of snowdrops or winter aconites.

Propagation

Division or seed.

Troubleshooting

Generally trouble-free.

Which variety?

A. europaeum tends to grow in clumps. You are most likely to come across it when visiting specialists. **A. caudatum**, another evergreen, has larger leaves and a more spreading habit so is a good choice for groundcover. **A. canadense** is herbaceous i.e. it dies down over winter. It has downy leaves that can irritate the skin.

Asphodeline

Asphodeline lutea

Shape and size

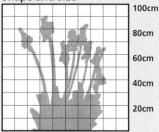

100cm
80cm
60cm
40cm
20cm

Position   Hardiness   Soil

WELL-DRAINED

Uses

Features calendar

Jan	Feb	Mar	Apr	May	June
				❋	❋

July	Aug	Sept	Oct	Nov	Dec
❋	❋				

Buying tips *If difficult to find in your area, try herbaceous specialists or specialist bulb companies (dormant rhizomes are usually despatched in autumn).*

Asphodeline lutea

Growing guide

Despite their exotic appeal, these plants are easy to grow.

A. lutea has blue-grey grassy leaves that are almost evergreen. Spikes of yellow, star-shaped flowers are borne on leafy, unbranched stems. The flowers open irregularly on the spike, which extends the flowering period from late spring to early summer. It has a slight fragrance and after flowering the stems retain attractive seedheads.

Asphodelines are moderately to very hardy, particularly if given a sunny spot with well-drained soil. Plant carefully so as not to damage the fleshy root or rhizome.

Good companions

A useful addition if you are trying to extend the period of interest of a border – interplant with later-flowering plants such as *Sedum spectabile*. It is also suitable for gravel bed plantings alongside phlomis and catmint or Acanthus, or for adding interest to the herb garden.

Propagation

Division or seed, in spring.

Troubleshooting

Generally trouble-free.

Which variety?

The species **A. lutea** is most widely sold, but you may come across a named variety **'Yellow Candle'** (syn. 'Gelbkerze'). **A. liburnica** is similar but is later flowering and has narrower leaves and more slender spikes.

Asphodelus

Growing guide

Asphodelus is closely related to Asphodeline and, like its cousin, needs plenty of sun and a well-drained soil to thrive. *A. ramosus* forms a fair specimen reaching 1.2m (4ft) and the foliage is bolder in outline and the flower spikes are branched. The flowers are white with buff/brown tints and orange anthers.

Good companions

As for *Asphodeline* (above).

Propagation

Division or seed.

Troubleshooting

Generally trouble-free.

Which variety?

A. ramosus (syn. *A. cerasiferus*, *A. lusitanicus*) is the most decorative. **A. albus** is 90x30cm (36x12in) with white flowers, tinted brown in early summer.

Asphodelus albus

Aster

Aster x frikartii 'Mönch'

Shape and size

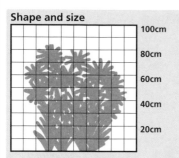

| | 100cm |
| 80cm |
| 60cm |
| 40cm |
| 20cm |

Position · Hardiness · Soil

MOIST

Uses

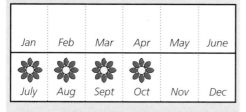

Features calendar

Jan	Feb	Mar	Apr	May	June
✿	✿	✿	✿		
July	Aug	Sept	Oct	Nov	Dec

Buying tips *Buy recently delivered stock in late summer to early autumn so you can select the flower colour you want.*

Aster amellus 'Violet Queen'

Aster x frikartii 'Mönch' and Rudbeckia fulgida 'Deamii'

Growing guide

Strictly speaking, Michaelmas daisies are *A. novi-belgii* and its varieties. These are well-known but require a lot of attention, so it is worth considering other asters instead.

Asters offer autumn flowers – usually from mid-September to the end of October but some, such as *A. x frikartii*, start flowering earlier. Others, like *A. pringlei* 'Monte Cassino', flower until November. Plant all but the mat-forming types in groups of at least three plants so you get a bold splash of colour – it makes staking easier too if this is needed.

All asters do well in sun or light shade, most reasonable soils are suitable, but most asters need to be kept well-watered in dry soils.

Good companions

Asters can be planted in summer to fill gaps left by early flowering plants – their flowers look lovely in silvery, grey or pastel schemes. They are an essential ingredient of beds devoted to plants with autumn colour. Combine with hardy chrysanthemums or Japanese anemones or let autumn foliage and berries form a backdrop to the mauve-pink flowers.

Propagation

Division.

Troubleshooting

A. novi-belgii plants are especially prone to the Michaelmas daisy mite. The flowers are replaced by rosettes of tiny green leaves in September – you may also notice rough, brown scars along the stems. Plants become stunted too. The tiny, cream mites are difficult to spot because they live among the flower buds. Remove and burn infested plants – *A. amellus* and *A. novae-angliae* varieties flower normally when attacked.

Powdery mildew is a problem on some asters, especially in dry, hot spells. Pick off and burn affected parts then spray with systemic fungicide – you may need to repeat spray. Cut down to 10cm (4in) in autumn and burn debris.

Which variety?

For a trouble-free, long-flowering aster for the border we recommend ***A. x frikartii 'Mönch'**. It bears lavender-blue flowers from July to October, 75–90cm (30–36in) tall. Other *A. x frikartii* varieties include: ***'Wunder von Stäfa'** paler flowers, may need staking; and **'Flora's Delight'** 40cm (16in) a newish dwarf aster with lilac flowers and grey foliage. There are many other good asters worth considering. Those marked with ***** flowered well in recent *Gardening Which?* trials.

ITALIAN ASTERS

(*A. amellus*) most 60cm (24in), and flower from August to November: ***'Brilliant'** bright pink; ***'King George'** violet blue; ***'Pink Zenith'** (syn 'Rosa Erfüllung') pink. ***'Violet Queen'** (syn. 'Veilchenkönigin') very attractive blue-violet flowers. Height 50–60 cm (20–25in).

A. cordifolius 1.2m (4ft) needs staking. Star-shaped silvery-blue flowers, August to October.

*A. divaricatus (syn *A. corymbosus*) white, July to September, 60x60cm (24x24in) floppy habit.

HEATH ASTERS

(*A. ericoides*) **'Blue Star'** pale lavender-blue; **'Brimstone'** creamy-yellow; **'Erlkönig'** violet blue; and **'Pink Cloud'** pale lilac-pink. 'Pink Cloud' grows to 1.2–1.5m (4–5ft) but does not need staking.

*A. lateriflorus 'Horizontalis' is 60cm (24in) white, flushed pink in late summer, coppery-purple autumn tints. ***'Prince'** 75cm (30in) dark maroon stems and pink flowers in autumn.

NEW ENGLAND ASTERS

(*A. novae-angliae*) varieties to look out for include: **'Andenken an Alma Pötschke'** cerise-magenta, September to October, 90cm (36in); and **'Autumn Snow'** (syn. 'Herbstschnee') white, August to September, 1.2m (4ft).

MICHAELMAS DAISIES

(*A. novi-belgii*) have drawbacks – apart from pest and disease problems, they can be invasive and self-seed. For the best flowers, divide every two years in spring. Go for the following dwarf varieties: **'Audrey'** light lavender-blue, 40cm (16in); **'Blandie'** semi-double, pure white, 120cm (48in). **'Heinz Richard'** pink, 30cm (12in). **'Jenny'** red-purple, 30cm (12in). **'Lady in Blue'** semi-double, lavender-blue flowers that last only two weeks, 25cm (10in). **'Little Pink Beauty'** mauve-pink, 40cm (16in); **'Marie Ballard'** double, light blue flowers, 90cm (36in). ***'Winston Churchill'** one of the best varieties with a long display of ruby-red flowers, 75cm (30in).

*A. pringlei 'Monte Cassino' (syn. *A. ericoides* 'Monte Cassino') is used in the cut flower trade, but is worth a place in the garden for its habit and late flowering. The bush-like plants at 90–100cm (36–40in) high have masses of pretty, small, white flowers from September to November.

A. sedifolius (syn. *A. acris*) Blue-lilac, 75–120cm (30–48in), needs staking. The variety **'Nanus'** is more compact at 45cm (18in).

*A. thomsonii 'Nanus' is like a miniature *A. x frikartii* with all its merits. Height 50–60cm (20–24 in).

Aster amellus 'King George'

Aster cordifolius

Aster novi-belgii 'Marie Ballard'

Aster 'Winston Churchill'

Astilbe
Astilbe chinensis 'Pumila'

Shape and size

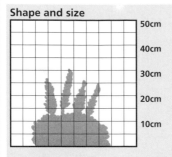

50cm
40cm
30cm
20cm
10cm

Position   Hardiness Soil

MOIST

Uses

Features calendar

Jan	Feb	Mar	Apr	May	June
July	Aug	Sept	Oct	Nov	Dec

Buying tips *Healthy plants reduced in price after flowering or at the end of the season are worth buying as astilbes are hardy and do well when planted in the autumn.*

Astilbe arendsii 'Fanal'

Astilbe chinensis 'Pumila'

Growing guide

Astilbes are one of the best plants for brightening up a moist, lightly shaded spot. Their delicate, feathery plumes in colours ranging from creamy-white through lilac and pink to red, rise above neat mounds of deeply cut foliage in summer. The foliage often has attractive tints and the flowering plumes can be left for winter interest.

Given the right site, they are easy perennials, being very hardy and requiring no support. The vigorous varieties make effective groundcover plants, too. Although most thrive in moist or boggy ground, A. *chinensis* 'Pumila' and A. 'Superba' can cope with drier soils. Astilbes do best in a rich soil and in partial shade – a woodland location between shrubs or by a pond would be ideal. They can tolerate sun if the ground is kept moist by mulching.

Plant in drifts 45–90cm (18–36in) apart depending on whether they are dwarf or vigorous varieties. Shade newly-planted astilbes and water freely until they get established.

Good companions

Combine different varieties to extend the flowering season. Or use the feathery plumes as highlights between foliage bog plants, such as hostas or *Rodgersias*.

Propagation

Divide roots every two to three years.

Troubleshooting

Generally trouble-free, although they dislike chalky soils.

Astilbe 'William Buchanan'

Astilbe 'Deutschland'

Which variety?

We've chosen **A. chinensis 'Pumila'** (syn. *A. pumila*) as a desirable variety that is easy to find. It has pinkish-purple flowers from August to September and is only 30cm (12in) high.

There are many other varieties but specific ones can be hard to track down, so it is best to decide on a flower colour and height and see what varieties you can get.

WHITE

The variety **'Bridal Veil'** (syn. 'Brautschleier') produces open sprays of white flowers which fade to cream, from June to August (75cm/30in). **'Deutschland'** dense spikes from June to August, 60cm (24in). **'Irrlicht'** white flowers from June to August with dark foliage, 60cm (24in). **'Snowdrift'** white flowers from June to August with fresh green foliage, 90cm (36in). **'White Glory'** ('Weisse Gloria') creamy white flowers from June to August, 90cm (36in). **'William Buchanan'** creamy-white to pale pink flowers from June to August with red tints to the foliage, only 25cm (9in).

LILAC

Lilac-rose **'Amethyst'** flowers from June to August, 90cm (36in). **'Superba'** (syn. *A. chinensis taquetii* 'Superba') magenta-mauve blooms in August, dark foliage, 1.2m (4ft).

PINK

Try **'Aphrodite'** for its deep pink flowers from July to September and bronze-green foliage, 35cm (14in). **'Bressingham Beauty'** rich pink flowers from June to August, 90cm (36in). **'Bronze Elegance'** rose-pink flowers from July to September with pretty dark foliage, only 30cm (12in). **'Perkeo'** pink flowers from June to August, 30cm (12in). **'Sprite'** arching sprays of pearl-pink flowers from July to September, 30cm (12in). **'Ostrich Plume'** (syn. 'Straussenfeder') rich coral-pink arching plumes from June to August, 90cm (36in).

RED

Dark crimson **'Fanal'** flowers from June to August, 60cm (24in). **'Federsee'** rose-red from June to August, can tolerate drier areas, 60cm (24in). **'Feuer'** (syn. 'Fire', 'Cherry Ripe') coral-red flowers from July to September, 90cm (36in).

Astilbe x arendsii 'Federsee'

Astrantia

Astrantia major 'Sunningdale Variegated'

Shape and size

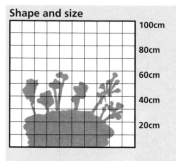

				100cm
				80cm
				60cm
				40cm
				20cm

Position Hardiness Soil

ANY

Uses

Features calendar

Jan	Feb	Mar	Apr	May	June
			🌿	🌿	✿

July	Aug	Sept	Oct	Nov	Dec
✿	✿				

Buying tips Look in garden centres for the ones we have mentioned but for the more unusual varieties try a herbaceous specialist.

Astrantia major involucrata 'Shaggy'

Astrantia major 'Sunningdale Variegated' with crocosmia

Growing guide

Astrantias are dainty-looking plants, with their basal clumps of divided foliage topped with small flowers, usually of whitish-green or blush-pink. At 60cm (24in) high they are an ideal height for the middle of a border. They are easy to please, growing in any soil in either sun or partial shade.

As very few herbaceous perennials boast bright spring foliage, *A. major* 'Sunningdale Variegated' is particularly valued for its new leaves which are splashed with white and yellow. Plant in a sunny spot for the best leaf colour. The markings fade as the leaves age, so by autumn the leaves are green – this can be prevented if you remove the flowers.

Good companions

Most astrantias have soft, quiet colours which fit into most colour schemes. *A. major* 'Sunningdale Variegated' contrasts well with the purple foliage of *Viola labradorica* in spring.

Propagation

Division or seed (variegated forms do not come true from seed).

Troubleshooting

Generally trouble-free.

Which variety?

We've chosen **A. major 'Sunningdale Variegated'** (syn. *A. major* 'Variegata') for its bright spring foliage. You may also come across: **A. major involucrata 'Shaggy'** (syn. 'Margery Fish') which has white flowers with a collar of extra long petals and **A. major 'Rubra'** with plum-coloured flowers.

A. maxima (syn. *A. helleborifolia*) has particularly good pink flowers but it needs a fertile soil.

Baptisia

Baptisia australis

Shape and size

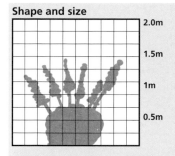

2.0m
1.5m
1m
0.5m

Position Hardiness Soil

MOIST

Uses

Features calendar

Jan	Feb	Mar	Apr	May	June
July	Aug	Sept	Oct	Nov	Dec

Buying tips *Not widely available as plants, although it is stocked by specialists. It can be bought as seed from mail-order seed suppliers.*

Choose a sunny site for Baptisia australis

Baptisia australis

Growing guide

This plant deserves to be more widely grown. It looks a bit like a blue lupin and is an unusual back-of-the-border plant if you can provide the right conditions. It offers early summer interest with its blue-green leaves and summer flowers. The foliage blackens with the first frosts, but the dark grey seed pods can be cut for dried flower arrangements.

This plant does not like being moved, so position it carefully. It is drought-tolerant, but needs plenty of well-rotted organic matter dug in before planting to help the roots penetrate deep into the soil. Avoid chalky soils and shade. The ideal site is a sunny, well-drained spot.

Good companions

As an early summer-flowering plant, put it behind autumn-interest plants such as asters or dahlias.

Propagation

Division or seed.

Troubleshooting

Generally trouble-free if grown in the right conditions and left undisturbed.

Which variety?

B. australis is the best and the one you are most likely to find. Two other species with creamy-white flowers are ***B. lactea*** (syn. *B. leucantha*) and ***B. pendula***. For a dry, wild garden try ***B. tinctoria*** (wild indigo), bright yellow flowers on branched spikes.

Bergenia

Bergenia 'Sunningdale'

Shape and size

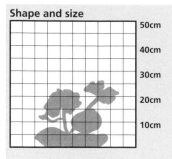

50cm
40cm
30cm
20cm
10cm

Position

Hardiness   Soil

ANY

Uses

Features calendar

| Jan | Feb | Mar | Apr | May | June |

| July | Aug | Sept | Oct | Nov | Dec |

Buying tips *You are most likely to come across B. cordifolia – a dull choice compared with the named varieties recommended here, so it is worth going to a large garden centre or a specialist.*

For winter foliage colour: Bergenia purpurascens

'Sunningdale' combines a neat habit with excellent flowers and winter tints

Growing guide

Bergenias are one of the best groundcover perennials. Their thick, leathery, rounded evergreen leaves pack densely together to suppress weed growth. The leaves are glossy, either dark green or purple, depending on variety, and many take on autumn and winter tints, too. In spring, pink or white flower spikes are produced and add much needed colour to the garden.

Bergenias are tough plants, tolerant of neglect and inhospitable sites. They will grow in any soil from dry to heavy clay and most are completely hardy. Those that can be damaged by frost are best planted away from frost pockets and given a winter mulch of chipped bark, garden compost or well-rotted manure.

In early spring, clear away any dead leaves around the base of the plant then sprinkle a handful of general fertiliser such as growmore around each plant. After flowering, cut out the faded spikes and topdress the plant with growmore at about 30g per sq m (1oz per sq yd).

Early-flowering varieties can be potted up and brought into a cold greenhouse or conservatory for display. Bergenia foliage is useful in winter flower arrangements; the leaves can be treated with glycerine to keep them flexible.

Good companions

Use the bold, evergreen foliage as a permanent edging to a border. The large leaves contrast well with fine-textured plants. Interplant with early spring bulbs such as snowdrops or dwarf narcissi.

Propagation

Division. On a heavy soil, divide in spring.

Troubleshooting

Generally trouble-free, but some varieties can be damaged by frost. Rejuvenate an old specimen by lifting and dividing using secateurs. Replant selected healthy young rhizomes.

'Morning Red' often has a second flush of blooms in September

Bergenia 'Silberlicht' with Stipa calamagrostis

Which variety?

We've chosen **'Sunningdale'** for its excellent winter foliage. It also has carmine flowers on red flower stalks. A hardy variety, it is related to *B. purpurascens* but flowers longer and is a better groundcover plant. Many other colourful varieties exist.

FOR FOLIAGE

All bergenias are ideal foliage plants, but **'Ballawley Hybrids'** have leaves 23cm (9in) across which turn dark red in winter. They are less hardy than most. *B. ciliata* has large, hairy leaves but needs winter protection. **'Baby Doll'** has neat rosettes of leaves only 6.5cm (2½in) across, and is a compact, free-flowering form.

FOR WINTER COLOUR

The foliage of many bergenias develops rich red, bronze or purple shades in winter. In late spring they turn back to green. Colourful choices are *B. purpurascens* (syn. *B. beesiana*, *B. delavayi*), **'Bressingham Ruby'** and **'Eric Smith'**. The latter is hard to obtain.

FOR FLOWERS

Bergenias have much to offer as early-flowering plants but the flowers can be damaged by hard frosts. *B.* x *schmidtii* (syn. *B. crassifolia* 'Orbicularis') with soft pink flowers starts to bloom in January or February and is worth seeking out although it needs shelter. By March, there is **'Evening Glow'** (syn. 'Abendglut') with deep crimson flowers above maroon foliage or **'Morning Red'** (syn. 'Morgenröte') which often has a second flush of flowers in September. Most bergenias flower from April to May. One of the best if you can find it is the large-flowered **'Snow Queen'** (syn. 'Schneekönigin') an excellent groundcover plant. Any of the 'composer' series produce showy flowers (e.g. **'Beethoven'** and **'Brahms'**) but they are not widely available. If you want a white-flowered bergenia, like **'Bressingham White'** or **'Silberlicht'**, remember all-white varieties tend to darken to pink during warmer weather.

'Ballawley Hybrids', one of the best for large leaves

'Brahms' is worth searching out for its flowers

Brunnera

Brunnera macrophylla 'Hadspen Cream'

Shape and size

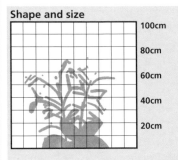

100cm
80cm
60cm
40cm
20cm

Position

Hardiness

Soil

MOIST

Uses

Features calendar

Jan	Feb	Mar	Apr	May	June
			✿	✿	

July	Aug	Sept	Oct	Nov	Dec

Brunnera macrophylla

Buying tips *'Hadspen Cream' is worth tracking down but you may have to go to a specialist nursery. Make sure plants have not been allowed to dry out in the pots. Tip the plant out and inspect the roots.*

Brunnera macrophylla 'Hadspen Cream' has interesting foliage

Growing guide

Brunnera bears intense blue, forget-me-not-like flowers on dark, wiry stems in April and May. These contrast well with the heart-shaped foliage beneath – particularly if a variegated variety is chosen.

This perennial is easy to grow and makes an interesting groundcover in shady or semi-shaded areas. It prefers a soil that does not dry out, so if yours is very free-draining add well-rotted organic matter to the soil before planting. Divide every 2 or 3 years to keep under control and replant young, healthy sections 45cm (18in) apart.

Good companions

Useful as an early-flowering plant in the front of the border. Plant in front or alongside perennials such as Hemerocallis or irises, as their foliage provides an eye-catching contrast to the brunnera's heart-shaped leaves.

Propagation

Division, root cuttings or seed.

Troubleshooting

Generally trouble-free. With variegated forms, remove any reverted green shoots.

Which variety?

We've chosen the fairly new introduction **'Hadspen Cream'** for the extra interest provided by the cream-edged leaves. But the plain-leaved species **B. macrophylla** (syn. *Anchusa myosotidiflora*) is worth growing for its flowers. You may also come across the varieties **'Dawson's White'** (syn. 'Variegata') which will thrive if given a cool, sheltered spot and **'Langtrees'** (syn. 'Aluminium Spot') with silver-grey spots on the leaves.

Caltha

Caltha palustris

Shape and size

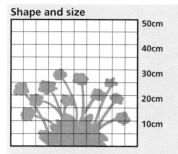

50cm
40cm
30cm
20cm
10cm

Position

Hardiness

Soil

MOIST

Uses

Features calendar

Jan	Feb	Mar	Apr ✿	May ✿	June
July	Aug	Sept	Oct	Nov	Dec

Buying tips *Calthas are best bought early in spring either from an aquatic centre or by mail order from a pond-plant specialist.*

Caltha palustris 'Flore Pleno'

Caltha palustris

Growing guide

Calthas produce large, buttercup-like flowers in early spring that literally glow against a backdrop of dark, rounded leaves. They are hardy plants that grow well in wet, boggy soil or in shallow water up to 15cm (6in) deep. They prefer a neutral to slightly acid soil and a sunny spot but can cope with shade, especially in areas where the soil dries out slightly in the summer.

Plant in autumn or early spring – for impact plant in groups or drifts. The main season of interest is in the spring when the yellow flowers brighten up the pond side or border. After flowering remove any foliage that looks tatty.

Good companions

They make a fine single subject at the side of a pond. Or combine with water irises for a contrast of form.

Propagation

Division from May to June or seed (not double varieties).

Troubleshooting

Generally trouble-free.

Which variety?

Caltha palustris is widely available and one of the best for the naturalness of its single flowers. At 30x40cm (12x16in) it has a neat habit. **C. palustris radicans 'Flore Pleno'** is a double, yellow-flowered variety reaching 15x20cm (6x8in). **C. palustris 'Palustris'** (syn. *C. laeta*) is commonly known as the giant marigold. It is 75cm (30in) tall with large yellow flowers.

You may also come across the variety **'Alba'** 20cm (8in) which has single, white flowers from March to May, which combine well with primulas.

Campanula

Campanula lactiflora 'Prichard's Variety'

Shape and size

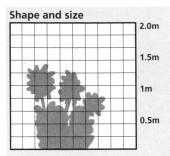

2.0m
1.5m
1m
0.5m

Position

Hardiness   Soil

ANY

Uses

Features calendar

Jan	Feb	Mar	Apr	May	June
✿	✿	✿	✿		
July	Aug	Sept	Oct	Nov	Dec

Buying tips *For the best varieties, you may have to wait until they are sold in larger pots in flower later in the year or buy from a specialist nursery in autumn.*

Campanula lactiflora 'Alba'

Campanula lactiflora 'Prichard's Variety'

Growing guide

Campanulas come in sizes ranging from the delicate harebell to the giant chimney bellflower that tops 2.1m (7ft) – most of the taller ones need staking.

The border campanulas are tolerant of many soils and will thrive in sun or partial shade. The flowers are blue, white or pinkish and the length of the flowering period varies enormously. While some like *C. lactiflora* 'Prichard's Variety' can flower continuously for 11 weeks, other campanulas flower for only three to four weeks.

Good companions

They combine well with other cottage garden plants such as white lilies and deep red peonies. They are ideal partners for shrub roses with pink or cream flowers.

Propagation

Division, seed or basal cuttings.

Troubleshooting

Slugs and snails can be a problem especially when plants are young. Some varieties, such as 'Alba Flore Pleno', 'Bernice' and 'Chettle Charm', are prone to rust. Prevent problems by spacing plants out and getting rid of the weed groundsel, as it acts as an alternative host. A protective spray of dilute Bordeaux mixture is worthwhile on susceptible varieties. Destroy plants that become infected with rust.

Which variety?

Gardening Which? trials have found that **C. lactiflora** and many of its varieties have the most to offer for flowering impact. They have large trusses of flowers that last two to three months. The following were

Campanula lactiflora 'Loddon Anna'

Campanula glomerata 'Dahurica'

outstanding, all are 1.2–1.5m (4–5ft) and need staking. **C. lactiflora**, pale blue flowers from July to August. The variety **'Alba'** has white flowers from July to September. **'Loddon Anna'**, pale pink flowers from July to October. Widely available. **'Prichard's Variety'** lavender-blue flowers from July to October. Widely available.

NO STAKING REQUIRED

If you do not want to stake plants, concentrate on these smaller ones. **C. 'Burghaltii'**, unusual lilac-grey flowers in July to August, 60–70cm (24–30in). The flowers of this variety would combine well with ferns or evergreen shrubs. **C. alliariifolia 'Ivory Bells'**, long white bells from July to August, 60–70cm (24–30in). **C. glomerata 'Dahurica'**, the best cluster-flowered campanula with deep purple flowers from June to July, 70–80cm (30–34in).

OTHERS TO CONSIDER

Below are some campanulas that we have not trialed that you might come across. **C. cochleariifolia 'Elizabeth Oliver'**, pale blue, double flowers, 60cm (24in). **C. garganica 'Dickson's Gold'**, pale blue flowers and golden foliage, 60cm (24in). **C. 'Elizabeth'** is a recent introduction with arching stems of purplish-pink bells from July to September. It makes a 60cm (24in) tall mound, the foliage is light green. **C. 'Kent Belle'**, large blue-violet flowers, often promoted in garden centres, 45cm (18in).

C. lactiflora 'Blue Cross', a new variety with light blue flowers from June to August, 1.2m (4ft). The variety **'Pouffe'** is a dwarf one at 30cm (12in) with a mound-like habit. The flowers are pale blue and last from June to October.

Campanula lactiflora 'Pouffe', a useful dwarf variety

Catananche

Catananche caerulea

Shape and size

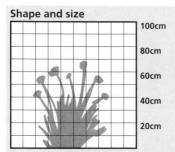

	100cm
	80cm
	60cm
	40cm
	20cm

Position Hardiness Soil

WELL-DRAINED

Uses

Features calendar

Jan	Feb	Mar	Apr	May	June
✿	✿				
July	Aug	Sept	Oct	Nov	Dec

Buying tips *Not widely sold in garden centres, so try herbaceous specialists for plants. However, they can be bought as seed from mail-order seed suppliers.*

Catananche caerulea 'Alba'

Catananche caerulea with Anthemis tinctoria 'E.C. Buxton'

Growing guide

This delightful plant bears a continuous display of cornflower-blue, daisy-like blooms all summer long. The blooms are held on wiry stems up to 75cm (30in) tall and are ideal for cutting and using either fresh or dried in floral arrangements. The plant itself is unobtrusive, forming grassy clumps of grey-green leaves.

Catananches are easy to grow, preferring a sunny spot with good drainage. They are very hardy but tend to be short-lived. Plant in spring or early autumn.

Use them in the middle of a border surrounded by plants that will help support the flowers.

Good companions

Catananche is an ideal plant to include in a cottage-garden style display. Elsewhere, it can look rather sparse, so combine it with silver or grey-leaved foliage plants, such as *Artemisia perovskia* that will help support the wiry flower stems.

Propagation

Seed, but as you can lose the original colours of named varieties, increase these by root cuttings.

Troubleshooting

Generally trouble-free.

Which variety?

The species, **C. caerulea**, produces blue flowers. Height and spread usually 60–75x40–45cm (24–30x16–18in). Other reliable varieties: **'Alba'** has white flowers; **'Bicolor'** is white with purple centres, but varies in height from 45–70cm (18–28in) depending on the source of the plant; **'Major'** is a lavender-blue colour.

Centaurea

Centaurea hypoleuca 'John Coutts'

Shape and size

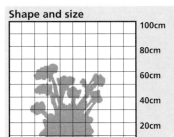

	100cm
	80cm
	60cm
	40cm
	20cm

Position   Hardiness   Soil

Uses

Features calendar

Jan	Feb	Mar	Apr	May ✿	June ✿
July ✿	Aug	Sept ✿	Oct	Nov	Dec

Buying tips *C. macrocephala can be bought cheaply in small pots in early spring, but the more unusual varieties will have to be purchased later on or from specialists.*

Centaurea montana with Papaver orientale

Centaurea hypoleuca 'John Coutts'

Growing guide

These are easy-to-please plants that will thrive in sunny spots on most soils. A fairly dry, poor soil is preferable as they can be invasive in rich, moisture-retentive soils.

The colours range from blue to lilac, pink, white or even yellow. Some are low, carpeting plants for the front of a border, for edging or groundcover. But there are taller ones for the middle of the border and some with thistle-like flowers are suitable for a wild garden.

All *Centaureas* will flower for longer if regularly dead-headed. *C. hypoleuca* should be trimmed after flowering to encourage new growth at the centre of the plant.

Good companions

Those with silver-tinged foliage and blue, pink or white flowers look lovely planted in front of silver foliage plants. Those with yellow, thistle-like flowers can be teamed with purple flowers such as *Salvia* x *superba* or the deep red valerian.

In a wild garden, the British natives can be planted in grass to act as a source of nectar for butterflies and bees. Or you could create a cornfield effect by combining them with poppies, corncockle and white ox-eye daisies.

Propagation

Division, seed or heeled cuttings.

Troubleshooting

To prevent vigorous spreaders taking over a border, lift and split clumps every two to three years in spring. Treat powdery mildew promptly with a suitable fungicide.

Which variety?

We've chosen **C. hypoleuca 'John Coutts'** (syn. *C. dealbata* 'John Coutts') for its grey-green foliage and large rose-pink flowers with a yellow centre. It flowers from May to July and again in early autumn. It is not invasive and does not need staking, 60cm (24in). Others worth considering are:

FRONT OF BORDER
The straggly **C. montana** needs staking but is good for chalky soils. Deep blue flowers May-June, 45x60cm (18x24in). Named varieties in white, pink or lavender from specialists. **C. pulcherrima** has a neat, clump-forming habit and does not need staking. Bright pink blooms June–July, 60x30cm (24x12in).

MID-BORDER
The spreading **C. dealbata** has grey-green foliage and lilac-pink flowers June-July. 75x60cm (30x24in). Needs staking. **'Steenbergii'** has reddish-pink flowers with a white centre. Spreading and invasive, 75x60cm (30x24in). **C. macrocephala** has yellow, thistle-like blooms that can be dried for floral arrangements. 120x60cm (48x24in).

EDGING/GROUNDCOVER
Well-behaved **C. bella** has grey foliage and pink flowers May–August. 23x45cm (9x18in). **C. simplicicaulis** has grey foliage and pink flowers May–June. 23x23cm (9x9in). Can be invasive in moist soils. **C. triumfettii cana 'Rosea'** forms 60cm (24in) wide mats of narrow, silver leaves and mauve flowers May–June.

WILD GARDEN
Black knapweed, **C. nigra**, red-purple thistles, July-September, 60x30cm (24x12in). **C. scabiosa** (greater knapweed) is similar but with lobed foliage.

Centranthus (Kentranthus)
Centranthus ruber

Shape and size

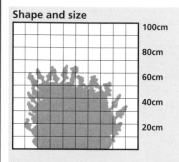

100cm
80cm
60cm
40cm
20cm

Position Hardiness Soil

WELL-DRAINED

Uses

Features calendar

Jan	Feb	Mar	Apr	May	June
✿	✿	✿	✿		
July	Aug	Sept	Oct	Nov	Dec

Buying tips *Buy in small pots in early spring. Grown from seed, it should flower in the first year. Try herbaceous specialists for more unusual varieties.*

Centranthus ruber with Alchemilla mollis

Centranthus ruber 'Atrococcineus' is worth searching for

Growing guide

The deep reddish-pink clusters of star-shaped flowers of red valerian give it a very informal look in planting schemes. At 60x45cm (24x18in), the plants can be placed at the front or in the middle of borders where the most can be made of their long flowering period. The leaves are a grey-green and have a distinctive odour if crushed.

Red valerian is a familiar sight in summer growing out of walls, on stony ground and chalky soils. This inherent toughness makes it a good choice for seaside gardens with poor, well-drained soils, but they do need sun to flower well. Plant in early to mid-spring. Cut down dead growth in autumn. If self-seeding is a problem, cut back hard in July after their first flowering.

Good companions

Combine with golden rod (*Solidago*) or knapweeds (*Centaurea*) in a wild garden or use as a cottage garden plant. In a more formal setting, they can be planted to make repeated groups along the length of a border, with other plants such as *Nepeta* and *Monarda*.

Propagation

Seed (saved seed often gives a mixture of shades).

Troubleshooting

Generally trouble-free.

Which variety?

C. ruber and the white form **'Albus'** are widely available. You may also come across red varieties such as **'Atrococcineus'** and **'Coccineus'** in specialist nursery catalogues.

Chelone

Chelone obliqua

Shape and size

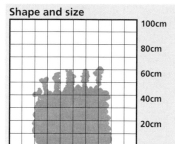

Position

Hardiness

Soil

 MOIST

Uses

Features calendar

Jan	Feb	Mar	Apr	May	June
July	Aug	Sept	Oct	Nov	Dec

Buying tips *Buy a few, small plants – they will soon increase rapidly from the roots, or try growing from seed.*

Chelone lyonii

Chelone obliqua

Growing guide

A distinctive plant that can be relied upon to provide interesting late summer colour. Each flower is said to look like a turtle's head or snapdragon. Growing to around 60cm (24in), this plant is ideal for the centre of a border. It has a stiff, upright habit and spikes of rose-pink flowers from August to October. In the wild, these plants are to be found in waterside areas in eastern North America. However, in gardens they will tolerate a wider ranges of soils. Most borders or beds where the soil has been improved and mulched will provide sufficient moisture in late spring to summer.

Chelones are easy to grow in sun or partial shade and they prefer a deep, moist soil.

Good companions

Useful as a filler between other autumn-flowering plants such as asters and sedums. Alternatively, add a few plants to a herb garden to provide end-of-season interest. Chelone was used by native Indians and settlers in North America as a tonic.

Propagation

Division in spring or autumn. Or raise from seed either under glass in early spring or outdoors in early summer.

Troubleshooting

They may need staking in exposed borders but are otherwise trouble-free.

Which variety?

C. obliqua is widely available but you may come across **C. lyonii** which is taller at 90cm (36in) with clusters of pink flowers.

Cimicifuga

Cimicifuga racemosa

Shape and size

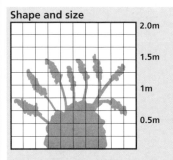

2.0m
1.5m
1m
0.5m

Position   Hardiness   Soil

MOIST

Uses

Features calendar

Jan	Feb	Mar	Apr	May	June
✿	✿	✿			
July	Aug	Sept	Oct	Nov	Dec

Cimicifuga racemosa flowers from July to September

Buying tips Check the plants have not been allowed to dry out in their pots. Inspect the roots before buying.

Cimicifuga simplex 'White Pearl'

Growing guide

These unusual plants have white or cream flower heads that look like bottle brushes and elegant foliage. They are sturdy and easy to grow – even the tallest species, which top 2.1m (7ft), do not need staking.

Give them a cool, moist position such as by a pond. They are perennials that are best left undisturbed once planted. The only regular care they need is a generous dressing of leafmould or garden compost in spring.

Good companions

Use as a background plant to the vivid colours of phlox. The purple-leaved bugbane would enhance a late aconitum such as
A. carmichaelli 'Arendsii' or a golden-leaved grass like
Hakonechloa macra 'Aureola'.

Propagation

Division, every four years.

Troubleshooting

Generally trouble-free.

Which variety?

C. racemosa is a stunning species that can be obtained from a number of specialists. There are others that flower later in September to October. These include the shorter **C. simplex** and its varieties at 120x60cm (48x24in). **'Atropurpurea Group'** (syn. *C. racemosa* 'Purpurea') is widely available with the bonus of dark purple foliage to contrast with the flowers. You may also come across named varieties like **'White Pearl'** and **'Elstead's Variety'**, the latter has purplish buds before the white flowers.

Cirsium

Cirsium rivulare 'Atropurpureum'

Shape and size

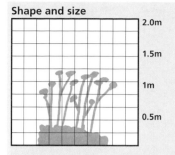

- 2.0m
- 1.5m
- 1m
- 0.5m

Position

Hardiness

Soil

MOIST

Uses

Features calendar

Jan	Feb	Mar	Apr	May	June
✿	✿				
July	Aug	Sept	Oct	Nov	Dec

Buying tips *You are unlikely to find cirsiums at garden centres. Try wild flower or native plant specialists or grow from seed.*

Meadow thistle (Cirsium dissectum)

Cirsium rivulare 'Atropurpureum'

Growing guide

Cirsiums are a group of thistle-type plants useful when planting a wildlife garden. Some of the named varieties could be included in a border where their pink or crimson thistles would be a talking point.

The plants will grow in most soils except those that remain wet. They will tolerate quite dry conditions, but do best in a moist soil. They prefer sun but will grow in partial shade.

Good companions

Combine with other summer-flowering wild flowers, such as *Monarda*, red or white flowered valerian or with pale blue flowers.

Propagation

Division, root cuttings or seed.

Troubleshooting

Generally trouble-free but the roots can be invasive. Some are self-seeding.

Which variety?

C. rivulare 'Atropurpureum' for its crimson thistles. You may also come across varieties of **C. japonicum** such as **'Pink Beauty'**, **'Rose Beauty'** and **'Strawberry Ripple'** which have long been used in Japan as cut flowers.

Wild flower specialists may stock meadow thistle (**C. dissectum**) which is 60cm (24in) tall with purple flowers from June to August. The melancholy thistle, **C. heterophyllum** (syn. *C. helenioides*), is 50cm (20in) and starts flowering a month later with mauve thistles.

Clematis (herbaceous)

Clematis heracleifolia 'Davidiana'

Shape and size

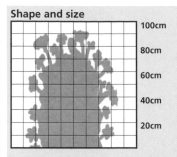

100cm
80cm
60cm
40cm
20cm

Position   Hardiness   Soil

WELL-DRAINED

Uses

Features calendar

Jan	Feb	Mar	Apr	May	June
✶	✶	✶	⚘	⚘	
July	Aug	Sept	Oct	Nov	Dec

Buying tips *For herbaceous clematis you will probably need to go to a herbaceous or clematis specialist.*

Many varieties produce attractive seedheads

Clematis heracleifolia 'Davidiana'

Growing guide

Unlike their well-known large-flowered climbing cousins, these herbaceous clematis grow to only 90cm (36in). In late autumn or spring, cut back stems to 15cm (6in) above the ground.

They produce scrambling stems that do not climb, but can look most effective trained through a neighbouring shrub or allowed to sprawl over evergreen groundcover. The plant can be supported with twiggy sticks.

In late summer clusters of blue flower heads are borne along the trailing stems and are followed by silky seedheads in autumn. The flowers are also useful for cutting.

They like a sunny position but any fertile, well-drained soil will suit them and they thrive in chalky soils.

Good companions

Grey-leaved shrubs enhance the blue flowers and provide reliable support. Yellow crocosmias would contrast well.

Propagation

Take basal cuttings in April or May.

Troubleshooting

They are subject to the same problems as the climbing clematis, namely slugs, wilt and powdery mildew.

Which variety?

C. heracleifolia **'Davidiana', 'Côte d'Azur'** and **'Wyevale'** have scented, small blue flowers with attractive seedheads, on plants 90cm (36in) high. **C. x durandii** has 7.5cm (3in) flowers of deep blue. It grows 1.5m (5ft) but has a non-clinging semi-herbaceous habit. **C. integrifolia** and its varieties are 75cm (30in) high with 5cm (2in) flowers that are scented and are followed by attractive seedheads. The species is dark blue, but there are named varieties in other colours such as the pink **'Rosea'**.

Codonopsis

Codonopsis clematidea

Shape and size

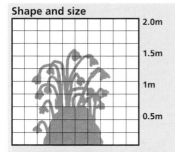

2.0m
1.5m
1m
0.5m

Position   Hardiness   Soil

MOIST

Uses

Features calendar

Jan	Feb	Mar	Apr	May	June
✿	✿	✿			
July	Aug	Sept	Oct	Nov	Dec

Buying tips *You will have to go to a nursery specialising in unusual plants. Most codonopsis are sold as small plants and can be expensive. Check the plant is healthy and well-rooted.*

Codonopsis convolvulacea

Codonopsis clematidea

Growing guide

This unusual hardy perennial is almost, but not quite, a climber. It has a twining habit allowing it to be grown against a pergola pillar or through a shrub. Alternatively, it can be grown in a border if supported by twiggy sticks.

To appreciate its lovely blue, bell-shaped flowers, plant it so you can look up at it – a raised bed by a patio would be ideal. However, some consider it to have an unpleasant smell.

This plant will grow in most conditions but prefers some shade and a humus-rich soil. Dig in plenty of garden compost or leafmould before planting. Once planted, leave undisturbed so it can establish itself. Dead stems can be cut down in autumn.

Good companions

Plant with other 'cool' coloured plants such as blue or white *Clematis alpina* or *C. macropetala*.

Propagation

Seed or cuttings.

Troubleshooting

Generally trouble-free.

Which variety?

The most commonly available, **C. clematidea**, has an orange and maroon centre to each bloom, but you need to lift the flowers up and look inside. **C. convolvulacea** and **C. vinciflora**, which is very similar, are both species that are worth searching for. Other codonopsis available do not twine and prefer a well-drained soil. These are generally blue-flowered perennials reaching 60x60cm (24x24in).

Convallaria

Convallaria majalis

Shape and size

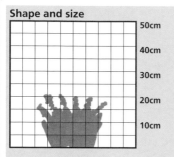

50cm
40cm
30cm
20cm
10cm

Position

Hardiness

Soil

MOIST

Uses

Features calendar

Jan	Feb	Mar	Apr	May	June
July	Aug	Sept	Oct	Nov	Dec

Buying tips *Offered by mail-order bulb companies as well as herbaceous specialists. Named varieties are much more expensive than the species.*

WARNING

All parts of this plant are poisonous.

Convallaria majalis

Growing guide

Lily-of-the-valley is a popular perfume yet the plant is not widely sold or planted these days. It will make a luxuriant carpet of fresh green in moist shade. In the border, it offers early flowers during April and May. Sometimes these are followed by small berries.

Lily-of-the-valley requires humus-rich, fairly moist soil to do well. It tolerates shade, especially beneath deciduous trees.

Good companions

Plant under or beside foliage plants that like moist shade such as hostas or arums. *Omphalodes cappadocica* with blue flowers in spring to summer would be an ideal flowering partner.

Propagation

Division.

Troubleshooting

After several years, the numbers of flowers on the plants may decrease.

In spring or autumn, lift and divide the rhizomes using a fork. Choose healthy, fist-sized crowns. Dig in 35g per sq m (1oz per sq yd) of growmore and replant the clumps 15cm (6in) apart. Topdress in spring with 30g per sq m (1oz per sq yd) of sulphate of potash before applying a mulch.

Which variety?

C. majalis is the native species which is perfectly suitable for the garden. You may come across the following named varieties. **'Fortin's Giant'** has large flowers which appear a week or two later than the species. **'Hardwick Hall'** blooms are larger still, with a pale-green margin on the leaves. **'Rosea'** has mauve-pink flowers.

C. majalis **'Variegata'** has golden stripes on its leaves – best if given some sun, if there is too much shade the leaves will turn plain green.

Coreopsis
Coreopsis verticillata 'Grandiflora'

Shape and size

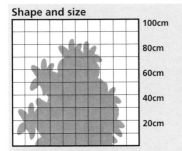

Position Hardiness Soil

Uses

Features calendar

Jan	Feb	Mar	Apr	May	June
✿	✿	✿	✿		
July	Aug	Sept	Oct	Nov	Dec

Buying tips *C. verticillata 'Grandiflora' is available at larger garden centres and specialists. Make sure, however, that you do not get the inferior C. grandiflora by mistake.*

'American Dream'

Coreopsis verticillata 'Grandiflora'

Growing guide

Coreopsis are easy to grow and quickly make excellent fillers that will flower all summer. Their yellow, daisy-like flowers are a valuable source of pollen and nectar so are popular with bees and butterflies.

The foliage is attractive too: finely cut and feathery, ranging in colour from bright green to grey depending on the variety.

Some, such as the *C. verticillata* varieties make reliable perennials as they will last through the winter, but others such as the *C. grandiflora* varieties are best grown as showy annuals.

Grow in a sunny place. They prefer a well-drained soil and one that does not dry out in summer. Most do not need staking, apart from *C. grandiflora* 'Mayfield Giant'. All can be cut for use in floral arrangements.

Good companions

These are ideal plants for front- or mid-border, depending on size. Their soft outlines make a fine contrast with bolder plants such as bronze-leaved cannas or phormiums.

Propagation

Division or seed.

Troubleshooting

Generally trouble-free, but the perennial ones are easiest.

Which variety?

Gardening Which? trials of nine varieties found that for flowering impact nothing can beat *C. verticillata* 'Grandiflora'. This plant is 70–90cm (28–36in) high with large flowers.

Other *C. verticillata* varieties also did well in the trial, although their flowers were smaller. These varieties have fine feathery foliage. **'Moonbeam'** has soft yellow flowers and is 50–70cm (20–28in) high with a lax habit. **'Zagreb'** has bright yellow flowers and a dwarf habit at 25–30cm (10–12in).

You may come across the pink-flowered **C. rosea**. This is a dwarf plant at 25–30cm (10–12in) that flowers from August to September. The variety **'American Dream'** is very similar but flowers for a month longer.

Corydalis
Corydalis flexuosa

Shape and size

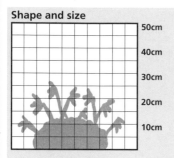

50cm
40cm
30cm
20cm
10cm

Position

Hardiness

Soil

MOIST

Uses

Features calendar

Jan	Feb	Mar	Apr	May	June
		✿	✿		
July	Aug	Sept	Oct	Nov	Dec

Buying tips *You may find young plants in the alpine section at garden centres as well as with the perennials.*

Corydalis solida transsylvanica 'George Baker'

Corydalis flexuosa 'Père David'

Growing guide

Corydalis are small plants with delicate, fern-like foliage, which is topped with small, spurred flowers – usually yellow or blue depending on the species. They are ideal for using to soften paving, rockeries and garden walls. The common corydalis (*C. lutea*) is often seen self-seeding in such situations.

The growing conditions they require depend on the species. *C. flexuosa* does best in shade in a humus-rich soil, while some species like *C. cashmeriana* prefer to be in an alpine house. *C. lutea* is less fussy and grows anywhere.

Good companions

C. flexuosa combines well with other woodland-type plants such as arums and lily-of-the-valley and can be used to carpet ground between shrubs and trees. *C. flexuosa* makes an attractive container plant.

Propagation

Seed (use as fresh as possible).

Troubleshooting

Generally trouble-free, but you will need to pull up those that self-seed.

Which variety?

Corydalis flexuosa is widely available from specialists and so are many of its varieties such as **'China Blue'**, **'Père David'** and **'Purple Leaf'**. These are very similar, the plants are 30–45cm (12–18in) tall with blue flowers in spring, but there are slight differences in the foliage. These all make interesting garden plants and are easy to grow. **C. cashmeriana** has blue flowers and is only 15cm (6in). It is difficult to grow outdoors in southern England as it needs cool, humid conditions and a humus-rich soil free of lime. **C. cheilanthifolia** has yellow flowers, it self-seeds like *C. lutea*, but has better, fern-like foliage. Height 15–25cm (6–10in). **C. solida** is 15cm (6in) tall, has murky red flowers and self-seeds. There are many named varieties.

Crambe

Crambe cordifolia

Shape and size

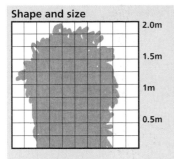

2.0m
1.5m
1m
0.5m

Position   Hardiness

Soil   Uses

WELL-DRAINED

Features calendar

Jan	Feb	Mar	Apr	May	June
July	Aug	Sept	Oct	Nov	Dec

Buying tips *If you cannot find plants on sale you can buy seakale as seed, root cuttings ('thongs') or crowns by mail order.*

Vegetable seakale (Crambe maritima)

Crambe cordifolia erupts with billowing clouds of tiny flowers in early summer

Growing guide

If you have got the space, there is little to equal the impact of giant seakale in full bloom. Huge billowing clouds of tiny white flowers reaching up to 2.4m (8ft) high and 1.5m wide are borne in early summer. It is best grown behind other plants where its rather dull mound of rough leaves are hidden from view.

Choose a sheltered spot. A light soil in full sun is best but it can cope with partial shade. Cut down to ground level in autumn and mulch the root area in spring.

Good companions

Use as a backdrop to plants with large flowers or plant it in front of plants you want to hide in summer – a spring-flowering shrub, for instance.

Propagation

Seed (takes three years to flower) or root cuttings.

Troubleshooting

Watch out for slugs, snails, caterpillars and whitefly.

Which variety?

If you have the room, go for **C. cordifolia** – it is the best species and is widely available.

For something smaller, vegetable seakale (**C. maritima**) is worth growing as an ornamental plant. When in flower it reaches 90cm (36in) and has glaucous leaves with crinkled edges.

Crocosmia

Crocosmia 'Lucifer'

Shape and size

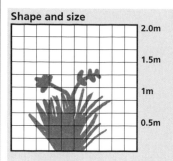

2.0m
1.5m
1m
0.5m

Position

Hardiness

Soil

MOIST

Uses

Features calendar

Jan	Feb	Mar	Apr	May	June
July	Aug	Sept	Oct	Nov	Dec

(June and July marked with flower symbols)

Buying tips *Buy established plants in pots or get bare-rooted plants from mail-order specialists. Avoid plants with flecked or discoloured foliage and those that have been allowed to dry out in their pots.*

'Canary Bird'

Crocosmia 'Lucifer' adds fiery highlights to a summer border

Growing guide

Crocosmias in bloom provide intense colour in high summer and have grassy or sword-like foliage. They look stunning from a distance but the flowers are also interesting close to and make ideal cut flowers.

They tolerate most types of soil but need protecting from drought by mulching and extra watering if the soil is free-draining. The site should catch the sun or be in partial shade. Not all varieties are hardy in all areas, if in doubt provide an insulating mulch of chipped bark over winter or grow in pots under cover. Planting is best done in late spring.

Good companions

Red and orange varieties combine well with flowering plants such as heleniums, coreopsis and red hot pokers, or with silver foliage plants. The yellow varieties are softer and work well with blue flowers such as eryngiums and blue salvias. Or combine with purple foliage plants.

Propagation

Division, every 3–4 years.

Troubleshooting

Generally trouble-free but not all are fully hardy and *C.* x *crocosmiiflora* can be invasive.

Which variety?

We've chosen **'Lucifer'**, a fully hardy variety . It is very imposing, standing 120x30cm (48x12in) tall with intense red flowers.

If you live in a cold area, concentrate on red or red-orange varieties as these are hardier than the pinks and yellows. One exception is 'Jenny Bloom' one of the few hardy yellows. Widely available varieties tend to be tougher than unusual varieties. In mild areas most varieties will be hardy once established except perhaps 'Solfatarre'.

Crocosmia 'Vulcan'

All the following flower from July to August unless otherwise stated.

RED
'Lucifer' bright red flowers from June to July, 120cm (48in). **'Vulcan'** burnt-red flowers, 75cm (30in).

YELLOW
'Canary Bird' yellow flowers, 75cm (30in). **'Jenny Bloom'** pale yellow flowers, 90cm (36in). One of the few hardy yellow varieties.
'Citronella' (plants labelled as this could be 'Golden Fleece', 'George Davidson', 'Rowden Chrome') golden yellow flowers, 75cm (30in).
'Norwich Canary' (syn. 'Lady Wilson') pure yellow flowers, 60cm (24in). **'Solfatarre'** pale-apricot yellow flowers from July to September with bronze-coloured foliage, 60cm (24in).

ORANGE-RED/ORANGE-YELLOW
'Emberglow' orange-red flowers, 75cm (30in). **'Emily McKenzie'** (syn. 'Lady McKenzie) dark orange flowers with a red centre August to October, 60cm (24in). **'Firebird'** orange-red flowers from July to September, 60cm (24in).
'Jackanapes' (syn. 'Fire King') orange and yellow flowers July to September, 60cm (24in). **'James Coey'** orange-red flowers August to September 75 cm (30in). **'Lady Hamilton'** soft orange flowers with an apricot eye, 90cm (36in). **C. masoniorum** bright orange flowers, 75cm (30in).
C. paniculata (syn. *Curtonus paniculatus, Antholyza paniculata*) orange-red flowers July to September, 120cm (48in). **'Severn Sunrise'** orange flowers tinged with pink as they fade from August to September, 60cm (24in). **'Spitfire'** orange-red flowers July to September, 75cm (30in). **'Star of the East'** reddish buds opening to soft apricot-orange flowers, 60cm (24in).

PINK
C. Rosea (syn. *Tritonia rubrolucens*) soft pink flowers, 60cm (24in).

Crocosmia masoniorum

Crocosmia 'Jackanapes'

Cynara

Cynara cardunculus

Shape and size

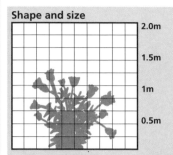

2.0m
1.5m
1m
0.5m

Position   Hardiness   Soil

MOIST

Uses

Features calendar

Jan	Feb	Mar	Apr	May	June
July	Aug	Sept	Oct	Nov	Dec

Buying tips *If you cannot get hold of plants locally, look for cardoons and globe artichokes in the vegetable section of seed catalogues.*

Cynara cardunculus

Cynara scolymus

Growing guide

This group of thistle-like plants includes the cardoon and globe artichoke. Both are perennial vegetables, but also make stately specimens for the large border. They produce handsome foliage and dramatic purple thistle flower heads. Foliage and flowers are both useful for floral arrangements – the flowers can be cut and dried for winter decorations, too.

The cardoon is the best choice for foliage interest in the garden. The leaves reach up to 1.2m (4ft) long, and are deeply cut with a distinctive silvery sheen, yet they are not prickly. To get the most impressive foliage display, remove the flowering stems in summer.

The cardoon and the globe artichoke need to be planted in spring in a sunny, well-drained site. Give them plenty of room – at least a 1.2m (4ft) square. Dig in lots of well-rotted organic matter. Except in mild areas, protect the crowns with a 15cm (6in) layer of straw, or use a cloche. Mulch well the following spring.

Good companions

Try growing them at the back of a border to add summer interest to spring-flowering shrubs. This will also hide the gap that appears when their foliage dies down. Alternatively, allow them to grow up through a mixture of dainty cottage garden plants, such as aquilegias and honesty.

Propagation

Division, root cuttings or seed.

Troubleshooting

Generally trouble-free.

Which variety?

The cardoon (**C. cardunculus**) produces the best display of foliage and in summer the thistles can reach 2.1m (7ft). The globe artichoke (**C. scolymus**) is similar, but the foliage is less decorative. Both are widely available.

Dactylorhiza

Dactylorhiza foliosa

Shape and size

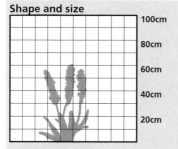

100cm
80cm
60cm
40cm
20cm

Position

Hardiness

Soil

WELL-DRAINED

Uses

Features calendar

Jan	Feb	Mar	Apr	May	June
July	Aug	Sept	Oct	Nov	Dec

Buying tips *Hardy orchids are expensive and in short supply. This can encourage unscrupulous collectors to dig them up from the wild and sell them. Contact Fauna & Flora International on 01223 461471 for* The Good Bulb Guide *which lists suppliers that raise their own plants.*

Dactylorhiza elata

Dactylorhiza foliosa

Growing guide

The marsh orchid (*Dactylorhiza*) includes several species that make good perennials for the border or which can be naturalised in a meadow if their requirements can be met. These are hardy terrestrial orchids so are easy to grow. The main feature is the clusters of purple flowers on stout stems in early summer.

They need normal garden soil supplemented with garden compost. Most species will not grow well in clay, chalk or sandy soils and all need partial shade. However, some species, such as the common spotted orchid (*D. fuchsii*) can be found naturally in meadows on chalk downland.

They grow from tubers, which duplicate themselves each year. Plant 23–25cm (9–10in) apart and 8cm (3in) deep.

Good companions

If you grow them in a border, combine with dainty, soft-textured plants such as violas or *Corydalis*.

Propagation

Division of the tubers in early spring.

Troubleshooting

Generally trouble-free.

Which variety?

We pick **D. foliosa** (Madeira orchid) which has pale purple flowers, 60cm (24in). **D. elata** is similar with darker blooms. **D. fuchsii** (common spotted orchid) lilac flowers, spotted leaves, 60cm (24in). Found on chalk downland. **D. incarnata** a smaller orchid at only 25–40cm high (10–16in) with pink/lilac flowers. **D. maculata** (heath spotted orchid) white, pink, mauve or red flowers, spotted leaves. **D. majalis** (marsh orchid) purple flowers, 45cm (18in) or more.

Delphinium
Delphinium 'Blue Nile'

Shape and size

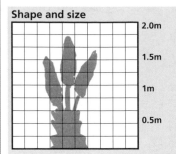

2.0m
1.5m
1m
0.5m

Position · **Hardiness** · **Soil**

WELL-DRAINED

Uses

Features calendar

Jan	Feb	Mar	Apr	May	June
					✿
July	Aug	Sept	Oct	Nov	Dec
✿					

Delphinium 'Blue Nile'

Buying tips *The cheaper delphiniums sold in garden centres as 'Pacific Hybrids' or as 'Black Knight', 'Guinevere' and 'King Arthur' are fairly short-lived perennials. Either raise your own plants from seed or buy named varieties from specialist nurseries.*

'Fenella'

Growing guide

Delphiniums are a magnificent sight and one of the most admired cottage garden plants. In mid-summer they throw up towering spires in every shade of blue, but there are also white, cream, lilac, purple and pink varieties.

They grow best in full sun or where they will get sunshine for at least half the day. They can be grown in a wide range of soils, but will rot over winter if the soil becomes waterlogged. In summer, they will thrive if given as much water as possible and a good supply of nutrients. By digging in plenty of garden compost or well-rotted manure prior to planting, you will improve the soil's ability to hold water without waterlogging. A sheltered site is best, as this will prevent wind damage to the flower spikes. Some delphiniums, such as 'Mighty Atom', 'Lord Butler' and 'Loch Leven' have spikes that can cope quite well with windy conditions .

Spring is the ideal time to plant rooted cuttings. Rake in 100g per sq m (4oz per sq yd) of a general fertiliser such as growmore before planting. Space plants 75cm (30in) apart.

Once the plants reach 30cm (12in), mulch the surrounding soil, but do not let the mulch build up around the stems or they may rot. At this time, cut off any extra shoots, leaving just five to ten to grow into big spikes. For lighter, more graceful spikes, pinch out the tips when they are about 30cm (12in) high to encourage side shoots. Stake plants well. After flowering remove faded spikes promptly to encourage later-flowering shoots to develop.

Delphiniums make impressive cut flowers, and can be dried too, but take care when handling them as they can be an irritant.

Good companions

The best companion for a stunning flowering combination must surely be roses. However, in a mixed border it is worth growing late-flowering plants such as asters, dahlias and Japanese anemones around delphiniums to extend the display. Achilleas cover up the spent delphiniums well too.

Propagation

Seed, or heeled basal cuttings in early spring.

Troubleshooting

Slugs are the worst problem so apply slug pellets after planting and early in spring. Powdery mildew may be a problem in late summer, spray with a systemic fungicide at the first sign of the disease. Taller forms will need staking.

'Sungleam'

'Michael Ayres'

Which variety?

It is worth buying named varieties from a specialist nursery, as the plants will last for three or four years and you will be able to choose from a wider range of sizes and colours. We recommend the *D. elatum* varieties, they range in height from 0.9–1.8m (3–6ft) and are available in white, cream, pink and purple as well as blue. We've picked the variety **'Blue Nile'** as one of the best examples. It has pure mid-blue flowers and is a mid-season variety that reaches 1.2–1.5m (4–5ft) in height. Other good *D. elatum* hybrids to look out for (all are mid-season and around 1.5m (5ft) unless otherwise stated) are as follows:

BLUES

'Blue Dawn' late; **'Faust'**; **'Fenella'**; **'Gillian Dallas'** late, needs thinning to obtain good blooms, has large florets, do not overfeed; **'Gordon Forsyth'** late, susceptible to mildew but has large florets; **'Loch Leven'** early to mid-season; **'Lord Butler'** only 1.2m (4ft); **'Mighty Atom'** late, 1.2m (4ft), susceptible to mildew but has large florets, do not overfeed; **'Pericles'**; **'Spindrift'** an early variety with large, turquoise florets.

PURPLES

'Bruce' susceptible to mildew but has large florets; **'Cassius'** late; **'Emily Hawkins'**; **'Fanfare'** early; **'Michael Ayres'** early to mid-season, 1.8m (6ft); **'Min'** pale lavender with dark veins; **'Nimrod'** up to 1.8m (6ft); **'Nobility'**; **'Tiddles'** almost double flowers.

PINKS

'Rosemary Brock' needs thinning to obtain the best blooms; **'Royal Flush'** 1.2–1.5m (4–5ft).

CREAMS/WHITES

'Olive Poppleton' early, needs thinning to obtain good blooms; **'Sandpiper'** early to mid-season, 1.2–1.5m (4–5ft), large florets; **'Sungleam'** creamy yellow, 1.2–1.5m (4–5ft), needs thinning to obtain good blooms.

Another type to look out for are the **Belladonna** forms. These make compact plants that are ideal for informal plantings. If they are deadheaded they will flower through summer into autumn. The following are all 75cm (30in) high. **'Casa Blanca'**, white flowers from June to October; **'Cliveden Beauty'**, light blue flowers from July to October; **'Piccolo'**, gentian-blue flowers from June to October.

'Lord Butler'

'Gillian Dallas'

Dendranthema
Dendranthema 'Clara Curtis'

Shape and size

100cm
80cm
60cm
40cm
20cm

Position   Hardiness   Soil

WELL-DRAINED

Uses

Features calendar

Jan	Feb	Mar	Apr	May	June
July	Aug	Sept	Oct	Nov	Dec

(flowers shown in Sept and Oct)

Buying tips *Not widely sold in garden centres, you may need to order from a herbaceous specialist.*

'Anastasia'

Dendranthema 'Clara Curtis'

Growing guide

A superb range of colours and a long flowering display late in the year has kept chrysanthemums (now called *Dendranthema*) one of Britain's favourite plants. Although many chrysanthemums need to be lifted and stored over the winter, the *D. zawadskii* hybrids are hardy in most areas. They make bushy plants 45–75cm (18–30in) high and they come in a variety of colours to suit any border. Flowering usually starts in late summer and continues through to October, but some varieties such as 'Emperor of China' flower for eight weeks from October.

These plants need a position in full sun, with reasonable drainage and a fertile soil, so a well-manured border and additional feeds are important. Once flowering is over, cut the plants to the ground in December.

They make good cut flowers, but take care when handling all chrysanthemums as the sap can be an irritant.

Good companions

Much depends on the colour of chrysanthemum you choose, but lily turf (*Liriope muscari*) would be an interesting contrast of form with its spire-like flowers in autumn. Also consider the later-flowering red-hot pokers, such as 'Border Ballet' or pale yellow 'Little Maid'.

Propagation

Division or cuttings.

Troubleshooting

Divide regularly in spring to keep them in tip-top condition.

Keep an eye out for white rust – this begins as tiny yellow spots on the surface and underside of the leaves. It affects all types of chrysanthemums and cannot be cured. Remove and burn infected leaves and spray the rest of the plant with a suitable fungicide as soon as you notice the problem.

Wiggly lines on the leaves are a sign of leaf miner – picking off affected leaves is usually sufficient to control this pest. Spray with a systemic insecticide.

'Mei-kyo'

Mottled leaves, shrivelled or discoloured flower petals suggest a thrips problem. Spray with a systemic insecticide.

Flowers and leaves may be eaten by earwigs or caterpillars. For the former use traps made from upturned plant pots filled with newspaper; for the latter pick off by hand or spray with a suitable insecticide.

Which variety?

There are lots of varieties from which to choose, unfortunately, apart from the clear pink **'Clara Curtis'**, some of the best ones are not easy to obtain. The following are among the best of the most widely available varieties. **'Anastasia'** lilac-pink pompon flowers from October to November, 60cm (24in). **'Dr Tom Parr'** is similar but a coppery-brown. Slightly later and smaller is the deep lilac **'Mei-kyo'** and its coppery relative **'Bronze Elegance'**. **'Duchess of Edinburgh'** has cinnabar-red flowers. **'Ruby Mound'** is a rich crimson and **'Mary Stoker'**

has creamy flowers which develop a pink tinge as they age. **'Paul Boissier'** is coppery-bronze. **'Emperor of China'** (syn. 'Cottage Pink') silvery pink flowers from October to mid-December, often accompanied by crimson tints to the foliage. At 1.2m (4ft), it is taller than most so needs staking. **'Innocence'** pale pink flowers in early autumn, 60cm (24in).

Korean chrysanthemums are also reliable autumn-flowering, hardy perennials about 60–90cm (24–36in) high. There are many varieties, such as **'Nancy Perry'** with clear pink flowers and **'Wedding Day'** which has white flowers with a green centre.

You may see plants described as 'Yoder mums' or 'Yoder chrysanths'. These are fairly hardy, cushion-shaped, dwarf plants that grow to about 30cm (12in), they can be used in containers as well as in borders. They will bear some blooms in June, but most of the floral display is produced from August onwards.

'Mary Stoker'

Dianthus
Dianthus 'Doris'

Shape and size

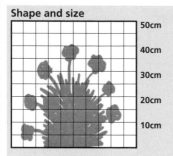

Position

Hardiness

Soil

WELL-DRAINED

Uses

Features calendar

Jan	Feb	Mar	Apr	May	June
July	Aug	Sept	Oct	Nov	Dec

Buying tips *From February to May, you may find named varieties of pinks such as 'Doris', 'Haytor White' and 'Laced Monarch' available as 'tot' plants at garden centres. Or, you can buy pinks by mail order from specialists. If you get very small plants or rooted cuttings, grow them on in a coldframe or unheated greenhouse before planting them out.*

'Bookham Perfume'

'Doris'

Growing guide

Dianthus is a large genus that includes florists' carnations, alpine and bedding pinks as well as garden or border pinks.

Most border or garden pinks grow 23–45cm (9–18in) tall and have attractive evergreen, grey-green foliage. The flowers appear in June or July and many have a spicy scent. Some of the modern varieties will flower for a second time in autumn. They make long-lasting cut flowers, especially those that are scented.

Despite popular belief, you do not need an alkaline soil to grow any of the dianthus, but a sunny spot with well-drained soil is essential. If your soil is heavy clay, grow them in tubs or troughs. Flowers can become flattened by wind or heavy rain.

Plant border pinks in March or April. A group of three or four plants will soon form a decent-sized clump. Although they like a well-drained soil, you must water them in dry weather until their roots are established. In April, young plants may start to produce flower buds at the expense of the side shoots. To encourage a more bushy plant, break off the main flowering shoots just above a leaf joint. Some of the taller varieties may need staking. You may need to protect plants from winter wet, and do not mulch too near the stems.

Good companions

Pinks, with their evergreen foliage, make an informal edging to flower or herb beds, near paths or paved areas. They look particularly effective accompanied by thrifts, violas or veronicas. In the border they can be used in combination with irises and roses.

Propagation

Take cuttings from non-flowering side shoots in summer. Pot up and keep cool in a coldframe until rooted – usually within a month. Pot up and grow on before planting out.

Troubleshooting

Modern pinks do become untidy and bare in the centre after three or four years, even the old-fashioned ones will become like this after five or six years. The answer is to take cuttings every couple of years so you can replace old plants cheaply.

Watch out for aphids and powdery mildew and spray with a suitable product as soon as possible.

Which variety?

We've concentrated on the border or garden pinks. These can be divided into two groups, modern and old-fashioned varieties.

The modern pinks tend to flower more reliably and for longer than the old-fashioned ones with their main flush in June or July then inter-mittently with a second flush in September. Deadhead the first flush to ensure a reasonable second display. If your priority is scent, opt for one of the older varieties, which usually have their main flowering period from June to July.

MODERN VARIETIES

We've chosen **'Doris'** as a widely available, garden-worthy variety with salmon-pink flowers and a red eye. It is easy to grow, with sturdy stems and a fine scent.

Other varieties to look out for include the following: **'Diane'**, strong flower stems up to 38cm (15in) tall with salmon-red flowers fading to deep pink; **'Haytor White'** (syn. 'Haytor'), strong, vigorous plant with flower stems up to 45cm (18in), white flowers with a pleasant perfume; **'Houndspool Ruby'** (syn. 'Ruby Doris'), very bushy plant with 40cm (16in) flower stems, flowers are reddish-purple with deeper red eye and can flower as early as May; **'Monica Wyatt'**, bushy habit with strong flower stems 30cm (12in) tall, pink flowers with a ruby eye; **'Gran's Favourite'**, spreading habit with flower stems about 35cm (14in) long, flowers are white laced with light purple and have a red eye, flowers from mid-May; **'Laced Monarch'**, a bushy plant with pink, scented flowers with chestnut lacing on stems. It is 38cm (15in) tall.

OLD-FASHIONED VARIETIES

'Brympton Red', tidy plant with attractive blue-grey foliage. The rigid flower stems are 23cm (9in) tall and have single, raspberry-red flowers with darker lacing and eye.
'Inchmery' has a tidy habit and flowering stems up to 23cm (9in) tall. The open-centred flowers are

'Musgrave's Pink'

double and rose-pink fading to almost white with a sweet scent. **'Mrs Sinkins'** is a vigorous, tumbling, cushion-like plant with strong flowering stems 25cm (10in) long. The double, white flowers are heavily scented. **'Musgrave's Pink'** is a neat, compact plant with single, white flowers with a green eye on stems just 20cm (8in) tall. It can be difficult to grow. **'Sam Barlow'** is a vigorous, compact variety with 23cm (9in) stems of white flowers each with a purple eye.

You may also come across border carnations – these need careful staking and last only a couple of years, so are more work than garden pinks. However, **'Bookham Perfume'** (rich crimson) and **'Lavender Clove'** are worth searching out for their clove-like perfume. They flower from July to August.

There are also annual carnations and Indian pinks (both are used as bedding or container plants) as well as a wide range of alpine pinks – all available from alpine specialists and seed companies. Most have a height and spread of 45x30cm (18x12in) and flower from July until the first frosts.

'Inchmery'

'Monica Wyatt'

Dicentra
Dicentra spectabilis

Shape and size

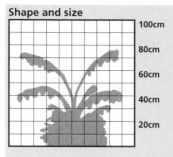

Position

Hardiness   Soil

MOIST

Uses

Features calendar

Jan	Feb	Mar	Apr	May	June
				✹	✹

July	Aug	Sept	Oct	Nov	Dec

Buying tips In early February and March you may find D. spectabilis on sale as pre-packed plants in boxes. They can be worth trying as a cheap alternative to container-grown plants, so long as they have not dried out in the pack.

'Stuart Boothman'

Dicentra spectabilis is stocked by most garden centres in spring

Growing guide

These are elegant plants with fern-like foliage and heart-shaped blooms on arching stems. They are very easy to grow and flower early, from late April, peaking in May.

Dicentras can grow in sun or shade and in most soils, but they will do best in a sheltered area, in partial shade and a moist soil. By keeping them out of the midday sun and keeping the ground moist, the flowering season will extend into the summer. They make good cut flowers.

Most dicentras die down naturally in late summer. In dry conditions they may die down earlier, although when this happens, they will often reappear and flower again in the autumn. It is important not to disturb the soil around their roots as they are shallow-rooting and easily damaged.

Good companions

The taller dicentras like D. spectabilis have arching flower stems that combine well with low-growing plants such as London pride, mossy saxifrages, ivies and hellebores. Other good companions are hostas and hardy geraniums, or any other plant that can provide interest later on in the season.

The smaller dicentras could be grown with astilbes, Solomon's seal, foxgloves or taller campanulas.

Propagation

D. eximia and D. formosa can be lifted and divided in March. D. spectabilis can be propagated by leaf and stem cuttings. You can also raise dicentras from seed, but it takes two years.

Troubleshooting

Dicentras can die back after flowering, particularly if they are allowed to dry out.

'Snowflakes'

Which variety?

D. spectabilis and **D. 'Bountiful'** are widely available in garden centres, but for a broader range of varieties you will have to buy from a herbaceous specialist.

D. spectabilis is taller than most dicentras growing up to 70cm (28in) tall with sprays of pink flowers. The variety **'Alba'** has lighter green foliage and ivory-white flowers.

Varieties derived from **D. eximia** or **D. formosa** are more compact, growing to only 45cm (18in) high. They have a long flowering period that starts in May and can continue on into October. Among the best varieties to look out for are:

'Stuart Boothman' (syn. 'Boothman's Variety') which has particularly attractive foliage and soft pink flowers. **'Bacchanal'** the darkest red dicentra. **'Bountiful'** pink. **'Langtrees'** grey-tinged foliage, white flowers with pink tips. **'Pearl Drops'** is similar. **'Luxuriant'** has rich-red flowers with compact mounds of fresh green foliage. **'Snowflakes'** is a fairly new one with graceful sprays of white flowers. It often flowers until October and can tolerate drier conditions.

'Bacchanal'

'Bountiful'

'Pearl Drops'

Dictamnus

Dictamnus albus

Shape and size

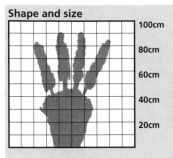

100cm
80cm
60cm
40cm
20cm

Position   Hardiness   Soil

WELL-DRAINED

Uses

Features calendar

Jan	Feb	Mar	Apr	May	June
July	Aug	Sept	Oct	Nov	Dec

Buying tips If you cannot find plants on sale in garden centres, try growing it from fresh seed from a neighbour or friend. You can also buy seed from mail-order seed suppliers.

Dictamnus albus 'Purpureus'

Dictamnus albus

Growing guide

This fascinating plant is known as the burning bush because on hot days, when the seed pods are ripening, it releases volatile oils that can be ignited by a burning match held at the base of the spike.

It is an easy-to-grow perennial with aromatic leaves. In early summer, it bears attractive 90cm (36in) high, loose spikes of pure white flowers, followed by seedpods from mid-summer onwards.

Grow in any well-drained soil, especially chalky soils, in a sunny position. However, plants can be difficult to establish and resent being moved, so are best left to establish large clumps. Cut back the stems to the base in autumn.

Beware, dictamnus can cause skin irritation in bright sunlight.

Good companions

Combines well with other early summer perennials such as irises.

Propagation

Seed, but this may take several years to reach flowering size. The seed needs a cold spell to encourage germination. Sow seed in small pots and leave in a coldframe over winter.

Troubleshooting

Generally trouble-free, but attracts slugs. Apply slug pellets after planting and early in the spring.

Which variety?

D. albus (syn. *D. fraxinella*) is widely available and has white or pink flowers. You may also come across the variety **'Purpureus'** which has lilac-mauve flowers, with darker veins.

Dierama

Dierama pulcherrimum

Shape and size

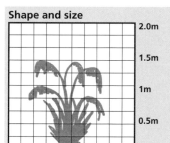

- 2.0m
- 1.5m
- 1m
- 0.5m

Position   Hardiness   Soil

MOIST

Uses

Features calendar

Jan	Feb	Mar	Apr	May	June
July	Aug	Sept	Oct	Nov	Dec

Buying tips Best bought as growing plants in spring rather than as corms or ask a friend for a self-sown seedling and grow it on.

Close up of graceful flower of Dierama pulcherrimum

Dierama pulcherrimum

Growing guide

This plant is grown mainly for its gracefully arching flowering stems which create a fountain effect with spires of small, bell-shaped flowers at the end of each stem. Despite being a tall plant, the stems are wiry and there is no need for staking. The rest of the foliage is grassy and evergreen, but not particularly eye-catching.

Plant in spring, choosing a warm, sunny position in a soil that is light but able to retain moisture. In very cold areas, the plant will need protecting over winter with a layer of bracken or bark chips.

Good companions

This makes a good specimen near a pond where its stems will be reflected in the water. Alternatively, position it at the end of a border planted next to drifts of bold-leaved plants such as hostas. *Dierama* should stand out above lower-growing plants. It looks effective growing in courtyards and paved areas.

Propagation

Division in spring. Plants can also self-seed.

Troubleshooting

Generally trouble-free, but not always hardy in cold areas.

Which variety?

D. pulcherrimum is the only species that is widely available. The flower colour can vary from pink to white or purple, although sometimes you may also find named varieties with specific colours. You may come across **D. dracomontanum** (syn. *D. pendulum* 'Pumilum') which is a dwarf version at 60x30cm (24x12in) with more upright growth.

Digitalis
Digitalis grandiflora

Shape and size

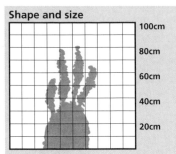

100cm
80cm
60cm
40cm
20cm

Position

Hardiness

Soil

ANY

Uses

Features calendar

Jan	Feb	Mar	Apr	May	June
					✺
July	Aug	Sept	Oct	Nov	Dec
✺					

WARNING
All parts of the foxglove are poisonous, including the smoke from burning its foliage. Foxgloves are grown commercially to produce digitalin to treat heart disease.

Digitalis grandiflora

Growing guide

Most people are familiar with the native *D. purpurea* and its varieties which are biennials, but there are more choice perennial species that are worth seeking out. These have larger flowers in some lovely colours including soft yellow, dusky pink and chocolate brown.

Foxgloves will grow in most soils, but they won't tolerate drying out in late summer. Grow them in sun or shade and they will self-seed freely if they are in a favourable spot. Cut down the main spike as it fades, this will encourage the growth of flowering side shoots.

Good companions

Use with other cottage garden plants or plant in drifts among roses, shrubs or trees.

Propagation

Division of the perennial types every two to three years after planting. Most are easy to grow from seed.

Troubleshooting

Fairly trouble-free, but foxgloves might hybridise with native plants, giving you lots of purple foxgloves after a few years. To prevent this, weed out seedlings with red-stained leaf stems.

In very wet soils, the roots or the crown may rot.

Which variety?

D. grandiflora (syn. *D. ambigua*) is one of the best. It has soft yellow flowers from June to July and a clump of evergreen leaves. At 60x80cm (24x32in) it has a good habit for a border plant. **'Temple Bells'** has larger flowers on a more compact plant.

D. x mertonensis is also worth considering as it has large flowers the colour of crushed strawberries. Height 60–90cm (24–36in).

Other perennial foxgloves you may encounter include the following:

Digitalis x mertonensis

Digitalis 'Sutton's Apricot'

D. ferruginea with rust-brown flowers forming very upright spires, 90–150cm (36–60in). **D. lanata** (syn. *D. lamarckii)* and **D. lutea** (syn. *D. eriostachya*) are both perennial yellow foxgloves. **D. parviflora** is an unusual chocolate-brown foxglove that flowers from July to August and is 60–80cm (24–32in) high.
D. viridiflora has yellowish-green flowers from June to July that are highly sought after for flower arranging. Height 60–80cm (24–32in).

Good biennials are as follows.
'Excelsior Hybrids' a pastel mixture flowering from May to July. Height 1.2–1.5m (4–5ft). **'Foxy'** a dwarf pastel mix 80–90cm (32–36in) high. It can be grown as an annual: sow in February, plant out in April and it should flower from July to August.
'Sutton's Apricot' is a lovely creamy pink from May to July. Height 90–150cm (36–60in).

Digitalis ferruginea

Digitalis lanata

Doronicum

Doronicum 'Miss Mason'

Shape and size

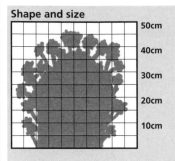

Position

Hardiness Soil

ANY

Uses

Features calendar

Jan	Feb	Mar	Apr ✿	May ✿	June
July	Aug	Sept	Oct	Nov	Dec

Doronicum 'Miss Mason'

Growing guide

These plants are worth a place in the garden for their cheerful-looking yellow, daisy-like flowers from April to May. They vary in height from 15–23cm (6–9in) dwarf plants ideal for rock gardens, to back-of-the-border types up to 1.2m (4ft) high.

Doronicums are very easy to grow, being hardy and suitable for any soil or position except dense shade. Spring is the best time to plant, even if they are in flower. There is no need to stake them. It is worth deadheading to get a second flush of bloom in September, although the plants will not flower as well the following spring.

Flowers of all types are suitable for use in floral arrangements.

Good companions

The small doronicums could be grown in a rock garden with purple-red primulas. Or grown at the base of a wall smothered with purple aubrieta. Medium-sized doronicums could be used in spring bedding schemes with white tulips and grape hyacinths. Larger doronicums are ideal for softening the sword-like leaves of yellow-variegated irises.

Propagation

Division after flowering.

Troubleshooting

Slugs can be a problem, so it is worth applying slug pellets when the leaves first emerge. You might find the rhizomes grow out of the soil, especially with *D. plantagineum* 'Excelsum' which can leave a gap in the middle of the plant. If this happens, split up the plant and replant healthy outer sections.

Which variety?

We pick **'Miss Mason'** as an easy-to-get variety that forms impressive clumps. It bears deep yellow flowers on 45cm (15m) stems from mid-April. The smallest dwarf variety is **D. columnae** (syn. *D. cordatum*) at 15–20cm (6–8in) high. It starts flowering in March and continues until May.

Another pretty medium-sized variety **D. orientale** (syn. *D. caucasicum*) with flowers that start off a pale gold then fade to lemon, height 30cm (12in). The double-flowered doronicum, **D. 'Spring Beauty'** (syn. 'Frühlingspracht') at 30cm (12in) high resembles a high-class dandelion.

The tallest variety is **D. x excelsum 'Harpur Crewe'** (syn. *D. plantagineum* 'Excelsum') with flower stems 90–120cm (36–48in), April to June. **D. orientale 'Magnificum'** is 60cm (24in).

Echinacea
Echinacea purpurea

Shape and size

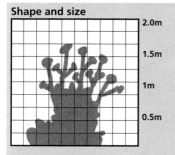

2.0m
1.5m
1m
0.5m

Position   Hardiness   Soil

Uses

Features calendar

Jan	Feb	Mar	Apr	May	June
✻	✻	✻			
July	Aug	Sept	Oct	Nov	Dec

Buying tips *It is worth trying varieties such as 'White Swan' from seed. Plants of named varieties are available from herbaceous specialists.*

'White Swan'

Echinacea purpurea

Growing guide

Echinacea are stately plants with stiff, branching stems. Their main feature is their striking daisy-like flowers which last all summer. When first in flower, the petals form a flat circle around the prominent central cone or 'boss'. Later, the petals bend down making the boss even more prominent and creating a very eye-catching profile.

Their height makes *Echinacea* effective back-of-the-border plants, but the flowers are attractive to look at close up, so it is worth cutting a few for indoors too.

Echinacea are sun-loving perennials. *E. purpurea* is native to the eastern USA and likes a moist but well-drained, fertile soil. Other *Echinacea* grow in drier areas.

Good companions

Cone flowers can be used to great effect against more diffuse flowers and foliage. They attract bees and butterflies so would add impact in a butterfly border alongside globe thistle (*Echinops*) and *Monarda*.

Some varieties have rich colours that can be combined with fuchsias, blue salvias or *Sidalcea*. The whites would complement tall, slender blue plants.

Propagation

Division, root cuttings, or seed.

Troubleshooting

Generally trouble-free.

Which variety?

E. purpurea (syn. *Rudbeckia purpurea*) with mauve-crimson petals around a brown boss, is easy to find. You might come across several named varieties: **'Magnus'** has purple flowers and an orange boss; **'Robert Bloom'** is similar but rich mauve-pink; and **'White Swan'** is a warm white with an orange-brown boss.

Cone flower

83

Echinops

Echinops bannaticus 'Taplow Blue'

Shape and size

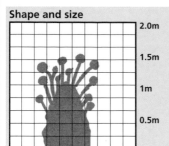

Position   Hardiness   Soil

WELL-DRAINED

Uses

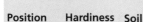

Features calendar

Jan	Feb	Mar	Apr	May	June
✿	✿				
July	Aug	Sept	Oct	Nov	Dec

Buying tips *Worth growing from seed. E. bannaticus 'Taplow Blue' is available from some garden centres, but for other varieties try a wildflower or a herbaceous specialist.*

Close up of E. bannaticus drumstick flowerheads

Echinops bannaticus 'Taplow Blue'

Growing guide

Globe thistles are statuesque plants that form substantial clumps of prickly grey-green foliage topped with 'drumstick' flower heads. They look most striking just before they open when the distinctive drumstick shape is most eye-catching.

These are ideal perennials for a sunny garden on poor soil such as thin chalk or sand, although they can be grown on well-drained, fertile soils too.

The flowers are interesting subjects for cutting and drying – pick before they start to open.

Good companions

Ideal in a wildlife garden as they attract bees and butterflies, the blue flowers would combine well with white *Scabiosa*. In a gravel garden globe thistles look striking with bold foliage plants such as phormiums.

Propagation

Division or seed.

Troubleshooting

Generally trouble-free, but if soil is wet over winter, spring planting is recommended. Fairly prickly.

Which variety?

We've chosen **E. bannaticus 'Taplow Blue'** (syn. *E. ritro* 'Taplow Blue') as it is a reliable and easily available plant. There are more choice relatives – these usually have better coloured foliage. For example, **E. 'Nivalis'** (syn. *E. albus*) has lovely grey foliage with grey-white drumsticks, **E. ritro 'Ruthenicus'** has dark green leaves with white undersides and bright blue flowers.

Epilobium

Epilobium fleischeri

Shape and size

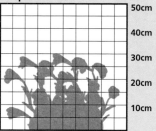

	50cm
	40cm
	30cm
	20cm
	10cm

Position   Hardiness   Soil

WELL-DRAINED

Uses

Features calendar

Jan	Feb	Mar	Apr	May	June
					❁
July	Aug	Sept	Oct	Nov	Dec
❁	❁	⚘	⚘		

Epilobium fleischeri

Epilobium glabellum

Growing guide

Epilobiums offer a long flowering display of pink or white blooms that are loved by bees and butterflies. The flowers are followed by fluffy seedheads.

They are sun-loving plants that need a well-drained soil. *E. fleischeri* forms a small clump, 30x30cm (12x12in), and, unlike other species, is not invasive. It has small, grey leaves and mauve-pink blooms.

Epilobiums are members of the evening primrose family and among their relatives are rose-bay willow herb and the Californian fuchsia (*Zauschneria californica*).

Good companions

E. fleischeri would suit a sunny rockery or the front of a border. It could also be used to brighten up a herb garden or a wildlife garden. It combines particularly well with named varieties of *Festuca glauca*.

Propagation

Division or seed.

Troubleshooting

Some species are invasive, notably the rose-bay willow herb (*E. angustifolium*) which seeds around waste ground, but also *E. dodonaei* which has spreading rhizomes.

Which variety?

E. fleischeri is a dainty, non-invasive plant. ***E. dodonaei*** (syn. *E. rosmarinifolium*) is similar but less well-behaved. Avoid taller *E. angustifolium* – it is far too invasive, **'Album'** is a white form that is less of a problem.

E. glabellum with white flowers is smaller at 23x30cm (9x12in) and is considered a rock garden plant.

Epimedium

Epimedium perralderianum

Shape and size

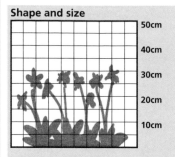

50cm
40cm
30cm
20cm
10cm

Position

Hardiness Soil

WELL-DRAINED

Uses

Features calendar

Jan	Feb	Mar	Apr	May	June

July	Aug	Sept	Oct	Nov	Dec

Buying tips *Most garden centres will stock some epimediums – if you want the new varieties you will need a specialist.*

Epimedium x versicolor 'Sulphureum'

Epimedium perralderianum

Growing guide

Epimediums are mainly grown for their attractive foliage that forms a dense, weed-suppressing groundcover. They also produce dainty sprays of pink, white or yellow blooms in spring. The leaves are shaped liked arrows or hearts and when young have a bronze or red flush or markings. Some, like *E. perralderianum* are evergreen and develop red or bronze tints in winter. The deciduous ones offer golden autumn colour and if the winter is not too cold they will keep their leaves. The leaves are highly valued by flower arrangers, too, for winter displays. The spring flowers are like small stars and they attract bees.

Most epimediums are hardy and easy to grow but they appreciate protection from spring frosts and cold winds which can cut back or scorch young flowers and leaves. A woodland situation is ideal – partial shade and a well-drained soil that has plenty of leafmould or garden compost dug in. Most can tolerate a chalky soil if leafmould is added but some like *E. grandiflorum* and *E. x youngianum* require an acid soil. Epimediums can be grown in containers. They can also be 'forced'. Lift and divide in autumn, bring into an unheated greenhouse in the new year, when the young flowers and foliage can be appreciated without the problem of frost damage.

In late February to early March, trim away old leaves if they detract from the young growth.

Good companions

Grow them with other woodland plants including ferns and spring-flowering bulbs. Or use them as an underplanting around euphorbias or phormiums. They make an effective groundcover or a border edging – plant 45cm (18in) apart.

Propagation

Division or seed.

Troubleshooting

Generally trouble-free but vine

Epimedium pinnatum 'Colchicum'

weevil grubs and poor drainage can damage the roots. Divide the clump-forming species like *E. grandiflorum* regularly – every three years. If this is not done, they can exhaust the soil and flowering and leaf size will be reduced.

Which variety?

We would recommend the evergreen **E. perralderianum** for winter and spring interest. As one of the taller ones it is particularly colourful in the border. It has deep green leaves over winter. In spring, the new foliage bears coppery-red markings and bright yellow flowers.

The following epimediums are 30cm (12in) high with yellow flowers from April to May and need partial shade unless otherwise stated. **E. grandiflorum**, deciduous with red tinge, flowers crimson, white, rose and yellow. Named varieties like **'Rose Queen'** have particularly attractive pink flowers. **E. x perralchicum 'Fröhnleiten'** is 25cm (10in) high with evergreen,

marbled foliage with prominent, bronzed edges, one of the best varieties for containers.
E. pinnatum 'Colchicum' is 35cm (14in) high with evergreen leaves that are bronze, then green.
E. x rubrum is just 25cm (10in) high, deciduous with bronze-red foliage and crimson flowers in May.
E. x versicolor 'Sulphureum' is deciduous, with a purple-bronze tinge – it can cope with sun more easily than other species and flowers earlier in March to April.
E. x warleyense is evergreen, with light green foliage and orange-yellow flowers. **E. x youngianum 'Niveum'** is only 20cm (8in) high, deciduous, with purple-bronze tinge and white flowers. **'Roseum'** is similar, but has pink flowers. Both these would be suitable for a rock garden.

Many new species will become more available to gardeners as material collected from China is evaluated for garden use and propagated by nurseries.

Epimedium x youngianum 'Roseum'

Epimedium grandiflorum 'Rose Queen'

Erigeron

Erigeron 'Darkest of All'

Shape and size

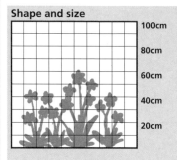

100cm
80cm
60cm
40cm
20cm

Position   Hardiness   Soil

WELL-DRAINED

Uses

Features calendar

Jan	Feb	Mar	Apr	May	June
					✿
✿	✿				
July	Aug	Sept	Oct	Nov	Dec

Buying tips *Choose a named variety rather than an unnamed plant or species because they have a better shape and better flowers.*

Erigeron 'Dimity'

Erigeron 'Darkest of All'

Growing guide

These sun-loving plants produce daisy-like blooms for most of the summer that attract bees and butterflies. They are easy to grow and do well in gardens if given a reasonably fertile soil. Fleabane can also be used as cut flowers.

The plants usually need some support – twiggy sticks will do. Regular deadheading will ensure longer flowering. In autumn, cut down to the ground.

Good companions

Grow in informal cottage garden beds. They can be used as fillers between spire-shaped plants such as lupins.

Propagation

Division or seed.

Troubleshooting

Generally trouble-free.

Which variety?

There are many varieties – height, flower colour and season all vary, so look around for one that suits your planting schemes. We've chosen **'Darkest of All'** (syn. 'Dunkelste Aller') for its deep violet flowers with yellow centres. It is 60cm (24in) tall and flowers from June to August.

The following are the same height and flowering time unless otherwise stated.

'Dignity' violet-mauve flowers, 50cm (20in) tall. **'Dimity'** a dwarf pink at 25cm (10in). **'Foersters Liebling'** a pink, semi-double, 45cm (18in) tall. **'Quakeress'** white flushed pale pink flowers from June to July. **'Wuppertal'** semi-double, light violet flowers.

E. karvinskianus (syn. *E. mucronatus*) is a low-growing spreading plant with flowers that look just like the daisies in a lawn. It is only 15x30cm (6x12in) and flowers from June to October so is a possible candidate for container planting. It can also be allowed to grow between cracks in paving – it seeds itself around.

Erodium

Erodium manescavii

Shape and size

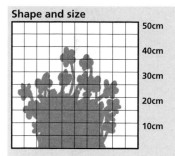

50cm
40cm
30cm
20cm
10cm

Position   Hardiness   Soil

WELL-DRAINED

Uses

Features calendar

Jan	Feb	Mar	Apr	May	June
			🌿	🌿	✳
July	Aug	Sept	Oct	Nov	Dec
✳	✳				

Buying tips *A good garden centre may have some Erodium. Check the alpine section as well as the perennial beds. Otherwise, you will have to order from a specialist. Seed can be obtained from alpine societies.*

Erodium reichardii

Erodium manescavii

Growing guide

Erodium look very much like hardy geraniums and make attractive border or rockery plants. They offer summer flowers and some have handsome foliage, too.

Coming originally from warm, dry regions they need a sunny position and well-drained soil to do well, though most are hardy. They thrive on chalky soil.

The larger *Erodium* are the most useful in borders, while the mat-forming types make long-lived plants for the rockery. When growing them in rock gardens, a topping of gravel or stone chippings helps to set off the plants and keep them clean.

Erodium with very hairy leaves need protection from winter rain – grow them in pots in a coldframe.

Good companions

E. manescavii is an ideal choice for the front of a border with low-growing foliage plants such as the black, grass-like *Ophiopogon planiscapus* 'Nigrescens', and the golden form of creeping Jenny (*Lysimachia nummularia* 'Aurea'). Dainty alpine pinks are an ideal companion for rockery *Erodium*. The smaller ones add summer colour to a rockery.

Propagation

Cuttings from new shoots in April. Root cuttings for *E. reichardii*. Seed.

Troubleshooting

Generally trouble-free outdoors but greenfly and spider mite can attack plants kept under glass. Some, like *E. manescavii*, tend to self-seed.

Which variety?

We've chosen **Erodium manescavii** *(syn. E. manescaui)* as it is one of the larger ones at 40x45cm (16x18in) and is widely available. A clump-forming plant, it has fern-like foliage and magenta flowers from June to the end of August.

Others you may come across: **E. chrysanthum**, primrose-yellow flowers from June to September on separate male and female plants, may only produce a few flowers but is valued for the grey-green foliage, small clump-forming plant 15x30cm (6x12in); **E. pelargoni-iflorum** has flowers that resemble a trailing geranium, white with purple spotting and last from June to the end of August, a clump-forming plant 30x30cm (12x12in) with heart-shaped downy leaves; **E. reichardii** (syn. *E. chamaedry-oides*), small mat-forming plant 5x23cm (2x9in) with white flowers, veined with pink from June to September.

There are many other worthwhile *Erodium* that are tuft or mat-like – around 8–10cm (3–4in) high and spreading 20–60cm (8–24in), but these are mostly rock garden plants.

Eryngium

Eryngium x tripartitum

Shape and size

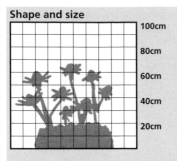

100cm
80cm
60cm
40cm
20cm

Position   Hardiness   Soil

WELL-DRAINED

Uses

Features calendar

Jan	Feb	Mar	Apr	May	June
July	Aug	Sept	Oct	Nov	Dec

Buying tips *Apart from E. planum, most will have to be obtained from specialists. Seed of E. alpinum is fairly widely available.*

Eryngium variifolium

Eryngium x tripartitum

Growing guide

Few plants can offer the metallic steel blues of the sea hollies and few plants look effective for so long. The teasel-like flower heads vary in size, colour and form. Some are like giant thimbles, others are pea-shaped and produced by the hundred. Most are shades of purple, blue or silver. The flowers can last for up to three months and, if left, the seedheads provide interest into the winter. Fresh or dry, they are interesting additions to cut flower arrangements.

Sea hollies need a sunny, well-drained site. Generally any soil will do but *E. alpinum* and *E. proteiflo-rum* need a rich, moisture-retentive soil to do really well. Most are hardy but *E. agavifolium* and *E. proteiflo-rum* need protection from frost except in mild areas. *E.* x *tripartitum* needs staking – insert twiggy sticks by mid-June. Also worth staking are *E.* x *oliverianum* and *E. planum*.

Good companions

Sea hollies growing 75–120cm (30–48in) tall are ideal candidates for the middle of the border. Their steely-blue colours are particularly attractive with orange lilies or yellow- or white-flowering perennials such as *Achillea*.

There are also many species (e.g. *E. alpinum* and *E. bourgatii*) that make lovely front-of-the-border plants and one (*E. eburneum*) for the back of a border. Again, choose colourful companions that set off their metallic flowers.

Propagation

Seed, either bought or lift self-sown seedlings. Root cuttings for named varieties. Propagation by division is not recommended as the plants do not like their roots disturbed.

Troubleshooting

Generally trouble-free, but they need full sun to develop the best colour. Very prickly.

Which variety?

We have chosen the widely available **Eryngium x tripartitum** for its masses of small flower heads in an intense metallic blue. At 75x60cm (30x24in) it is a useful size.

The other sea hollies have been listed according to their uses. All flower from July to September unless otherwise stated.

FRONT OF THE BORDER

All these are around 60x60cm (24x24in). **E. alpinum** has very large blue flower heads on blue flower stems. The flowers look prickly but, unlike other sea hollies, are soft to the touch. Many named varieties. **E. bourgatii** has particularly eye-catching foliage – finely divided and prickly with white marbling. Look out for the superior **'Oxford Blue'**; both flower until August. One of the best sea hollies is **E. x zabelii**, which combines the flowers of *E. alpinum* with the foliage of *E. bourgatii*. For year-round foliage interest try **E. variifolium** with its evergreen, white-veined leaves. The flowers are grey-blue and last until August.

MIDDLE OF THE BORDER

These sea hollies are 80–120cm (34–48in) unless otherwise stated. **E. x oliverianum** has flowers and stems of rich steely blue. **E. giganteum** is better known as 'Miss Willmott's Ghost'. It is a biennial, but self-seeds readily. Its flowers are silvery green and appear from August to September. **E. planum** with its masses of pale blue flower heads from July to August is widely available. There are also plenty of named varieties, including the dwarf **'Blue Dwarf'** (syn. 'Blauer Zwerg') at 60cm (24in). A new variety is **'Jos Eijking'**, a brighter, more intense lavender-blue than any other sea holly. It grows to around 70cm (28in).

BACK OF THE BORDER

Reaching 1.2m (4ft), **E. eburneum** (syn. *E. paniculatum*) produces arching, rapier-like leaves and tall, much-branched stems with pale green flower heads.

Eryngium x oliverianum

Eryngium x zabelii

SPECIMEN PLANTS

The **E. agavifolium** (syn. *E. bromeliifolium*) has a rosette of sword-shaped leaves, green flowers are borne on 1.2m (4ft) stems from July to August. Not reliably hardy. **E. proteiflorum** (syn. *E.* 'Delaroux') is an evergreen with sword-like leaves but is not reliably hardy. It has unusual cone-shaped, green flower heads. Height 90cm (36in).

Eryngium bourgatii

Erysimum

Erysimum 'Bowles' Mauve'

Shape and size

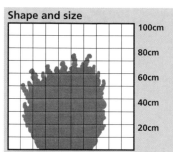

	100cm
	80cm
	60cm
	40cm
	20cm

Position   Hardiness   Soil

WELL-DRAINED

Uses

Features calendar

Jan	Feb	Mar ✿	Apr ✿	May ✿	June ✿
July ✿	Aug ✿	Sept ✿	Oct ✿	Nov ✿	Dec

Buying tips *Perennial wallflowers are unlikely to come true from seed. Try your local garden centre for 'Bowles' Mauve' – or ask for a cutting from a friend or neighbour. For the more unusual varieties go to a specialist supplier.*

Erysimum 'Wenlock Beauty'

Erysimum 'Bowles' Mauve'

Growing guide

Perennial wallflowers come in a wide range of colours and shapes, some offer attractive foliage, too. They do not need replacing every year like their biennial counterparts. Nearly all are evergreen.

To get the best from them, choose a sunny site on well-drained soil. Free-draining soils are best enriched with some garden compost when planting so they do not dry out in summer. To help keep plants neat and to prevent them quickly becoming bare in the centre, trim after flowering to remove faded flowers and any straggly shoots. The plants are fairly short-lived and need replacing every three years.

Good companions

The dark evergreen foliage contrasts well with paving and light-coloured stonework. Combine with silver-leaved Mediterranean-style plants and dwarf bulbs, and dress with pea gravel or stone chippings. The taller ones, such as E. 'Bowles' Mauve', add colour to shrub borders or to narrow beds besides paths.

Propagation

Basal cuttings in early summer.

Troubleshooting

Plants may show signs of viral infection which causes leaf yellowing and creamy flecking of the flowers. Affected plants should be destroyed.

Which variety?

We've chosen the easy and reliable **'Bowles' Mauve'** for its year-round value. It has grey-green, evergreen foliage and an extremely long flowering season. The spikes start flowering in March, peak in April and May but then it flowers inter-mittently until late autumn. It is one of the tallest at 75x45cm (30x18in). Other tall ones at 45–60x30cm (18–24x12in) include **E. cheiri 'Harpur Crewe'** with scented, double, golden-yellow flowers from April to May and **'Bloody Warrior'** with double, brown-red flowers with streaks of yellow from May to early June.

Two new additions are **'Plantworld Lemon'** and **'Plantworld Gold'**. They are unusual as they have a two-tone colour. The individual flowers in the cluster open as lemon or gold then age to mauve or purple. Flowering lasts from April to June. Plant height is 30–45cm (12–18in). **E. linifolium 'Variegatum'** (syn. E. 'Sissinghurst Variegated') has creamy-variegated leaves and lilac flowers from May to August. Height 30–45cm (12–18in).

There are also low-growing types that form rounded hummocks around 30x45cm (12x18in) high, **E. 'Wenlock Beauty'** is particularly compact and reliable. It has copper flowers fading to mauve that last from May to June. Carpeting *Erysimum* are ideal for rockeries.

Eupatorium

Eupatorium purpureum

Shape and size

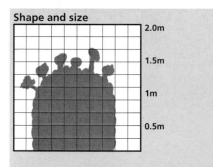

2.0m
1.5m
1m
0.5m

Position

Hardiness

Soil

MOIST

Uses

Features calendar

Jan	Feb	Mar	Apr	May	June
July	Aug ✿	Sept ✿	Oct	Nov	Dec

Buying tips *These plants are very prone to drying out, so check the compost is moist. Also the plants can be top-heavy, and stems can break easily, so check for damage before you buy if you want a good display the first year.*

Eupatorium purpureum 'Atropurpureum'

Eupatorium purpureum

Growing guide

This North American perennial is a dramatic and long-lived plant. At 1.8m (6ft) high with a distance of 75–90cm (30–36in) needed between plants, it requires careful placing, but the reward is a striking flowering display of purplish pink on dark purple stems.

It prefers a fertile, moist or boggy soil in sun or partial shade. Given enough moisture, it is easy to grow. Cut the stems down after flowering.

Good companions

Use at the back of a bog garden or as a specimen. Plant bold foliage in front of it such as the larger hostas, or use *Aruncus dioicus* or *Lythrum salicaria* to add flowering interest.

Propagation

Division.

Troubleshooting

Generally trouble-free.

Which variety?

Eupatorium purpureum is widely available and a fine plant. The variety **'Atropurpureum'** is even better because it offers more colour with its purple leaves and rose-lilac flowers. The hemp agrimony (*E. cannabinum*) is a weed but there are named varieties, such as **'Flore Pleno'**, with double purple-pink flowers from July to September. The white snake root (*E. rugosum*) at 1m (3ft) has green leaves and white flowers. It self-seeds freely.

93

Euphorbia
Euphorbia polychroma

Spurge

Shape and size

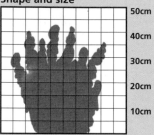

50cm
40cm
30cm
20cm
10cm

Position   Hardiness Soil

ANY

Uses

Features calendar

Jan	Feb	Mar	Apr	May	June
July	Aug	Sept	Oct	Nov	Dec

Buying tips *E. characias, E. polychroma and E. myrsinites are easy to find in garden centres, although the latter might be with the alpines. Those with either purple foliage or orange bracts are becoming more widely available. For the more unusual ones, try an unusual plant or herbaceous specialist.*

WARNING
All euphorbias are poisonous (except the Christmas houseplant poinsettia). Euphorbias produce milky sap when damaged. This can irritate the skin and, if eaten, can burn the mouth and cause stomach upset. Wear gloves when taking cuttings or dividing plants.

Euphorbia polychroma

Growing guide

Euphorbias are excellent plants for year-round interest and an essential ingredient in many gardens. Although they are a very diverse group that includes succulents and poinsettia, here we concentrate on the hardy types that make good border or container plants.

The true flowers are insignificant, but the eye-catching bracts make up for this when they appear in late spring or early summer. The garden euphorbias are mostly herbaceous, although some may become woody with age, and all are easy to grow.

In general, most prefer sun, but will tolerate partial shade. A few, like *E. palustris* and *E. amygdaloides* 'Robbiae' do well in shade. Euphorbias grow in most soils which do not become waterlogged, but on a free-draining soil they might spread too rapidly. For example, on woodland clay, *E. palustris* or *E. griffithii* 'Fireglow' or 'Dixter' would do well, but could be rather invasive on light soils.

Good companions
E. polychroma neatly fills the gap between spring bedding and the first flush of summer perennials. It combines well with *Geum rivale* 'Leonard's Variety' or with purple sage.

E. characias and the variety 'Wulfenii' can hold their own as specimen plants by a wall or in a gravel bed, but they also combine well with silvery or bluish foliage plants.

Propagation
Either seed (s), cuttings (c) or division (d) depending on the species. *E. amygdaloides* 'Robbiae' (d). *E. characias* (c, s). *E. griffithii* (d). *E. x martinii* (c). *E. myrsinites* (c, s). *E. nicaeensis* (s). *E. palustris* (d). *E. polychroma* (d). *E. schillingii* (d, s).

Troubleshooting
Some, like *E. cyparissias, E. lathyrus, E. dulcis* and *E. stricta* can be invasive – either because their roots run or because they self-seed. *E. amygdaloides* 'Purpurea' (syn. 'Rubra') is prone to mildew.

Euphorbia characias 'Wulfenii'

Which variety?

There are so many invaluable euphorbias, it is worth having several in the garden. We've chosen **Euphorbia polychroma** (syn. *E. epithymoides*) for its neat dome of bright yellow. Equally effective, although different in habit, is the taller **E. characias 'Wulfenii'**, which has blue-tinged foliage and green-yellow bracts.

Below, we suggest others based on their size. All have green-yellow bracts from March to May unless otherwise stated.

LARGER EUPHORBIAS

E. characias 'Wulfenii' is a superb evergreen that lasts all winter, height 1.8m (6ft). The species is similar but half the height. **E. x martinii** is smaller, at 75cm (30in) with maroon 'eyes' to the flower head.

E. griffithii is noted for its orange bracts in June. Height 1.2m (4ft). Two superior, named varieties are **'Fireglow'** with rich orange bracts and **'Dixter'** with deep apricot flowers. **E. palustris** has yellow bracts from May to June. Height and spread 1.2m (4ft). **E. schillingii** with upright stems to 80cm (34in) offers late summer and autumn interest with green and yellow bracts from August to October.

SMALLER EUPHORBIAS

E. nicaeensis flowers from July to September and is evergreen. Height 50cm (20in), but spreads to 90cm (36in). **E. polychroma** (syn. *E. epithymoides*) is one of the earliest to flower. It is non-spreading and suitable for the smallest gardens. Named varieties are available such as **'Candy'** (syn. 'Purpurea') with purple-flushed leaves. **E. myrsinites** has trailing stems and is suitable for the front of the border, a container or a rockery. It is an evergreen with succulent foliage. Height and spread 20x80cm (8x32in).

E. amygdaloides 'Robbiae' (syn. *E. robbiae*) is a spreading evergreen that is one of the few reliable groundcovers for dry shade. Height 45cm (18in), spreads indefinitely.

NEW VARIETIES

Many new varieties are being produced with variations in foliage colour and height. **E. cyparissias 'Fens Ruby'** is recent, with purple-red foliage that ages to grey-green. It is short at 25–30cm (10–12in) high, but spreads, so consider growing it in a pot.

Euphorbia palustris and Rheum australe

Euphorbia griffithii 'Dixter'

Euphorbia myrsinites

Filipendula

Filipendula ulmaria 'Aurea'

Shape and size

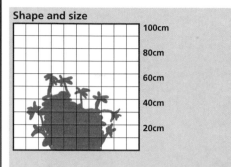

Position

Hardiness   Soil

Uses

MOIST

Features calendar

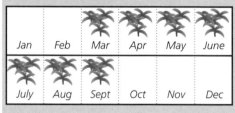

Jan	Feb	Mar	Apr	May	June
July	Aug	Sept	Oct	Nov	Dec

Buying tips *You will probably have to buy from a specialist. Check the compost is moist and the roots have not been allowed to dry out.*

Filipendula rubra 'Ventusa'

Filipendula ulmaria 'Aurea'

Growing guide

Most meadowsweets have flat, feathery flower heads in summer but *F. ulmaria* 'Aurea' is valued for its bright, golden-yellow spring foliage. This slowly turns yellow-green through summer and autumn.

Remove the flowering stems of *F. ulmaria* 'Aurea' when they start appearing in May, this will encourage the plant to keep producing fresh foliage. The flowers are insignificant and if you let them develop the leaves tend to go green.

Although they are bog plants, filipendulas will grow in any reasonably fertile soil that does not dry out over the summer – a good layer of mulch in spring will help retain moisture through the growing season. Partial shade or full shade is preferred in hot areas.

Good companions

The clumps of butter-yellow leaves would form a striking feature in a border. It could be used as part of a yellow scheme next to variegated shrubs, contrasted with a purple-leaved *Heuchera*, or underplanted with *Viola labradorica*. Filipendulas associate particularly well with ponds and other water features.

Propagation

Division.

Troubleshooting

If the plant is growing in dry or poor soil it can be prone to powdery mildew.

Which variety?

***Filipendula ulmaria* 'Aurea'** is the best for spring foliage. The species is the wild flower meadowsweet which has scented white flowers from June to August and is 60–90cm (24–36in) high. It can be naturalised in wet grass areas. Other named varieties of *F. ulmaria* are available but do not have as much to offer as *F. ulmaria* 'Aurea'.

F. purpurea (syn. *F. palmata* 'Purpurea') is an imposing plant for a rich, boggy area in partial shade. It offers both large, handsome foliage and flat heads of cerise-crimson flowers. Height and spread 120x60cm (48x24in). ***F. rubra* 'Venusta'** (syn. 'Venusta Magnifica') is an enormous plant at 1.8–2.4x1.2m (6–8x4ft) – quite spectacular if you have the room. It does not need staking and has pink summer blooms.

Foeniculum

Foeniculum vulgare 'Purpureum'

Shape and size

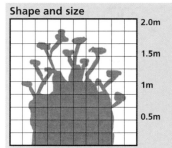

Position Hardiness Soil

WELL-DRAINED

Uses

Features calendar

Jan	Feb	Mar	Apr	May	June
July	Aug	Sept	Oct	Nov	Dec

Foeniculum vulgare 'Purpureum'

Buying tips *Although it is widely sold in small pots in the herb section, plants often fail to transplant well. It is easy to raise from seed, or ask a friend for a small self-sown seedling.*

Foeniculum vulgare

Growing guide

Although fennel is best known as an aniseed-flavoured herb, it is also a garden-worthy plant. It makes large clumps of feathery leaves and if allowed to flower it can reach 1.8m (6ft) high – ideal for the back of a border or as a prominent specimen in the early summer border. The purple-bronze form is more useful in the ornamental border.

Fennel needs a sunny, well-drained spot to thrive, but grows well in poor or fertile soil.

Cut the yellowish flowers off if you only want the foliage and to prevent self-seeding.

Good companions

Use it as a backdrop to create a haze for phloxes or oriental poppies, or as a feature plant in a herb garden. Here you may want it to self-seed so allow the flowers to develop. The seeds can be collected later.

Propagation

Seed.

Troubleshooting

Self-seeding in the border in hot summers is the main problem. Fennel is fairly short-lived and needs to be replaced after about three years.

Which variety?

Choose **Foeniculum vulgare 'Purpureum'** (syn. 'Bronze') the bronze-leaved form. It is just as tasty when used as a herb.

Gaillardia

Gaillardia 'Dazzler'

Shape and size

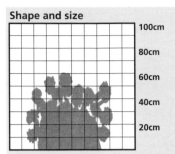

100cm
80cm
60cm
40cm
20cm

Position   Hardiness   Soil

WELL-DRAINED

Uses

Features calendar

Jan	Feb	Mar	Apr	May	June
✿	✿	✿			
July	Aug	Sept	Oct	Nov	Dec

Buying tips *It's well worth growing Gaillardia from seed. In* Gardening Which? *trials G. 'Goblin' ('Kobold') germinated within two weeks, flowered in its first year and bloomed profusely in its second year.*

Gaillardia 'Goblin'

Gaillardia 'Dazzler'

Growing guide

Gaillardia add cheerful reds and golds to give beds and borders a late summer boost. The daisy flowers last from July to September, but deadheading can prolong flowering into October.

The ones you are most likely to come across are hybrids bred from *G. aristata* and *G. pulchella*. Both species are from the dry, sunny prairies of North America, so their descendants thrive in sunny borders that are well-drained, such as sandy soils. However, they are worth trying in other positions as they are effective, cheap fillers.

Some of the taller hybrids, or those with large flowers, may need supporting with twiggy sticks as the flowers do not stand up to rain and wind well. Cut back the plants hard in early autumn to encourage new basal shoots.

Spare plants of the taller types can be grown in rows on the vegetable plot and used as cut flowers.

Good companions

Use them to fill in the spaces between newly planted shrubs. Or combine them with low-growing grasses. Gaillardia work well in 'hot' colour schemes with plants such as *Geum* and *Achillea*.

Propagation

All the varieties listed below can be raised from seed. Some rarer varieties like 'Mandarin' should be propagated by root cuttings.

Troubleshooting

Yellowing of the leaves can be due to downy mildew. Inspect the undersides of the leaves for a white downy growth. Destroy affected leaves and spray the remaining plant with a suitable fungicide.

Which variety?

We would recommend the aptly named variety **'Dazzler'** which is fairly easy to find. It has golden-yellow flowers with a red centre and is 60cm (24in) high. Another striking tall variety is **'Burgunder'** with wine-red flowers.

Dwarf varieties include **'Goblin'** (syn. 'Kobold') with yellow and red flowers usually 35cm (14in) tall, although height can be variable with some reaching 60cm (24in).

Galega
Galega officinalis

Shape and size

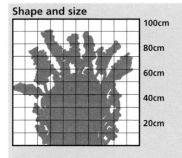

	100cm
	80cm
	60cm
	40cm
	20cm

Position

Hardiness

Soil

WELL-DRAINED

Uses

Features calendar

Jan	Feb	Mar	Apr	May	June
					✿
✿	✿	✿			
July	Aug	Sept	Oct	Nov	Dec

Buying tips *Galega officinalis is fairly easy to find. If you want named varieties, you will have to track down a specialist supplier.*

Galega officinalis 'Alba'

Galega officinalis 'His Majesty'

Growing guide

Galega (goat's rue) produces upright, branched spikes of pale lilac, pea-like flowers from mid-summer to early autumn. It is an ideal plant for adding a hazy colour wash to the back of a planting scheme. An undemanding perennial, it is very hardy and grows in any soil in sun or in light shade.

Galega is a tall, vigorous plant, with a tendency to sprawl. Allow plenty of room – 60–75cm (24–30in) between plants – and give it support so that it does not encroach on other plants. Cut down the flowering stems once they have finished.

Good companions

Use *Galega officinalis* as a background plant for pink daisy flowers or hybrid lilies. It also makes a subtle foil for peach or orange cluster-flowered (floribunda) roses. It can also be used to provide summer interest in a wildlife garden.

Propagation

Division or seed.

Troubleshooting

Generally-trouble free.

Which variety?

Galega officinalis is widely available and garden-worthy. You may also come across named varieties like **'Alba'** with white flowers, **'His Majesty'** (syn. 'Her Majesty') with soft lilac-blue flowers and **'Lady Wilson'** which is mauve and cream. **G. bicolor** has whitish-lilac flowers on 70cm (28in) stems.

G. orientalis is similar to *G. officinalis* but smaller with clear blue flowers. It can be invasive.

Gaura

Gaura lindheimeri

Shape and size

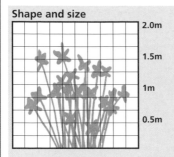

- 2.0m
- 1.5m
- 1m
- 0.5m

Position Hardiness Soil

WELL-DRAINED

Uses

Features calendar

Jan	Feb	Mar	Apr	May	June
✿	✿	✿	✿		
July	Aug	Sept	Oct	Nov	Dec

Gaura lindheimeri

Buying tips *Look for young, bushy plants in small pots. It is worth growing them from seed the autumn before, or take summer cuttings and overwinter if you want to grow it in drifts.*

Growing guide

This is an attractive, long-flowering plant, but for impact needs to be planted in bold drifts. Small white flowers tinged with pink are held on stiff branched stems. It flowers from early summer until the first frosts.

Plant young plants in a well-drained soil and a warm site. They self-seed, and need very little aftercare, but can be short-lived if the plants become woody.

Good companions

A graceful addition to borders and beds that can be used as a filler between bold flowering or foliage plants. Plant between sweet rocket (*Hesperis matronalis*) for colour in late summer. The foot of a sheltered wall can be a suitable site; plant with *Diascia* and silver-grey *Ballota*.

Propagation

Seed or cuttings in summer.

Troubleshooting

Generally trouble-free, but may not overwinter in cold, wet soils unless given winter protection. It self-seeds in favourable sites.

Which variety?

The species, ***Gaura lindheimeri***, is excellent. You may come across named varieties with golden-variegated foliage such as **'Corrie's Gold'** or **'Jo Adela'**. These are pretty plants, but not as hardy as the species.

Gentiana

Gentiana asclepiadea

Shape and size

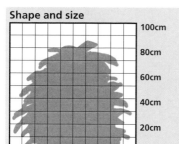

100cm
80cm
60cm
40cm
20cm

Position

Hardiness

Soil

MOIST

Uses

Features calendar

Jan	Feb	Mar	Apr	May	June
✿	✿				
July	Aug	Sept	Oct	Nov	Dec

Buying tips *Buy in flower as seedlings do not always come true to type. Try nurseries that specialise in shade or woodland plants.*

Gentiana sino-ornata

Gentiana asclepiadea

Growing guide

The gentians are a surprisingly varied group ranging from low-growing rockery plants to tall, graceful woodland dwellers – there is even a yellow one. Some prefer sun, others like shade but light shade suits most of them.

Gentians have a reputation for being difficult to grow but all you need to do is choose and prepare the planting site carefully. They cannot tolerate waterlogged soil – but the roots must not dry out either. Before planting, dig plenty of well-rotted organic matter, such as leafmould, into the soil. Alternatively, grow gentians in raised beds filled with a gritty topsoil or compost.

If *G. asclepiadea* is given dappled shade and moist soil it will be long-lived and need little attention.

Good companions

G. asclepiadea can be used to add summer interest to spring shrubs or planted up with ferns to create a cool, woodland planting. The autumn-flowering ones provide blue to contrast with the reds and oranges of autumn leaves and berries.

Propagation

Seed (when ripe).

Troubleshooting

Generally trouble-free if grown in suitable soil and left undisturbed.

Which variety?

We've chosen the summer-flowering **Gentiana asclepiadea**, as its arching stems make it an impressive gentian for the border. You may come across named varieties in different shades of blue or with white throats.

The following could be grown in containers or at the front of a border: **G. septemfida** is smaller at 30x30cm (12x12in), and is arguably the easiest to grow. **G. sino-ornata** has the most intense blue flowers in autumn, but it needs a lime-free soil and an adequate supply of lime-free water to keep it going. Height and spread 15x30cm (6x12in). There are many named varieties.

G. lutea is an unusual gentian that would make an impressive specimen plant. It has pale yellow flowers in summer and large ribbed leaves. It needs a sunny site with a deep, fertile soil. Height and spread 120x60cm (48x24in).

Willow gentian

Geranium

Geranium wallichianum 'Buxton's Variety'

Shape and size

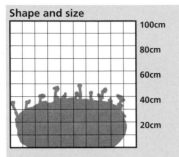

100cm
80cm
60cm
40cm
20cm

Position

Hardiness   Soil

ANY

Uses

Features calendar

Jan	Feb	Mar	Apr	May	June
✿	✿	✿	✿		
July	Aug	Sept	Oct	Nov	Dec

Buying tips *Most garden centres will offer a good selection. Buy as young plants in small pots – they soon establish into sizeable clumps. If you want a lot for groundcover, look out for large plants that can be divided up.*

'Russell Prichard'

Geranium 'Johnson's Blue'

Growing guide

Hardy geraniums are popular and versatile perennials, as useful in the modern garden as they are in cottage-style gardens. They are long-flowering yet require very little attention. Many are drought-tolerant and there are few problems with pests or diseases. Many have excellent foliage, and some are evergreen.

Once established, hardy geraniums can be relied upon to grow in virtually any situation, so use them in the tricky areas like dry, shady spots. Particularly good for dry shade are *G. macrorrhizum* 'Ingwersen's Variety', *G. nodosum*, *G. phaeum* or *G. gracile*. You do not need to prepare most garden soils before planting, but in dry shady areas some garden compost or well-rotted organic matter will help the soil retain moisture.

Good companions

The soft mound shapes need a partner with a strong outline – phormiums, tall alliums or irises work well. Hardy geraniums are also used as groundcover, on banks, between shrubs or under roses.

Propagation

Division or seed.

Troubleshooting

Generally trouble-free. Cut back in mid-summer if they start to look tatty or develop mildew.

Geranium wallichianum 'Buxton's Variety'

Geranium oxonianum 'Wargrave Pink'

Geranium 'Brookside'

Geranium psilostemon

Geranium nodosum

Which variety?

We've picked **Geranium wallichianum 'Buxton's Variety'** (syn. G. 'Buxton's Blue'), an old variety, still widely available, for its pretty blue flowers with white centres but there are many other recommended varieties.

FOR FLOWERS

'Ann Folkard' has a long period of interest, magenta flowers from May to October with a foil of yellowish young foliage ageing to light green. **G. oxonianum 'Wargrave Pink'** a well-known variety with pink flowers from May to September. For blue flowers from June to July there is another old favourite, **G. 'Johnson's Blue'. G. psilostemon** is a tall variety that may need support but is worth growing for its autumn colour and large flowers. The flowers are bright magenta with a dark centre and last from June until August.

FOR FOLIAGE

G. renardii has soft, round, sage-green leaves and white to pale pink flowers. It forms a low compact clump – ideal for the front of a border. **G. clarkei 'Kashmir Purple'** is a spreading plant with deeply and finely cut foliage. Hardy geraniums with brilliant autumn colour include: **G. sanguineum 'Striatum'** a low sprawler with deep pink flowers from May to August and **G. x magnificum** a taller plant with pale blue flowers from June to July. **G. nodosum** has bright green, glossy foliage, good autumn colour and pale lavender flowers from May to September. **G. macrorrhizum 'Ingwersen's Variety'** produces a dense carpet of aromatic, evergreen leaves and pale pink flowers from May to July. **G. procurrens** has light green, mottled leaves and dark pink-purple flowers but has a wayward habit

UNUSUAL VARIETIES

You will have greater variety if you order from a specialist. For example, **'Brookside'** is a good all-round plant with large purple flowers from May to July. **G. palmatum** is a tall evergreen with very large leaves and pink flowers from June to August. Needs winter protection. **G. x riversleaianum 'Russell Prichard'** has intense pink flowers from May until October and grey-green foliage. It prefers a sunny site and is best protected through the winter. In addition, there are many smaller hardy geraniums such as **G. cinereum 'Lawrence Flatman'** grown as rockery plants.

Geum
Geum 'Borisii'

Shape and size

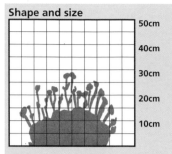

50cm
40cm
30cm
20cm
10cm

Position

Hardiness   Soil

ANY

Uses

Features calendar

Jan	Feb	Mar	Apr	May ✿	June ✿
July ✿	Aug ✿	Sept ✿	Oct	Nov	Dec

Buying tips *Geum 'Borisii' is widely available. 'Mrs J. Bradshaw' and 'Lady Stratheden' are well-known varieties widely sold in most garden centres, but you can save a lot of money by growing them from seed.*

'Mrs J. Bradshaw'

Geum 'Borisii'

Growing guide

Geum are easy to grow and have a long flowering period. They can be used in borders, containers or as cut flowers. In addition, some types can be used in rockeries and there are native species for wildflower gardens.

Most positions are suitable as they thrive in all but very heavy or waterlogged soils or dry, chalky soils. In a cold area, a well-drained soil is particularly important for the *G. chiloense* hybrids. *Geum* do well in sun or in partial shade.

The larger, clump-forming *Geum*, 30cm (12in) high or more, make easy border plants. They produce a main flush of flowers from late May until July and then intermittently through the year. To improve the later display, cut back the old stems after the first flowering. *Geum* often keep their leaves over winter. Staking is not usually necessary except in exposed positions.

Good companions

Geum contrast well with bold foliage plants like hostas, ferns and irises. The variety 'Borisii' with its luminous orange-scarlet flowers has enough impact to be a single subject in a terracotta pot, or in a border with blue veronicas, say. Yellow *Geum* can be used to brighten up dark-leaved shrubs such as smoke bush (*Cotinus coggygria*) or a purple berberis.

Propagation
Division.

Troubleshooting

The only pests likely to cause problems are sawfly larvae, which eat the edges of the leaves. Pick off the 'caterpillars' by hand and check the undersides of leaves.

If the plant loses its vigour, lift and divide the following spring or autumn. You will probably need to do this every two to three years in any case – every year for the *G. chiloense* hybrids.

Which variety?

We've chosen **'Borisii'** as it is widely available and has attractive, almost evergreen foliage and magnificent orange, single flowers. *G. chiloense* hybrids are nearly as impressive and offer a range of colours, but need good drainage in cold areas. **'Lady Stratheden'** (yellow) and **'Mrs J. Bradshaw'** (brick red) are widely sold, offering semi-double flowers from June until October on 45x30cm (18x12in) plants. **'Fire Opal'** with its orange-scarlet flowers is similar.

The water avens (**G. rivale**) is a native that can be used in wild gardens. It is a mat-forming plant 30–45cm (12–18in) in height and spread with pinky-cream, nodding flowers from May to October. Selected varieties such as the semi-double, coppery-pink **'Leonard's Variety'** could be used in borders.

Gunnera

Gunnera manicata

Shape and size

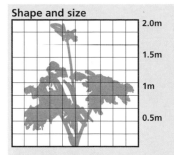

- 2.0m
- 1.5m
- 1m
- 0.5m

Position

Hardiness

Soil

MOIST

Uses

Features calendar

Jan	Feb	Mar	Apr	May	June
			🌿	✿	✿

July	Aug	Sept	Oct	Nov	Dec
✿	✿	✿	🌿	🌿	

Buying tips *Gunnera can be obtained from aquatic specialists as bare-rooted plants in autumn or as pot-grown plants in spring.*

Gunnera tinctoria

Gunnera manicata

Growing guide

The giant prickly rhubarb is one of the few Brazilian plants that can be grown outside in Britain. Its giant rhubarb-like leaves reach anything from 0.9–3m (3–10ft) and are carried on stems up to 3m (10ft) high, so it is suitable only for larger gardens. It is essentially a plant for moist soil, ideal for a bog garden or at the edge of a stream or pond. A deep, rich soil is needed, together with full sun and shelter from winds. When planting, dig a large hole and fill it with topsoil and well-rotted organic matter. Spring planting is best. Although it likes wet conditions, the crown should not be left waterlogged when dormant. It is possible to plant gunneras in a half-barrel, which keeps them more manageable.

Greenish flowers are produced in the summer. Plants may need watering in summer if not grown near water. In cooler districts, the crown of the plant must be well protected in the winter. As the leaves die down, fold them over the crown, then heap a pile of bracken or straw over them. Remove the protective covering in spring.

Good companions

Can be grown as a specimen on its own or used in a bog garden underplanted with *Iris pseudacorus*. Looks superb next to water.

Propagation

Division or seed.

Troubleshooting

Generally trouble-free if kept well watered and fed, and given protection over winter.

Which variety?

Gunnera manicata (syn. *G. brasiliensis*) is the main species, there are others such as **G. tinctoria** (syn. *G. chilensis*, *G. scabra*) which is similar, but smaller at 2.1m (7ft) and hardier. **G. magellanica** is a low, creeping plant with small round leaves suitable for damp spots.

Gypsophila

Gypsophila paniculata 'Compacta Plena'

Shape and size

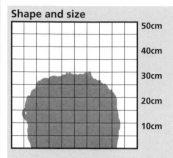

Position   Hardiness   Soil

WELL-DRAINED

Uses

Features calendar

Jan	Feb	Mar	Apr	May	June
✿	✿				
July	Aug	Sept	Oct	Nov	Dec

Buying tips *Despite being widely sold as a cut flower, you will probably have to visit a specialist if you want to buy plants.*

Gypsophila 'Rosy Veil'

Gypsophila paniculata 'Compacta Plena'

Growing guide

Gypsophila is perhaps best known as an ingredient for cut-flower arrangements, but it has lots to offer in the garden too. In summer, *Gypsophila paniculata* produces billowing white clouds of tiny flowers above a mound of lance-shaped foliage. Pale pink and double varieties are also available.

Gypsophila grows best in the warmer parts of the country. It needs full sun and a well-drained soil such as chalky or very stony ground. It has deep roots, so is best left to grow undisturbed – leave 60cm (24in) between plants. Twiggy supports may be needed for the taller types.

Good companions

Use *G. paniculata* to fill the gap left behind when spring bulbs, or early-flowering perennials such as poppies have finished.

Propagation

Sow seed *in situ*, during spring. Basal cuttings in spring.

Troubleshooting

Generally trouble-free, but can be short-lived in cold areas.

Which variety?

Gypsophila paniculata produces a froth of tiny white, single flowers. **'Bristol Fairy'** has white double flowers, **'Flamingo'** is a pale pink, double-flowered type.

More compact varieties are: **'Compacta Plena'**, double white 45cm(18in) tall; **'Rosy Veil'** (syn. 'Rosenschleier') only 30x45cm (12x18in) and has clear pink flowers. **'Festival White'** is 60cm (24in) tall and flowers from July to October. **'Festival Pink'** forms a low mound 45x50cm (18x20in).

Helenium

Helenium 'Moerheim Beauty'

Shape and size

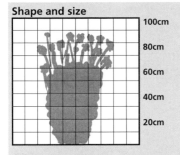

100cm
80cm
60cm
40cm
20cm

Position

Hardiness

Soil

MOIST

Uses

Features calendar

Jan	Feb	Mar	Apr	May	June
✿	✿	✿			
July	Aug	Sept	Oct	Nov	Dec

Buying tips *There are so many shades, heights and flowering times that it is worth looking at border collections in summer before you make your choice. Then order from a specialist for autumn planting.*

Helenium 'Butterpat'

Helenium 'Moerheim Beauty'

Growing guide

Heleniums are grown for their bright daisy-like flowers which appear from mid- to late summer, sometimes lasting into early autumn, depending on the variety. There are a number of colours and shades to choose from, including yellows, warm shades of coppery orange, bronzes and red-browns. Each flower has a prominent central disc. Heights vary from 60–150cm (24–60in), the taller ones need twiggy sticks, but you may get away without staking the dwarf ones.

Heleniums are easy to grow but they do best in a rich, fertile soil, and are an ideal choice for wet, sticky clay gardens. In poor, dry ground they will suffer unless you are prepared to improve the soil, feed, mulch and water during dry spells. Deadhead regularly to keep new flowers coming. Heleniums are useful as a cut flower.

Good companions

Combine them with bold foliage plants like white-flowered hostas, a grass, such as *Miscanthus sinensis* 'Silver Feather', or bergenias. If you want to use them with other flowering plants, choose ones with yellow, cream or white flowers.

Propagation

Division, in autumn or spring.

Troubleshooting

Be prepared to lift and divide them regularly to keep them flowering well. The plants may be eaten by slugs or tortrix caterpillars. A virus sometimes turns the flowers green. There is no cure, dig up and destroy affected plants. Replant with fresh stock elsewhere.

Which variety?

We would recommend **'Moerheim Beauty'**, a reliable, widely available variety. It has copper-red flowers from July to August/September and is 90cm (36in) high.

Others include the following (all are 90cm (36in) tall unless otherwise stated): **'Butterpat'** rich yellow flowers from mid-summer to early autumn; **'Bruno'** mahogany flowers from late summer to early autumn; **'Chipperfield Orange'** orange-yellow flowers, 1.5m (5ft) late summer to end autumn; **'The Bishop'** yellow flowers with a brown centre from June to September, 60cm (24in); **'Waltraut'** large flowers of golden brown from July to August; **'Wyndley'** coppery-orange flowers from June to August, 60cm (24in).

H. hoopesii looks similar to the above varieties, but its yellow flowers appear in June.

Helianthus

Helianthus salicifolius

Shape and size

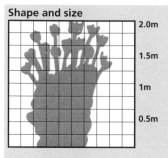

Position

Hardiness

Soil

WELL-DRAINED

Uses

Features calendar

Jan	Feb	Mar	Apr	May	June
July	Aug	Sept	Oct	Nov	Dec

In the calendar, flower symbols appear under Feb, Mar, and Apr.

Buying tips Most perennial sunflowers will have to be obtained from specialists. Look for healthy green foliage and moist compost.

Helianthus 'Loddon Gold'

Helianthus salicifolius

Growing guide

The perennial sunflower will provide a bright splash of late summer colour towards the back of a border where its rather coarse foliage can be hidden from view.

Helianthus salicifolius is a tall plant with small, yellow daisy-like blooms that last well into autumn. Unlike many of the other species, this one has reasonably attractive foliage which can be used as a backdrop to earlier-flowering plants.

Perennial sunflowers like a warm, sunny spot but are not that fussy about soil as long as the drainage is reasonable. The stems need support with canes or sticks and deadheading is required to prolong flowering. Once flowering is over, cut down stems to near ground level.

Good companions

Use as a backdrop to provide late summer interest when neighbouring plants are past their best. Try growing some in a wild garden, at the edge of woodland or in a shrubbery.

Propagation

Division.

Troubleshooting

Many perennial sunflowers have running roots which can be a nuisance in the wrong place.

Which variety?

We have chosen *Helianthus salicifolius (syn. H. orgyalis)* because it has willow-like leaves and flowers well into the autumn.

Varieties derived from *H. decapetalus* tend to have rather coarse foliage. For example, the variety **'Star'** is a cool, lemon-yellow and flowers from early August until September. It grows to 1.2m (4ft). **'Loddon Gold'** has golden-yellow, double flowers from July to September and can attain a height of 1.5m (5ft).

Heliopsis

Heliopsis scabra 'Summer Sun'

Shape and size

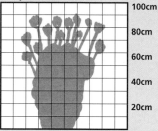

100cm
80cm
60cm
40cm
20cm

Position **Hardiness**

Soil **Uses**

WELL-DRAINED

Features calendar

Jan	Feb	Mar	Apr	May	June
✿	✿				
July	Aug	Sept	Oct	Nov	Dec

Buying tips *You are very unlikely to find this plant at garden centres. Try herbaceous specialists instead.*

Heliopsis scabra 'Summer Sun'

Growing guide

Heliopsis are closely related to perennial sunflowers and look very similar, but are easier to grow. They are not as popular as they deserve to be, yet they offer bright yellow, daisy-like flowers that are superb for providing highlights in a summer border. They are fairly compact and bushy, so staking should not be needed. Another bonus is that they do not need frequent lifting and dividing.

Just give them a reasonable garden soil and a sunny spot and they should flower from July to August. There should be plenty for cutting, too. At the end of the season cut down the flowering stems to the ground.

Good companions

These are bright, mid-border plants that team up well with the darker monardas and blue salvias.

Propagation

Division, every three years.

Troubleshooting

Generally trouble-free.

Which variety?

Most *Heliopsis* are shades of yellow. Some varieties are orange. There are single, semi-doubles or doubles. The most widely available variety of *Heliopsis scabra* is **'Summer Sun'** (syn. 'Sommersonne') which is listed by specialists and has golden, double flowers from July to August.

Helleborus
Helleborus orientalis hybrids

Shape and size

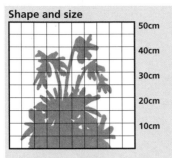

50cm
40cm
30cm
20cm
10cm

Position

Hardiness Soil Uses

MOIST

Features calendar

Jan	Feb	Mar	Apr	May	June
	✿	✿	✿		

July	Aug	Sept	Oct	Nov	Dec

Buying tips *Hellebores are fairly expensive. Buy in flower as the colours can vary greatly. Many hellebores, such as H. argutifolius, H. foetidus and H. niger are available in garden centres, but for the greatest choice of flower colour visit a hellebore specialist in early spring, when you can choose between two-year-old plants in flower or one-year-old seedlings.*

WARNING
All parts of the hellebore are poisonous if ingested. Care should also be taken to avoid getting the sap in the eyes. Wear gloves when handling this plant.

Helleborus orientalis 'Ashwood Garden Hybrids'

Growing guide

Hellebores are valued for their beautiful winter flowers, but many have very attractive foliage, too.

They are versatile plants, suitable for borders and raised beds of all sizes. They can be used as groundcover, or planted up as single subjects in containers.

The plants are tolerant of a range of soils, but will not thrive in waterlogged conditions. They like lime or chalk, but dig in plenty of well-rotted organic matter to improve moisture retention. You can grow hellebores on acidic soils provided you mulch with spent mushroom compost each spring. *H. foetidus* and its hybrids are the most tolerant of poor soil. The majority of hellebores will grow in either sun or shade. Before mulching, look for hellebore seedlings. These can be left if thinned or if there is a clump they can be lifted and replanted elsewhere. The larger hellebores may need staking.

Plants can be potted up and kept in a cold greenhouse or conservatory for even earlier flowers. Blooms, picked with 1cm (½in) of stem and floated in a bowl of water as part of a table decoration would be another way to appreciate their intricate markings.

Good companions

Hellebores can grow under trees, shrubs or beside walls if the ground is not too dry. Interplant hellebores with spring-flowering bulbs or hardy cyclamen for added interest. If growing hellebores in a border, team them with plants such as epimediums, hardy geraniums or pulmonarias, all of which will take over later in the season.

Grow hellebores in a mid-border position between deciduous shrubs or trees where they will be partially hidden from view for most of the year, but come to the fore in winter when surrounding plants lose their leaves.

Propagation

Division is possible but plants may be slow to recover. The best time for the *H. orientalis* hybrids is the end of August or early September. Look out for self-sown seedlings.

Troubleshooting

Hellebore leaf spot, a fungal disease that attacks leaves, flowers and stems, is the biggest problem. Remove and burn marked leaves in winter, to prevent the disease spreading from the leaves to the new flowers and to make the plants look less tatty. Spray remaining plants with a copper-based fungicide. Mice and slugs can damage young seedlings.

Helleborus foetidus

Helleborus lividus

Helleborus argutifolius

Helleborus niger 'Potter's Wheel'

Which variety?

We have chosen **H. orientalis** hybrids for their large flowers and colour range. **'Ashwood Garden Hybrids'** are new colour strains that have been bred from *H. orientalis*. The blooms range from white, pink, red, purple, black, yellow or green, each with attractive markings.

Other hellebores worth considering include: **H. argutifolius** (syn. *H. corsicus*), a tough plant reaching 90x90cm (36x36in) or more, best in full sun in well-drained soil. Greenish flowers from January to March. **H. foetidus** (stinking hellebore) is a British native with pale green flowers that thrives in moist soil in partial shade. It can reach 75x90cm (30x36in). **'Wester Flisk Group'** is an improved form of the species with purple-red stems, evergreen foliage and pale-green flowers in early spring. Height and spread is 38cm (15in). **'Chedglow'** is a new variety with golden foliage, height and spread 60x45cm (24x18in).

H. lividus is a desirable plant with attractive flowers and foliage, but it is hard to obtain and needs a sheltered position. Flowers have a pinkish or purple tint on green and last from December to March. Height about 38cm (15in). **H. niger** (Christmas rose) is well known but fairly fussy, and not easy to grow. It likes humus-rich, chalky soil in partial shade. Height 23–30cm (9–12in) with dark, evergreen leaves. White flowers appear from January to April. **'Potter's Wheel'** is a named form with large, white flowers and golden stamens. Buy plants while they are in flower as some strains are better than others.

Hemerocallis

Hemerocallis 'Hyperion'

Shape and size

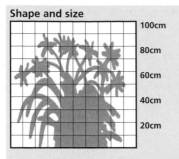

100cm
80cm
60cm
40cm
20cm

Position

Hardiness Soil

ANY

Uses

Features calendar

Jan	Feb	Mar	Apr	May	June
July	Aug	Sept	Oct	Nov	Dec

Buying tips *Although varieties vary in size, it is the quality of the flowers that is most important. It is worth visiting collections and looking at the flowers before you buy. As well as choosing colours you like and smelling them, note if the flowers are held well above the foliage, if they are still open in the afternoon and if there is rain damage or colour fading in sun. Be wary of buying expensive new introductions – if they stay the course they will be cheaper in a few years' time.*

Hemerocallis 'Hyperion'

Growing guide

These are first-class perennials, forming impressive clumps of grass-like foliage topped with flowers that are interesting close-to as well as from a distance. Although the individual flowers last only a day, plenty are produced over the summer. It is not worth picking them for arrangements, but the flowers and buds are edible and can be used to add a splash of colour to salads.

Day lilies are hardy, do not need staking and grow on all soils, even heavy clay. Clumps can be left for at least five years before they need dividing. They will grow in sun or partial shade – you will get the most flowers in sun but the darker colours, especially reds, may shrivel in really sunny spots.

Space the larger varieties 40–60cm (16–24in) apart; the new dwarf types only need 30–40cm (12–16in). Mulching will help retain moisture in the summer. Established plants on poor soil will benefit from a general fertiliser such as growmore in early spring. The dwarf types and those with ruffles or marked petals make excellent container plants. The older types make a useful weed-suppressing groundcover.

Good companions

Day lilies make good partners for daffodils as they help to hide the dying foliage. Yellow day lilies are effective with light blues or reds. The darker, richer day lilies go well with yellow or cream plants. Pink day lilies will add interest to silver or grey foliage plants.

Propagation

Division.

Troubleshooting

Generally trouble-free. However, hemerocallis gall midge, which first arrived in Britain a decade ago, seems to be an increasing problem. Flower buds swell abnormally and fail to open. Inside, you will find a white larva. The damage occurs between mid-May and mid-July. Destroy affected buds as soon as you see them.

'Pink Damask'

Which variety?

Hundreds of varieties exist and more are added each year, but very few are stocked by more than a few specialists. Some of the newer ones come from the USA and may not do that well in Britain. We have chosen the older variety **'Hyperion'** for its scented, yellow flowers from June to August, height 90cm (36in).

The following are listed by a number of specialists, all flower from June to August and are 90cm (36in) unless otherwise stated.

YELLOWS/ORANGES
'Burning Daylight' large flowers of deep orange. Height 75cm (30in). **'Cartwheels'** large, golden-yellow flowers. **'Cream Drop'** fragrant, creamy yellow flowers from June to July. Height 45cm (18in). **'Golden Chimes'** small flowers of golden yellow. Height 60cm (24in). **'Marion Vaughn'** fragrant light yellow flowers. **'Stella de Oro'** continuous blooms from June until October. Small, golden-yellow flowers. Height 55cm (22in). **'Whichford'** fragrant flowers of clear lemon-yellow. *H. dumortieri* very compact clump, up to 60cm (24in) high, brownish buds with orange flowers from May to June. A good choice for hot, dry spots. *H. lilioasphodelus* fragrant flowers of lemon-yellow that last a long time. Tolerates wet ground.

REDS
Most reds do not cope well with rain or cold. Here is our selection of the older, reliable varieties:

'Buzz Bomb' rich red flowers. Height 60cm (24in). **'Mallard'** large, ruby-red flowers. **'Sammy Russell'** small brick-red flowers. Height 70cm (28in). **'Stafford'** bright red flowers. **'Summer Wine'** maroon-red flowers. Height 60cm (24in).

PINKS/APRICOTS
Many pink varieties have intricate markings or ruffled petals.

'Catherine Woodbery' large flowers of lavender pink. **'Children's Festival'** a recent introduction that is becoming widely available, ruffled

'Stafford'

'Frans Hals'

apricot flowers from June to July. Height 55cm (22in). **'George Cunningham'** apricot flowers. **'Pink Damask'** deep pink flowers. Height 75cm (30in). **'Stoke Poges'** pale creamy pink on outside, pink flowers. Height 60cm (24in)

BICOLOR/PATTERNED
'Black Magic' deep ruby-mahogany with yellow. **'Bonanza'** buff flowers with brown from July to September. Height 75cm (30in). **'Frans Hals'** a bicolor of rust-red and yellow. **'Little Wine Cup'** burgundy and gold flowers from June to July. Height 50cm (20in). *H. fulva* **'Flore Pleno'** double orange flowers with red eye. Varieties with the prefix **'Siloam'** are from the USA, many are low-growing, small varieties that need a lot of sun to do well.

'Golden Chimes'

Hepatica

Hepatica nobilis

Shape and size

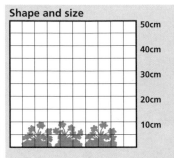

50cm
40cm
30cm
20cm
10cm

Position

Hardiness

Soil

MOIST

Uses

Features calendar

Jan	Feb	Mar	Apr	May	June
July	Aug	Sept	Oct	Nov	Dec

Buying tips *You are very unlikely to find this plant at garden centres. Try unusual plant specialists, they often sell them in flower in March/April.*

Hepatica transsilvanica

Hepatica nobilis

Growing guide

These are small perennials that bear blue, pink or white flowers in early spring. Their woodland origin makes them ideal for cheering up ground under shrubs and trees where many other flowering perennials would fail. A spot in shade or partial shade and a moist but well-drained soil is ideal. They do well on chalky soil, if moisture retention is improved. They can tolerate sun as long as the soil does not dry out.

Before planting, prepare the soil by adding leafmould or well-rotted garden compost. Thereafter, the plants can be left for many years without attention. When flowering declines, lift, divide and replant.

Good companions

Grow under deciduous shrubs and trees. Do not let them get swamped by taller plants. The early crocus *C. tomasinianus* and *Cyclamen coum* flower at the same time.

Propagation

Division or seed.

Troubleshooting

Generally trouble-free but they can seed themselves around. The seedlings may vary in colour from the parent.

Which variety?

Hepaticas are not widely available in garden centres but two species are worth seeking out from specialists. ***H. nobilis*** (syn. *H. triloba*) has blue, pink or white flowers depending on the form. There are also rare double forms. And ***H. transsilvanica*** (syn. *H. angulosa*) which is similar, but slightly taller with larger leaves and a more spreading habit.

Heuchera

Heuchera 'Pewter Moon'

Shape and size

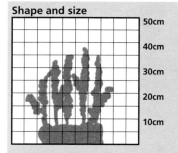

50cm
40cm
30cm
20cm
10cm

Position

Hardiness

Soil

WELL-DRAINED

Uses

Features calendar

Jan	Feb	Mar	Apr	May	June
July	Aug	Sept	Oct	Nov	Dec

Buying tips *There are lots of new varieties with interesting foliage tints. Visit a specialist in spring or autumn and select a colour you like.*

Heuchera micrantha 'Rachel'

Heuchera 'Pewter Moon'

Growing guide

Heucheras really earn their place in a garden as they offer foliage interest as well as attractive summer flowers. The foliage varies with the variety, but there are many unusual metallic hues in copper, purple and silver to choose from. They are almost evergreen and have a good weed-suppressing habit. Plant 30–45cm (12–18in) apart.

The flowers are borne on wiry stems held above the foliage mounds. They add a graceful, airy touch to plantings and are very effective in large drifts. Most are pink, red, white or green; the latter are popular with flower arrangers.

Heucheras like a well-drained but fertile soil in a sunny or lightly shaded spot. They do not like sticky, wet clay. If your soil is thin and poor, dig in plenty of well-rotted organic matter. Plant deeply, with only the crown above the ground and mulch well each spring.

Good companions

Heucheras are ideal at the front of a border or small divisions can be used as foliage foils in containers. The purple, silver-veined types look effective with silver foliage plants.

Propagation

Division. Some varieties like 'Palace Purple' can be raised from seed.

Troubleshooting

They need dividing every three years or so, or they become woody.

Which variety?

We've chosen **Heuchera parvifolia 'Pewter Moon'** for its attractive foliage: each leaf has a greyish sheen on top but deep maroon below. The pink flowers last from June to August.

Most of the following are 35cm (14in) high and flower from May to July, unless otherwise stated. **H. cylindrica 'Greenfinch'** has greenish-white flowers and silver foliage. It is a tall variety at 75cm (30in). **H. 'Green Ivory'** is similar. **H. micrantha diversifolia 'Palace Purple'** is widely available and offers the deepest foliage colour of purple bronze. Plants are 60cm (24in) and topped with white flowers. **H. micrantha 'Chocolate Ruffles'** has large brown and burgundy leaves. **'Persian Carpet'** has large red and purple foliage. **'Rachel'** has dark green foliage tinged with pink and coral pink flowers. **'Scintillation'** has masses of pink bells; it is eye-catching but hard to find. **'Stormy Seas'** boasts red foliage with a metallic sheen. **'Snow Storm'** is variegated with green/creamy white leaves. Grow in sun for the best foliage colour. Cerise-pink flowers.

There are also **x Heucherellas** which have more flowering impact but green foliage. The light pink **'Bridget Bloom'** can be obtained from specialists. **x H. tiarelloides** has golden-green foliage and pink flowers but is more difficult to find.

Hosta

Hosta sieboldiana 'Elegans'

Shape and size

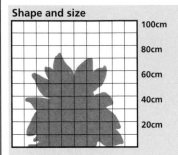

Position   Hardiness   Soil

MOIST

Uses

Features calendar

Jan	Feb	Mar	Apr	May	June
July	Aug	Sept	Oct	Nov	Dec

Buying tips *When choosing plants, remember the young foliage often has a different appearance to the mature foliage.*

Hosta 'Frances Williams'

Hosta sieboldiana 'Elegans'

Growing guide

Hostas are a large group of plants valued for their foliage. They are particularly versatile and form bold clumps that add structure and texture to borders, containers, underplantings and bog gardens. The ideal site is partial shade, especially where their roots have a moist, humus-rich soil. However, species and varieties vary in their tolerance and there is a hosta for most gardens. Some golden varieties with thin leaves can scorch in sun, yet thicker leaves develop a better colour in sun. Blue-leaved varieties generally prefer cool, shady spots.

To help hostas establish, it is worth digging plenty of well-rotted organic matter into the planting site. Mulch and water for the first two seasons. Clumps gradually increase in size reaching 60x45cm (24 x18in) in three years. For groundcover, plant 40cm (16in) apart, a little closer for small varieties and 45–60cm (18–24in) apart for large ones such as *H. sieboldiana* 'Elegans'. If growing in containers keep well-watered and feed with a balanced liquid feed. Hostas provide a lot of material for the flower arranger. The leaves can be used fresh or dried, the seed pods dried and the flowers fresh. Some hosta leaves colour up in the autumn.

Good companions

Hostas look particularly effective grouped together or can be used as a foil for spiky plants such as ornamental grasses and phormiums. Brighten up shady spots, such as north-facing fences, with variegated hostas, ferns and spring bulbs. Large specimen plants do not need companions – they are impressive on their own.

Propagation

Division works well but try to cut out a section from mature clumps. Hostas can also be topped (see right).

Troubleshooting

Slugs and snails can shred the leaves, so it is worth putting down slug pellets as a routine. Wind can damage and dry the leaves, making them look bedraggled. If rabbits are a problem, protect young leaves with wire netting for a few weeks. Grey mould can cause brown spotting on the leaves in wet years. Remove infected leaves.

Hosta lancifolia

Which variety?

We would recommend *H. sieboldiana* **'Elegans'** for its large blue-grey leaves. However, the following is a selection of the many widely available ones. All have lilac flowers unless otherwise stated.

'Frances Williams' (syn. 'Golden Circles') is like 'Elegans' but with a yellow margin. **'Halcyon'** has heart-shaped leaves of silvery-grey, and forms a small mound 45cm (18in) high. **'Honeybells'** is noted for its fragrant flowers. Pale pink in bud then white flowers over yellow-green leaves. One of the bigger ones at 90cm (36in).

H. aureomarginata **'Ventricosa'** (syn. *H.* 'Variegata') has dark green leaves edged with cream. *H. fortunei* **'Aureomarginata'** (syn. 'Yellow Edge', 'Obscura Marginata') is deep green, edged with yellow. *H. fortunei* **'Hyacinthina'** has grey-green foliage with a narrow grey edge. *H. lancifolia* narrow, glossy foliage with lovely deep purple flowers late in the year.

'Sum and Substance' has yellow leaves that do best in sun – it is said to be slug-proof. *H. undulata* **'Albomarginata'** (syn. 'Thomas Hogg') has glossy, green-and-cream leaves. Ideal for underplanting. *H. ventricosa* has heart-shaped, dark green, shiny leaves up to 90cm (36in) high. Violet flowers.

Hosta fortunei 'Aureomarginata'

Propagating hostas

Small plants can be propagated by a method called 'topping'.
First lift and wash a dormant crown (or buy a new plant). Divide into sections – each should have a plump bud. Cut the top third off the bud and cut a cross into

the base of the bud. Dust with a fungicide, pot up sections and cover with compost.
When signs of new growth appear in spring, knock out each section and split into four plants.

Houttuynia

Houttuynia cordata 'Chameleon'

Shape and size

50cm
40cm
30cm
20cm
10cm

Position   Hardiness   Soil

MOIST

Uses

Features calendar

Jan	Feb	Mar	Apr	May	June
July	Aug	Sept	Oct	Nov	Dec

Buying tips *You should not need to buy it! Just find a friend who has it in his or her garden and ask for a piece.*

Houttuynia cordata 'Flore Pleno'

Houttuynia cordata 'Chameleon'

Growing guide

This eye-catching plant is often bought on impulse for its multi-coloured foliage. It needs careful siting as it can be very invasive. Plant a small piece 8cm (3in) deep and it will form a low-growing mound, around 20cm (8in) high.

For the best foliage colour, it needs sun but the soil should be cool and moist for vigorous growth. Mulch well in early spring if the soil tends to dry out. It has white flowers in summer but these play second fiddle to the coloured, heart-shaped leaves.

Good companions

Do not let loose in a border, confine it in a container, where it makes a good single subject from late spring to autumn. Houttuynia is often used to excellent effect beside water, but could also be used to soften the edges of a bank, say.

Propagation

Divide rhizomes in spring.

Troubleshooting

This invasive plant can be a nuisance in the wrong place but it does not spread so much in a dry soil. The leaves of 'Chameleon' can revert to green if the plant is grown in shade; moving it to a sunnier spot should ensure the variegation returns the following growing season.

Which variety?

'Chameleon' (syn. 'Tricolor') is the one to go for, with its bright foliage of green, red and yellow. You may also come across **'Flore Pleno'** which has dark green leaves and more attractive white flowers.

Inula

Inula magnifica

Shape and size

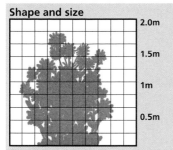

- 2.0m
- 1.5m
- 1m
- 0.5m

Position   Hardiness   Soil

MOIST

Uses

Features calendar

Jan	Feb	Mar	Apr	May	June
July	Aug	Sept	· Oct	Nov	Dec

(Aug and Sept show flower symbols)

Buying tips *You will probably have to buy from a specialist. Check the roots have not dried out.*

Inula hookeri

Inula magnifica

Growing guide

Inula magnifica tops 1.8m (6ft) and with its stout stems and golden yellow daisy-like flowers up to 15cm (6in) in diameter, it is a real show-stopper.

Given a moist, rich soil it will retain healthy foliage right down to the base, so could be used as a specimen. In less than ideal conditions, the lower leaves tend to look tatty and need something substantial like a clump of hemerocallis in front to hide them. It prefers a sunny site.

Good companions

Inula magnifica can be grown as a specimen in rough grass or in a bog garden. Use it to add colour to purple-leaved shrubs. For a bright border, use it at the back with crimson-red lythrums or phloxes in front.

Propagation

Division or seed.

Troubleshooting

Generally trouble-free if given enough space and a moist soil.

Which variety?

All have yellow daisy-like flowers either in summer or late summer, but they vary in height and coarseness of foliage. We have chosen **Inula magnifica** as it forms such an impressive specimen. Large yellow daisies from August to September. Height and spread 1.8x1m (6x3ft).

However, there are smaller ones which suit other situations better. **I. ensifolia** is a late summer-flowering dwarf plant at 30cm (12in). It has a dense habit, so is ideal for the front of a border. **'Gold Star'** has a neat habit at 60cm (24in) and flowers from June to August. **I. candida** is a new dwarf one, 30cm (12in) high with hairy, silver foliage, but it is not easy to get yet. **I. hookeri** spreads rapidly and has yellow flowers with brown centres from June to August on 60–75cm (24–28in) plants. **I. orientalis** (syn. *I. glandulosa*) has orange-yellow flowers in summer on 45cm (18in) plants. **I. racemosa** tops 2.7m (9ft) and has very coarse foliage, so it is suitable only for a wild garden.

Iris

Iris unguicularis

Shape and size

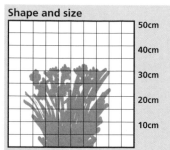

50cm
40cm
30cm
20cm
10cm

Position   Hardiness   Soil

WELL-DRAINED

Uses

Features calendar

Jan	Feb ✱	Mar ✱	Apr	May	June
July	Aug	Sept	Oct	Nov	Dec

Buying tips Check the rhizome is firm as overhead watering or poor compost can cause rot. For the widest selection of bearded irises you need to visit or order from a specialist. Autumn is the best time for planting.

Iris foetidissima showing autumn berries

Iris unguicularis

Growing guide

Iris is a large genus that includes some of the loveliest flowering perennials. Here we have concentrated on the ones with rhizomes that can be grown in a border. Rhizomatous irises include bearded and beardless types. The 'beard' refers to the hairs along the centre of the fall (lower) petals.

The rhizome needs to ripen in the sun each summer if it is to flower well the next year, so it is important that the upper surface of the rhizome is above soil level, with the fibrous roots deep in the soil. It helps to turn the rhizome (not the leaf fans necessarily) to get maximum sun during the day. Tall varieties can have their leaf fans trimmed to one-third of the total height to reduce wind-rock while the plants are getting established. Bearded irises hate waterlogged soil, but they will need watering until they establish. A general fertiliser can be forked in if the soil is poor. Make sure weeds and neighbouring plants do not shade the rhizome and hand-weed rather than apply a mulch.

Beardless irises often like the same conditions as the bearded irises, but there are exceptions. Pacific Coast irises are prized for cutting but need peaty soils in sun in cooler areas or lightly shaded areas in warmer regions. Water irises such as *I. ensata* (syn. *I. kaempferi*), *I. laevigata* and *I. pseudacorus* love the wet soils of bog gardens or pond margins. Siberian irises such as *I. sibirica* also prefer very moist soils.

Good companions

Grow *I. unguicularis* in a warm corner – perhaps a narrow border under a south-facing wall. Bearded irises are best grown towards the front of a border and combine well with crocosmias, hemerocallis, roses, peonies, hostas and hardy geraniums. Water irises can be grown with bog or marginal plants.

Propagation

Division, after flowering. August is the best time to divide the winter iris, but it takes several years to flower again. All rhizomatous irises can be raised from seed but may not come true

Troubleshooting

In wet spells, iris leaf spot can be a problem. You will notice it as brown, oval-shaped spots on the leaves. The disease spreads in raindrops so cut off any affected leaves as soon as possible. Spray neighbouring plants with a suitable fungicide. *I. sibirica* or bearded varieties like 'Cliffs of Dover', 'Jane Phillips', 'Ola Kala' and 'Stepping Stone' seem to show some resistance.

Guard against slugs and snails. Also, birds often peck the flowers of the winter iris. Late frosts may kill new growth, so remove blackened foliage to prevent disease.

Which variety?

Although it is very hard to select one iris, we have gone for **Iris unguicularis** for its winter flowers. The Algerian or winter iris, **I. unguicularis** (syn. *I. stylosa*), is valued for its lilac winter flowers that appear any time from mid-autumn to mid-spring. Buds can be picked as cut flowers. Give it a hot, dry place in rubbly soil and leave alone to form a mature clump. There are very many more; here is a brief guide to the best ones.

BEARDLESS

The Japanese iris, **I. ensata** (syn. *I. kaempferi*), has purplish flowers and narrow leaves, needs a moist, lime-free soil and a sunny spot. It comes in many varieties, including a variegated one. Flowers late in July and August. Height 30cm (12in).

I. foetidissima is an evergreen with purple and yellow flowers in June and scarlet-orange seeds from October to December. It tolerates full shade and almost any soil. It has a variegated form which contrasts well with bergenias but rarely flowers. Height 45cm (18in). **'Citrina'** (syn. 'Chinensis') has yellow flowers in June. **I. graminea** has reddish-purple flowers from June to July with a rich, fruity scent. Needs a sunny, well-drained site. Height 45cm (18in). **I. laevigata** is a marginal pond plant that will grow in shallow water with 5cm (2in) water over the rhizome. Many named varieties, but **'Variegata'** is the best as it combines green and white foliage with powder-blue flowers from early to mid-summer. **I. pallida 'Variegata'** has yellow-variegated leaves and lavender flowers from late spring to early summer. Height 90cm (36in). **'Argentea Variegata'** is a fine foliage plant with white and grey leaves in late spring to early summer. **I. pseudacorus** (yellow flag) is a native suitable for larger ponds and streams. Height 120cm (48in).

BEARDED

Use these to add flowering highlights to the border in late spring to early summer. In cool,

Iris sibirica 'Navy Brass'

Iris ensata 'Variegata'

Iris pseudacorus

cloudier parts of north-west England and Scotland, take local advice as not all varieties are reliable – beardless ones might be a better bet. Bearded irises are divided into groups depending on their height. **Tall Bearded** These vary from 68cm (27in) up to 120cm (48in). Early ones flower at the end of May, mid-season ones early to mid-June and late ones in late June. They may need staking in exposed gardens. **Border Bearded** at 40–68cm (16–27in) are scaled-down versions of Tall Bearded. **Intermediate** have the neat foliage, good flowers and ease of cultivation of the Standard Dwarfs, but are close in stature to Tall at 38–68cm (15–27in). They flower from May to early June. **Miniature** are tall, graceful plants with small dainty flowers on slender stems, useful for flower arranging. At 40–68cm (16–27in) they are ideal for small gardens and windy sites. They flower from late May to mid-June. **Standard Dwarf Bearded** are easy plants for spring colour at the front of a border. Prolific flowering on compact clumps. Height 20–38cm (8–15in), flowers from late April to late May.

There are so many varieties, we suggest you visit specialist nurseries when the flowering displays are out and choose ones you like. We have not covered the huge range of dwarf spring-flowering irises because they are bulbs.

Iris 'Jane Phillips'

Knautia
Knautia macedonica

Shape and size

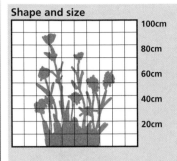

100cm
80cm
60cm
40cm
20cm

Position Hardiness Soil

WELL-DRAINED

Uses

Features calendar

Jan	Feb	Mar	Apr	May	June
					✿

July	Aug	Sept	Oct	Nov	Dec
✿	✿				

Buying tips *It is widely sold in specialist nurseries, but is easy to raise from seed and you should get flowers in the first year.*

Knautia macedonica

Knautia macedonica flower detail

Growing guide

This plant deserves to be more widely grown because it is easygoing and offers unusual, brightly coloured flowers. Although small, the blooms have a very intense crimson colour and are produced all summer.

The plant has a light, airy habit so can be planted at the front or in the middle of the border. It does tend to flop, unless supported with twiggy sticks or planted between more sturdy neighbours. Plant in a sunny spot in a well-drained soil.

Good companions

Often used in purple borders with clematis or delphiniums, but it would be equally at home with less highly bred flowers in a wildlife area. Worth considering at the base of climbing roses.

Propagation
Seed, or basal cuttings in spring.

Troubleshooting
Generally trouble-free.

Which variety?

You are only likely to find the species **Knautia macedonica** (syn. *Scabiosa rumelica*). The sweet scabious (*Scabiosa atropurpurea*) has the same dark red flowers but is grown as an annual or biennial. Height 90cm (36in), needs staking.

Kniphofia

Kniphofia 'Little Maid'

Shape and size

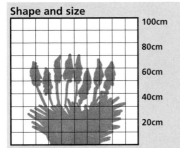

100cm
80cm
60cm
40cm
20cm

Position Hardiness Soil

WELL-DRAINED

Uses

Features calendar

Jan	Feb	Mar	Apr	May	June
July	Aug	Sept	Oct	Nov	Dec

Kniphofia 'Little Maid'

Buying tips
Garden centres often sell seed-raised plants that may be cheaper than named varieties, but will be more variable in size and flower colour. You will probably need to buy from a specialist if you want a particular named variety.

'Shining Sceptre'

Growing guide

The red-hot poker (*Kniphofia*) is one of the best known border plants because of its distinctive torch-like flowers in flaming reds and oranges. Although larger varieties can look scruffy if neglected, there are many excellent smaller ones and their colour range extends to yellow, cream, white, green and bronze.

Most of the modern varieties will survive over winter if the soil is not cold and wet. Although they like a soil to be well-drained, avoid it drying out in summer by digging in plenty of well-rotted organic matter in the autumn or winter. Then plant in late spring. If you have to plant in autumn, mulch the crown generously with straw or chipped bark. The essential thing is to position them where they will get lots of sun, or flowering will be reduced.

Good companions

Kniphofias work well as specimen plants in gravel beds surrounded by gazanias and succulents. They are often used as mid-border plants, with a large grass behind and a softening underplanting, such as *Alchemilla mollis* or geums, in front. The creamy-yellow ones such as 'Little Maid' combine well with steely-blue sea hollies.

Propagation

Division or seed (not named varieties).

Troubleshooting

Violet root rot causes stunted growth and yellowing. Look for roots covered with a purple fungus. Throw away infected plants.

Which variety?

Gardening Which? trials on a dozen of the most popular varieties show that the new compact varieties flower for longer. We recommend the following:

'Fiery Fred' at 90–120cm (36–48in) tall bears lots of light orange flowers that last from June to August. **'Ice Queen'** has pale yellow-green/cream flowers from July to October. Height 90–120cm (36–48in). **'Little Maid'** reaches only 50–70cm (18–28in) high. It has narrow spikes of yellow-green/cream flowers from August to October and grassy leaves. **'Shining Sceptre'** is taller at 90–120cm (36–48in) with broad leaves but it has great flowering impact with blooms of light orange/yellow lasting from June to August.

K. triangularis* 'Triangularis'** (syn. *K. galpinii*, *K. macowanii*, *K. nelsonii*) has deep orange blooms from August to September, height 60–80cm (24–34in). ***K. caulescens is worth growing for its blue-green, tropical foliage but it flowers late and rather sparsely. Height 90–120cm (36–48in).

Lamium

Lamium maculatum

Shape and size

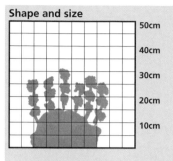

	50cm
	40cm
	30cm
	20cm
	10cm

Position

Hardiness   Soil

ANY

Uses

Features calendar

Jan	Feb	Mar	Apr	May	June
				✿	✿

July	Aug	Sept	Oct	Nov	Dec
✿					

Buying tips *Buy plants in small pots in the spring, they will soon bulk up.*

'Roseum'

Lamium maculatum 'Elizabeth de Haas'

Growing guide

These low-growing perennials are ideal for filling in areas of bare soil beneath or between larger plants such as shrubs. Although they are evergreen, the foliage can look a bit tatty over the winter months, but the new growth brings a welcome fresh look in spring. After flowering, plants can be cut back to encourage dense leaf cover.

They grow in any soil, in sun or shade although very golden or silver-leaved varieties can scorch in full sun. For groundcover, plant 30cm (12in) apart for a quick blanket of foliage, or 60cm (24in) apart if you can wait.

Good companions

They combine well with most plants; bugle (*Ajuga*) makes a good partner if you want groundcover in the shade.

Propagation

Division.

Troubleshooting

Generally trouble-free.

Which variety?

A recent *Gardening Which?* trial of 13 varieties of lamium revealed the value of some of the lesser-known ones. **'Elizabeth de Haas'** was outstanding for its long flowering period, mauve flowers are borne from May to November. Its foliage is a mix of green, silver and yellow. Another success was **'Roseum'**, a pretty variety with a white striped leaf and pale pink flowers. The following varieties also performed well:

'Beacon Silver' silver variegation, pink flowers, widely available; **'Chequers'** silver variegation, deep pink flowers; **'Pink Pewter'** silver variegation, pale pink flowers; **'White Nancy'** silver variegation, white flowers, widely available. These can be expected to flower intermittently for around ten weeks from May onwards. Some varieties such as **'Hermann's Pride'** and **'Silver Carpet'** scarcely flower. Others like *L. galeobdolon* 'Florentinum' and *L. album* are invasive.

Leucanthemum

L. x superbum 'Snowcap'

Shape and size

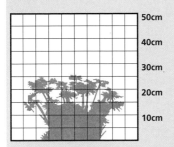

50cm
40cm
30cm
20cm
10cm

Position   Hardiness   Soil

MOIST

Uses

Features calendar

Jan	Feb	Mar	Apr	May	June
✺	✺				
July	Aug	Sept	Oct	Nov	Dec

Buying tips *'Wirral Supreme' is the easiest to find. Buy young plants in small pots as they will soon form a good-sized clump. You could find others in garden centres, otherwise try general herbaceous specialists.*

Leucanthemum x superbum 'Wirral Supreme'

'Snowcap' is a good dwarf variety

Growing guide

This is a group of hardy chrysanthemums that are valued for their summer flowers both in the garden and for cutting. They prefer a rich loam but can be grown on other soils if they are fertile and not too acidic.

A sunny site is essential. You will only need to stake if the flower stems tend to sprawl, so put in some twiggy sticks around clumps in May to provide support. Some varieties do not need staking.

Mulch around the plants in spring. Deadhead regularly to prolong flowering and cut down to the ground in autumn. Plants are best if lifted and divided every two years.

Good companions

Fits in well to the traditional herbaceous border where plants are grown for flowering impact. Recommended partners include varieties of *Campanula lactiflora* and penstemons.

Propagation

Division in early spring/late summer. Seed.

Troubleshooting

Shasta daisies are spared the greenhouse pests like whitefly and spider mite that can stunt the growth of tender chrysanthemums. However, they can be affected by chrysanthemum eelworm and slugs.

Which variety?

A recent *Gardening Which?* trial of nine Shasta daisy varieties and their parents came up with four winners that look good and do not need staking. **'Snowcap'** has full-sized single flowers on dwarf plants, in flower for six weeks, height 15–25cm (6–10in). **'Alaska'** the best single-flowered variety, in flower for eight weeks, height 70–90cm (28–36in). **'Bishopstone'** a robust plant with attractive feathery flowers, in flower for eight weeks, height 70–90cm (28–36in). ***L. vulgare*** (ox-eye daisy) dainty plants, in flower for seven weeks, self-seeds, height 40–50cm (16–20in).

Two well-known plants you might come across had drawbacks. **'Esther Read'** produces lots of semi-double flowers over nine weeks but then the plants look awful once the flowers die, height 50–60cm (20–24in). **'Wirral Supreme'** produces semi-double flowers for six weeks, a strong grower at a height of 70–90cm (28–36in), but it needs staking.

Liatris

Liatris spicata

Shape and size

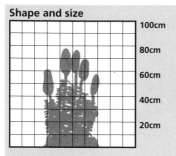

100cm
80cm
60cm
40cm
20cm

Position   Hardiness   Soil

MOIST

Uses

Features calendar

Jan	Feb	Mar	Apr	May	June
❀	❀	❀			
July	Aug	Sept	Oct	Nov	Dec

Buying tips *In late summer at the garden centre, look for new deliveries of liatris in large pots for instant colour. To save money, grow your own from seed.*

Liatris spicata

Liatris spicata 'Alba'

Growing guide

These are striking plants worth including in the border for high-summer colour or as cut flowers. The stout, leafy stems produce dense flower heads that look like bottle brushes. The flowers open at the top of the spike first; these can be removed when they have faded.

Despite their exotic appearance the plants are hardy. They do need sun, though. *L. spicata* is tolerant of heavy soils, but wet soils over winter can cause rotting.

The plants disappear below ground in winter and the foliage emerges late, so mark their positions to avoid damage from spring cultivation.

Good companions

Use bright-coloured ones in the middle of the border as summer highlights among purple-flowering plants. Use their shape as a contrast to dome-shaped plants such as hardy geraniums or *Monarda*.

Propagation

Division or seed.

Troubleshooting

Generally trouble-free, but protect the young shoots from slugs.

Which variety?

L. spicata (syn. *L. calllepsis*) and its varieties are the ones usually grown. Height is 80–90cm (32–36in) unless otherwise stated. **'Alba'** has white flowers, **'Floristan Violett'** is purple and **'Floristan Weiss'** bears long spikes of white blooms that are good for cutting. **'Goblin'** (syn. 'Kobold') produces bright mauve-pink flowers. Height 60cm (24in).

Ligularia

Ligularia 'The Rocket'

Shape and size

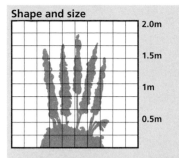

2.0m
1.5m
1m
0.5m

Position

Hardiness

Soil

MOIST

Uses

Features calendar

Jan	Feb	Mar	Apr	May	June
July	Aug	Sept	Oct	Nov	Dec

Ligularia dentata 'Desdemona'

Ligularia 'The Rocket'

Growing guide

This is an impressive perennial if you can provide it with moist soil and a sunny or lightly shaded spot. The large leaves form a striking clump but the highlight is the dark stems bearing spikes of yellow flowers in summer.

Plant it where it will have space to grow into a large clump, at a planting distance of 75–90cm (30–36in). If you are growing it in a moist border rather than a bog garden, mulch generously in spring and give extra water during periods of drought. Cut back the stems when flowering is over.

Good companions

It makes a good single subject, or planted in drifts between shrubs that also like a moist soil, such as dogwoods (*Cornus*). Use at the back of a bog garden alongside *Eupatorium* with astilbes or lythrum at the front of the group.

Propagation

Division, in spring or after flowering.

Troubleshooting

Generally trouble-free if the growing conditions are right.

Which variety?

We've chosen **'The Rocket'** for the way the foliage, stems and flowers combine together to create an impressive specimen plant. The following have a lot to offer too. *L.* **'Gregynog Gold'** is smaller at 60cm (24in) tall and has golden-yellow flowers with a bronze centre. *L. dentata* **'Desdemona'** has large, rounded leaves of brownish green, coloured purple underneath. Bright yellow flowers from July to August. Height 90cm (36in).

Limonium

Limonium platyphyllum

Shape and size

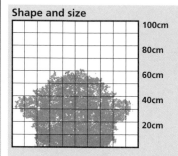

- 100cm
- 80cm
- 60cm
- 40cm
- 20cm

Position   Hardiness   Soil

WELL-DRAINED

Uses

Features calendar

Jan	Feb	Mar	Apr	May	June
❀	❀	❀			
July	Aug	Sept	Oct	Nov	Dec

Buying tips *Get named varieties from specialists or grow the species cheaply from seed in the spring.*

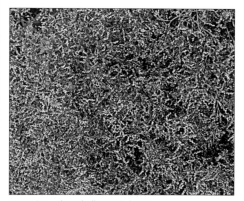

Limonium platyphyllum 'Violetta'

Limonium platyphyllum 'Robert Butler'

Growing guide

This is a hardy perennial version of the well-known dried flower statice. It has a well-branched habit and produces clouds of tiny lavender-blue flowers all summer. These can be picked and dried like statice.

Plant in full sun in a well-drained soil. An ideal subject for coastal gardens. The base becomes woody and there are rosettes of leathery evergreen leaves.

Good companions

Combine with silver foliage plants such as the curry plant (*Helichrysum angustifolium*) or Persian pyrethrum (*Tanacetum coccineum*), or it can be grown along one edge of the vegetable plot in rows and used for cutting.

Propagation

Division, root cuttings or seed (not named varieties).

Troubleshooting

Generally trouble-free, but grey mould may rot the stems and flowers.

Which variety?

The species, **L. platyphyllum** (syn. *L. latifolium*), is worth growing. Look for named varieties such as **'Robert Butler'**, a compact 45cm (18in) in height and spread with violet-blue flowers or **'Violetta'** with rich violet flowers.

Linaria

Linaria purpurea

Shape and size

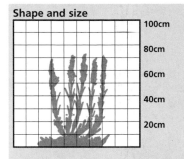

100cm
80cm
60cm
40cm
20cm

Position Hardiness Soil

WELL-DRAINED

Uses

Features calendar

Jan	Feb	Mar	Apr	May ✿	June ✿
July ✿	Aug ✿	Sept ✿	Oct	Nov	Dec

Buying tips *It is not often seen in garden centres. Try wildflower nurseries and cottage garden specialists as well as perennial specialists.*

Linaria triornithophora

Linaria purpurea 'Canon Went'

Growing guide

Purple toadflax is an easy perennial that will keep flowering from May to September. The tiny, snapdragon flowers are borne on slender spikes above tall, grey upright stems and covered in grey-green leaves. It is a versatile plant that is useful for filling gaps in the middle or back of a narrow border.

As it will self-seed freely, it is best suited to informal planting or wild corners, or allowed to grow in cracks in walls or paving.

Good companions

Use in informal plantings with erigerons and violas.

Propagation

Seed.

Troubleshooting

Generally trouble-free but self-seeds.

Which variety?

L. purpurea and its varieties are worth seeking out. Some of the best include: **'Canon Went'** pink flowers, height 60cm (24in); **'Springside White'** (syn. 'Alba', 'Radcliffe Innocence') white flowers, height 45cm (18in); **'Winifrid's Delight'** has blue-green foliage, and yellow flowers flushed with purple. Height 75cm (30in).

Other *Linaria* you may come across include: *L. x dominii* **'Yuppie Surprise'** which has pinkish-purple flowers with deeper veining that last from June to October. Height 60–90cm (24–36in); *L. triornithophora* is a sun-loving tender plant for mild areas. It bears deep lilac and yellow flowers, 90cm (36in). *L. vulgaris* is a native plant with yellow and orange flowers with a height of 60cm (24in).

Linum
Linum perenne

Shape and size

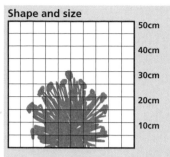

50cm
40cm
30cm
20cm
10cm

Position

Hardiness

Soil

WELL-DRAINED

Uses

Features calendar

Jan	Feb	Mar	Apr	May	June
					✿
✿	✿				
July	Aug	Sept	Oct	Nov	Dec

Buying tips *You can raise your own from seed, or buy named varieties as plants from specialists. At garden centres you might find them in the alpine section.*

Linum narbonense

Linum perenne growing in border with Euphorbia wallichii and Sambucus nigra

Growing guide

An attractive blue-flowered plant which is a relative of the flax. It is easy to grow given a well-drained sunny spot. Plant it in sizeable drifts to get full impact from the flowers. Being small, it is ideal for narrow borders, along walls and fences.

The only drawback is that it lives for only two to three years, but it is easy to replace by raising plants from seed or by basal cuttings in spring.

Good companions

Combine with other plants which thrive in dry, sunny spots like Dianthus 'Doris', Diascia, *Lychnis flos-jovis* or the grey-leaved Stachys.

Propagation

Cuttings or seed.

Troubleshooting

Generally trouble-free.

Which variety?

You are most likely to come across **Linum perenne** or one of its varieties, some of which are white. Other species can be found from specialists. **L. arboreum** has golden-yellow flowers in May and June. It needs warmth and shelter and is not hardy in cold areas. Height 30cm (12in).

L. flavum 'Compactum' has yellow flowers. Height 15cm (6in).
L. narbonense has the largest blue flowers at 2.5cm (1in) across. It needs shelter from cold and is almost evergreen in mild areas. Buy a named variety if you can. Height 45cm (18in).

Liriope

Liriope muscari

Shape and size

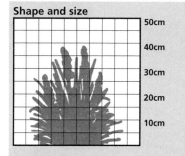

50cm
40cm
30cm
20cm
10cm

Position

Hardiness

Soil

Uses

Features calendar

| Jan | Feb | Mar | Apr | May | June |
| July | Aug | Sept | Oct | Nov | Dec |

Buying tips *Look for a decent-sized clump that you can split up before planting. Can be bought and planted any time.*

Liriope spicata

Liriope muscari

Growing guide

This is an underrated perennial that deserves to be more widely grown. All year round it provides a dense evergreen clump of strap-shaped leaves. In summer, they provide foliage contrast for large-leaved plants or summer flowering plants. But their great moment of beauty is autumn when their violet flowers appear.

If given a neutral to acid soil they are not fussy and can withstand drought, coastal winds and shade. They flower best in sun, however. Cut down old leaves to the ground each spring to encourage fresh, new foliage.

Good companions

For a contrast of flowers, combine them with bright pink *Nerine bowdenii* or colchicums. You could also establish clumps between spring-flowering shrubs where their foliage will add year-round interest.

Propagation

Division.

Troubleshooting

Some species are invasive, though *L. muscari* is not usually a problem.

Which variety?

The species, **Liriope muscari**, is widely available and a reliable, tough plant. Several named varieties are now available from specialists. Many have variegated foliage but are not as hardy as the species. There are white-flowered ones like **'Monroe White'** (syn. 'Alba'). **L. spicata** is more spreading, with white or pale lilac flowers. Height and spread 25x45cm (10x18in).

Lobelia

Lobelia 'Queen Victoria'

Shape and size

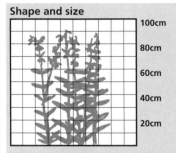

100cm
80cm
60cm
40cm
20cm

Position

Hardiness

(With mulch)

Soil

MOIST

Uses

Features calendar

Jan	Feb	Mar	Apr	May	June
✿	✿				
July	Aug	Sept	Oct	Nov	Dec

Buying tips *Often sold in flower in large pots in summer, lobelias make impressive gap-fillers if you water them in well. You can also raise some types from seed.*

'Russian Princess'

Lobelia 'Queen Victoria'

Growing guide

Perennial lobelias are quite different in habit and flower colour from the familiar blue bedding lobelia. They are tall, elegant plants with striking flowers in pink, red or purple – some have purple foliage, too.

They need a moist, fertile soil and will do well in bog gardens or ordinary borders if kept well watered. They have a reputation for not being hardy but *L. cardinalis* can tolerate cold (it originates from North America). However, it pays to grow them somewhere sheltered in full sun and to give them a thick winter mulch. Divide plants every two years in spring. Alternatively, take cuttings to overwinter in a greenhouse.

Good companions

L. 'Queen Victoria' is very striking – ideal for filling gaps left by early-flowering plants. Combine with plants like rudbeckia for late summer colour. In the bog garden it would contrast well with ligularia. Try it among shrubs that like moist soil such as the variegated dogwood, *Cornus alba* 'Elegantissima'.

Propagation

Cuttings, division or seed.

Troubleshooting

Watch out for slugs, not only when the young shoots emerge in the spring, but even when the plants reach full size. Plants sometimes collapse due to root rot. A virus can cause mottling of the foliage and distortion. Destroy any affected plants.

Which variety?

We've chosen **'Queen Victoria'** as it is widely available and has bright, beetroot-coloured foliage and stems and scarlet flowers. But there are some newer ones which claim to be easier to grow. All are 90cm (36in) unless otherwise stated.

HYBRIDS

'Compliment Scarlet' scarlet flowers, dark green foliage, one of the newer ones, often grown as a half-hardy annual. Also new is **'Dark Crusader'** dark red flowers, height 75–80cm (30–32in). **'Pink Flamingo'** ('Flamingo') warm pink flowers. **'Russian Princess'** pale pink flowers, each with a white spot, green foliage. **'Tania'** has crimson-purple flowers, brown stems and green foliage. Hardy.

OTHER SPECIES

L. cardinalis green foliage, scarlet flowers. **L. x gerardii** **'Vedrariensis'** (*L. vedrariensis*) purple-violet flowers, tender in many areas. **L. siphilitica** a very leafy one with clear blue flowers. **L. tupa** is a white variety, large plant that needs supporting. Red-brown flowers and downy, light green leaves. Height and spread 150x90cm (60x36in).

Lupinus

Shape and size

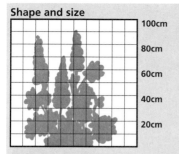

100cm
80cm
60cm
40cm
20cm

Position

Position   **Hardiness**   **Soil**

ANY

Uses

Features calendar

Jan	Feb	Mar	Apr	May	June
July	Aug	Sept	Oct	Nov	Dec

June is marked with a flower symbol.

Buying tips *Plants and seed labelled 'Russell Hybrids' are widely available and cheap but they do not always come true to type. It is better to buy plants raised from cuttings if you want a particular variety.*

'My Castle'

'Band of Nobles'

Growing guide

All lupins are ideal for herbaceous or mixed borders – the taller ones provide height and colour at the back, the smaller ones can be used as fillers. There are plenty of colours to choose from, so it is easy to use them as fillers whatever your colour scheme. Some of the better varieties are difficult to find.

The main drawbacks of lupins are their short flowering period, usually three to four weeks in June or sometimes July, and their scruffy appearance afterwards. So it is worth deadheading to encourage a second flush of flowers and to hide the shabby leaves with other plants.

Lupins will grow in sun or partial shade and on any soil. The large ones will require staking in exposed gardens and on very rich soil. They are short-lived and will need to be replaced every three years or so.

Good companions

Grow the tall ones at the back of the border with Japanese anemones to hide the lupin foliage later on in the summer. The smaller ones such as the 'Gallery Series' could be planted in between shrubs and evergreen groundcover.

Propagation

Cuttings or seed.

Troubleshooting

Young plants need protection from slugs. Lupins are very susceptible to viruses spread by aphids, so it is important to watch out for these pests and spray at the first sign of attack.

In dry summers, powdery mildew can be a problem unless you water the plants well. If you grow lupins as biennials, simply pull them up and destroy them if they get mildew after flowering.

Which variety?

There are many varieties, most are 90–120cm (36–48in) tall with a spread of 60–90cm (24–36in). Some are single colours, others are bicolours and there are also mixtures. Here are some of the more choice ones you are most likely to come across: **'Band of Nobles'** a mixture; **'Chandelier'** yellow shades; **'Gallery Series'** dwarf mixture, height 50cm (20in); **'Lulu'** ('Dwarf Lulu') dwarf mixture, height 60cm (24in); **'My Castle'** dark red; **'Noble Maiden'** white; **'Polar Princess'** white; **'The Chatelaine'** pink and salmon; **'The Governor'** blue and white.

133

Lychnis
Lychnis chalcedonica

Shape and size

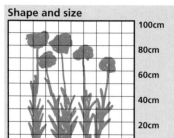

100cm
80cm
60cm
40cm
20cm

Position Hardiness Soil

ANY

Uses

Features calendar

Jan	Feb	Mar	Apr	May	June
					✿
July	Aug	Sept	Oct	Nov	Dec
✿	✿				

Buying tips Lychnis chalcedonica *is widely available in garden centres. Try to buy as young plants in small pots, or grow from seed. Other lychnis species and varieties will probably have to be obtained from specialists.*

Lychnis x arkwrightii

Lychnis chalcedonica

Growing guide

This traditional garden plant bears flat heads of bright red flowers which can be used in hot colour schemes or simply to brighten up dull borders.

It needs a sunny position and a fertile soil with reasonable drainage. The stems usually need staking. Flowering may last only a couple of weeks, but regular deadheading will keep the flowers coming. Cut down in the autumn and mulch in spring.

Good companions

The scarlet colour can be hard to place, but it would combine well with blue-purple flowers such as *Salvia nemorosa*. Or use it to add interest to a red berberis or a grey-leaved shrub like *Teucrium chamaedrys*.

Propagation

Division or seed.

Troubleshooting

Watch out for aphids. Mottling of the leaves could be a virus – dig up and destroy affected plants.

Which variety?

We've chosen **Lychnis chalcedonica** as it is widely available. The white form **'Albiflora'** and named varieties such as **'Rosea'** (a pale pink) are not as strongly coloured as the species.

L. x arkwrightii is very eye-catching, with scarlet flowers from June to July and dark maroon foliage. A short-lived plant that prefers a well-drained soil. Height 30cm (12in). A named variety, **'Vesuvius'**, has brighter flowers.
L. coronaria (rose campion) has silvery-grey leaves and magenta flowers. It does best on dry, poor soils. Although it is short-lived it self-seeds. Height 45–60cm (18–24in), spread 45cm (18in). There are many named varieties including a white-flowered one (**'Alba'**) and a new blush-pink called **'Angel's Blush'**.
L. flos-cuculi (ragged robin) has pink flowers in May to June and is 60cm (24in) high. It can be grown with other wildflowers in wet soils and tolerates partial shade.

Lysimachia

Lysimachia ciliata 'Firecracker'

Shape and size

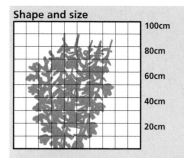

100cm
80cm
60cm
40cm
20cm

Position

Hardiness Soil

MOIST

Uses

Features calendar

Jan	Feb	Mar	Apr	May	June
✾	✾				
July	Aug	Sept	Oct	Nov	Dec

Buying tips
You may find L. ciliata 'Firecracker' promoted at garden centres in the summer. Creeping Jenny and L. punctata are widely available from garden centres, but for the others, buy from a specialist.

Lysimachia punctata

Lysimachia ciliata 'Firecracker'

Growing guide

Lysimachias are a reliable way of highlighting a border display in summer. They bear tall spires of white or yellow flowers, and some have coloured foliage too. There is one with a low, creeping habit that can be used as a trailing plant in containers.

A few are invasive, so you need to choose the species – and where to grow them – carefully.

Most lysimachias need a moist soil and a position in the sun or partial shade. They need little aftercare, although you may want to mulch plants in spring to cut down on the watering. If they are encroaching on neighbouring plants, they can be lifted and divided and small portions replanted.

Good companions

L. ciliata 'Firecracker' would combine well with *Iris sibirica* varieties in a moist border or pond planting.

Propagation

Division or seed.

Troubleshooting

Generally trouble-free if planted in the right place.

Which variety?

We've chosen a recent introduction *Lysimachia ciliata* **'Firecracker'** (*L. ciliata* 'Purpurea') as it is less invasive than the better-known yellow or garden loosestrife (*L. punctata*). It has star-shaped yellow flowers in summer which contrast well with the dark foliage. 90x45cm (36x18in).

L. clethroides is useful for late-summer interest as its arching, white flower spikes last from July to September. It needs a moist soil and plenty of space. 90x60cm (36x24in).
L. ephemerum is a tall, graceful plant with spires of white flowers, each with a purple eye. The flowers open over a long period in summer and are followed by knobbly seed pods. It has greyish foliage and has the advantage of not being invasive. Height 90cm (36in).
L. nummularia **'Aurea'** (Creeping Jenny) is a low-growing, spreading plant cultivated for its yellow foliage. Useful at the edge of ponds or in containers, it can cope with dry soils. 8x45cm (3x18in).

L. punctata is an invasive plant with yellow flowers, which might be useful in a wild garden. Height 90cm (36in).

Lythrum

L. salicaria 'Firecandle'

Shape and size

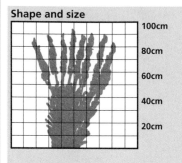

100cm
80cm
60cm
40cm
20cm

Position Hardiness Soil

MOIST

Uses

Features calendar

Jan	Feb	Mar	Apr	May	June
July	Aug	Sept	Oct	Nov	Dec

Buying tips L. salicaria *is widely available but it is worth getting a named variety. Check the compost is moist and the plants are well-rooted.*

Lythrum salicaria 'Firecandle'

Lythrum salicaria 'Robert'

Growing guide

These are easy, reliable perennials that look effective planted in drifts at repeated intervals along a border. They can also be used in bog gardens or near a pond where they would add summer colour to large-leaved foliage plants. The flower spikes last a long time and are liked by butterflies and bees.

Lythrums need moist soil in sun or partial shade, but by digging in plenty of well-rotted organic matter and regular mulching, most garden soil will be suitable. Cut back in autumn.

Good companions

Their rich cerise-pink and crimson-red colours can be used as a contrast to golden-yellow flowers, such as *Inula hookeri* or with a pink-flowered phlox. In a bog garden, they could also be used as plants to follow on after astilbes.

Propagation

Seed, cuttings or division.

Troubleshooting

Generally trouble-free.

Which variety?

The one you are most likely to come across is ***Lythrum salicaria*** or one of its varieties. **'Firecandle'** (syn. 'Feuerkerze') is prized for its intense rose-red flowers, while **'Blush'** is a new variety with blush-pink flowers. Far shorter at 60cm (24in) is the variety **'Robert'** which has bright pink flowers.

L. virgatum varieties are similar to *L. salicaria* varieties but only 60cm (24in) high so they could be worth searching out if space is limited.

Macleaya
Macleaya cordata

Shape and size

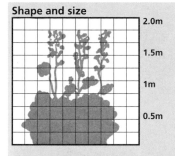

2.0m
1.5m
1m
0.5m

Position   Hardiness   Soil

WELL-DRAINED

Uses

Features calendar

Jan	Feb	Mar	Apr	May	June
July	Aug	Sept	Oct	Nov	Dec

Buying tips *You'll probably have to buy this from a herbaceous or foliage specialist. Buy a small plant – it will soon grow.*

Macleaya microcarpa 'Kelway's Coral Plume'

Macleaya cordata

Growing guide

This plant is one for foliage lovers, each leaf is beautifully shaped – like an oak leaf only with more graceful lobes. The leaves are greyish, and slightly whiter on the undersides. When the plant sways in the breeze, you can see the different colour rippling up and down the stems. In mid-summer, graceful plumes of creamy-white to beige flowers waft above the foliage.

It needs plenty of space, at least an area 60cm (24in) square. The best site would be somewhere sunny with a good depth of fertile soil.

Good companions

This is best planted on its own as a specimen, rather than hidden at the back of a border, so you can see the foliage all the way up the stems.

Propagation

Division or cuttings. It is also possible to detach outer shoots with a few roots attached in spring.

Troubleshooting

It can be invasive, especially on sandy soils where its underground suckers can spread easily.

Which variety?

The main species is **Macleaya cordata** but it is often confused with **M. microcarpa** which is similar. Two varieties you might come across are **'Flamingo'** and **'Kelway's Coral Plume'**; these have pinker flowers than the species.

Malva
Malva moschata

Shape and size

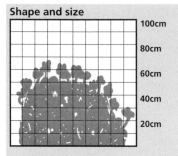

100cm
80cm
60cm
40cm
20cm

Position   Hardiness   Soil

WELL-DRAINED

Uses

Features calendar

Jan	Feb	Mar	Apr	May	June
					✿
✿	✿	✿			
July	Aug	Sept	Oct	Nov	Dec

Buying tips *You are unlikely to find them at garden centres, and few specialists offer them for sale as plants. Try growing them from seed instead.*

Malva sylvestris 'Primley Blue'

Malva moschata 'Alba'

Growing guide

These are long-flowering plants that are easy to grow on poor, dry soils. The flower looks like a lavatera and is usually pink, but there is a white version. When the fern-like leaves are crushed they release a musky smell, which is why it is sometimes known as musk mallow.

As a native plant it could be used for naturalising, or you could use it on dry banks, borders or as a cut flower. In fertile, moist soil it tends to produce a lot of growth that needs staking with twiggy sticks. It can be short-lived, although it seeds itself around.

Good companions

It could be used in the middle of a border with *Thalictrum* behind or catmint (*Nepeta*) in front. In a naturalised planting use it with meadow cranesbill (*Geranium pratense*) or white campions (*Silene alba*).

Propagation

Cuttings or seed.

Troubleshooting

Generally trouble-free, although some suffer from rust. This is first noticed as orange pustules on the leaves or stems. Pick off and destroy or throw away affected parts. Spray remaining plants with a suitable fungicide.

Which variety?

We selected **Malva moschata** and its white form (**'Alba'**) as its flowers and foliage go well together and because it is widely available. You may also come across **M. sylvestris** (common mallow) with reddish-purple flowers, which is only worth growing in a wild garden to attract bees.

More worthwhile is **'Mauritian'** with rich magenta, semi-double flowers on tall, sparse stems. Although short-lived, it makes a strong vertical shape for linking a border to a climbing backdrop, say. **'Primley Blue'** has lavender-blue flowers and is only 30cm (12in) high, but is a vigorous variety spreading to 75cm (30in).

Meconopsis

Meconopsis betonicifolia

Shape and size

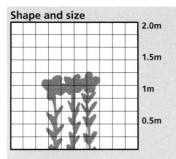

- 2.0m
- 1.5m
- 1m
- 0.5m

Position

Hardiness

Soil

MOIST

Uses

Features calendar

Jan	Feb	Mar	Apr	May	June ✿
✿ July	Aug	Sept	Oct	Nov	Dec

Buying tips *Look for good-sized specimens and check the compost has not dried out. Avoid buying small plants in flower.*

Meconopsis cambrica

Meconopsis betonicifolia

Growing guide

When you come across these sky-blue poppies with their golden stamens, you'll gasp at their beauty. Be warned, however, you need to give them precise conditions for them to do well.

They like cool, moist air during the summer and dry winters. The soil must be lime-free. In the south, grow them in partial shade in a moist bed enriched with plenty of leafmould or garden compost.

Staking will probably be necessary, and deadheading will prolong flowering. They are prone to rot if the soil is waterlogged over winter; in wet winters, place an open cloche over them. Mulch each spring with chipped bark.

Good companions

Grow among shrubs in a woodland setting with yellow or white primulas. Welsh poppies (*M. cambrica*) can be grown on poor stony ground to brighten up herbs.

Propagation

Division or seed (but it is difficult).

Troubleshooting

The plants often die after flowering in their first year, so remove buds before they open. Avoid damaging the crown as this is prone to rotting.

Which variety?

We've chosen **M. betonicifolia** as it is the blue-flowered one that is most widely available. There are named varieties, including a white-flowered one. **M. grandis** is similar. **M. x sheldonii** is a hybrid of these two species and has large blue flowers.

Not all *Meconopsis* have blue flowers; the following are all 1.2–1.5m (4–5ft) unless otherwise stated: **M. cambrica** (Welsh poppy) is a native that is much easier to grow and will seed itself around. Long-lasting flowers in yellow and orange provide colour from spring to autumn. Height 30–45cm (12–18in). **M. napaulensis** (syn. *M. wallichii*) has pale blue or pink flowers. **M. quintuplinervia** (harebell poppy) is a small one at 45cm (18in) with lavender flowers from May to June.

Melissa
Melissa officinalis

Shape and size

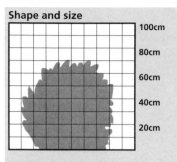

100cm
80cm
60cm
40cm
20cm

Position

Hardiness Soil Uses

  ANY

Features calendar

Jan	Feb	Mar	Apr	May	June
July	Aug	Sept	Oct	Nov	Dec

Buying tips *You may find it in the herb section at large garden centres but it is more easily found at most herb nurseries.*

Lemon balm (Melissa officinalis)

Melissa officinalis 'Aurea'

Growing guide

Lemon balm is an easy-to-grow foliage plant, whose leaves release a lemon scent when crushed. Although the individual leaves are not distinctive, there are golden and variegated forms. So much leaf is produced over a long season that it can be used both as a foliage filler in a border, or in containers, and it can be harvested for use indoors. Fresh leaves can be added to salads or drinks, dried leaves are a useful ingredient of pot-pourri.

Lemon balm will grow in almost any soil or position, although the foliage can scorch in hot, sunny spots. The green species and its golden and variegated varieties self-seed and the seedlings revert to the green form. If you want to keep the golden or variegated forms, cut back the plant to 15cm (6in) above the ground before the flowers set seed (usually in June). Cutting back the plant like this also encourages fresh leaf growth which is a better colour than older leaves, which tend to fade. In autumn, cut down the plant. In cold areas, cover the roots with insulating material or grow in a container and bring in under cover.

Good companions
Use lemon balm at the front of a border with plants such as purple sage or low-growing hyssops.

Propagation
Division or seed.

Troubleshooting
It self-seeds freely which can be a nuisance.

Which variety?

The species **M. officinalis** produces a lot of leaf for pot-pourri. For colourful garden plants, however, seek out two varieties which boast more eye-catching foliage **'All Gold'** and **'Aurea'** (syn. 'Variegata').

Mimulus

Mimulus cardinalis

Shape and size

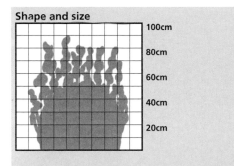

Position

Hardiness

Soil

MOIST

Uses

Features calendar

Jan	Feb	Mar	Apr	May	June
					✱
July	Aug	Sept	Oct	Nov	Dec
✱	✱	✱			

Buying tips *These plants are not always found with other herbaceous perennials. For the smaller ones, try rockery (or alpine) sections or specialists. For the ones which like wet conditions try pond plant specialists.*

'Andean Nymph'

Mimulus cardinalis

Growing guide

Mimulus have cheerful snapdragon flowers that can be used to brighten up wet or moist borders in sun or partial shade. Although the most familiar ones are sold as bedding plants, there are also semi-hardy shrubby forms and herbaceous perennials that make a useful contribution to the garden display. They are found naturally in boggy conditions, but in the garden they could also be used in a moist border, beside pools or in containers.

Hardiness varies so you need to check this out. However, there is the option of growing them in containers or covering them with cloches over winter. Many of the perennial types are quite short-lived, although you can get round this by taking cuttings.

Good companions

Much depends on where they are growing but mimulus at the front of a border combine well with almost any foliage plant, such as hostas or bugles. Near water they could be grown with *Iris sibirica*.

Propagation

Division, seed or cuttings (in April).

Troubleshooting

Generally trouble-free.

Which variety?

We suggest **M. cardinalis** as it is a hardy perennial that can tolerate drier soils. It is an upright plant with a height and spread of 90x60cm (36x24in) and bears red flowers. Hardy in most areas but needs shelter.

You may also come across the following (all flower from June to September unless otherwise stated): **'Andean Nymph'** creeping habit with soft pink flowers. Comes true from seed. **M. aurantiacus** shrubby, orange flowers. Grow in mild, sunny areas (it is not reliably hardy). Drought tolerant, 1.2m (4ft) tall. **M. cupreus 'Whitecroft Scarlet'** small creeping plant just 10cm (4in) high with bright orange-scarlet flowers. **M. lewisii** very hardy, with deep pink flowers. Does not need moist soil. Floppy habit with a height and spread of 30–60cmx40cm (12–24inx16in). **M. luteus** a perennial mimulus now naturalised near water. Yellow flowers with red markings. Height varies greatly from 10cm (4in) to 60cm (24in). **M. guttatus** (syn. *M. langsdorffii*) is similar. **M. ringens** is a very hardy marginal pond plant that can also cope with moist borders. It grows up to 75cm (30in) high and has lavender-blue flowers from August to September.

Monarda

Monarda 'Libra'

Shape and size

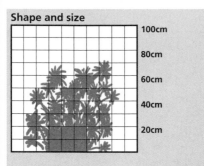

100cm
80cm
60cm
40cm
20cm

Position

Hardiness

Soil

MOIST

Uses

Features calendar

Jan	Feb	Mar	Apr	May	June
✿	✿	✿			
July	Aug	Sept	Oct	Nov	Dec

Buying tips *Older varieties like 'Cambridge Scarlet' and 'Croftway Pink' can be found in most garden centres. However, for specific varieties you will need a herbaceous specialist.*

'Cambridge Scarlet'

Monarda 'Libra'

Growing guide

The bergamots offer long-lasting flowers for the border and are liked by bees and butterflies. Their shaggy whorls of flowers in white, shades of pink, red or purple are produced from late June and last right through to September in ideal conditions. They are related to mint and have aromatic leaves.

Bergamots thrive in soils that retain moisture over summer and they appreciate some shelter from hot midday sun. In drier soils, a cool, shady position will be needed and a thick mulch in spring, otherwise flowering times will be reduced and the lower foliage will look tatty. Soils which are cold and wet over winter need to be improved by digging in plenty of well-rotted organic matter.

The taller varieties may need staking. Wait until the end of the flowering season before removing flower stems as subsequent flowers are produced on new growth made through the centre of the first flower. Fresh or dried leaves can be used to flavour tea or added to water as a drink. Leaves picked just before flowering will have the strongest flavour.

Good companions

Plant bergamots in the middle of the border in groups of at least three plants. Pink varieties can be combined with white-edged hostas or used as a backdrop to a carpet of pink-flowered hardy geraniums. The red varieties can be used as a backdrop for yellow-leaved frontal plants like *Tolmiea menziesii* 'Taff's Gold'. The purple colours can be combined with yellow day lilies.

Propagation

Division or cuttings from young growth in early April.

Troubleshooting

Powdery mildew may be a problem, but can be controlled by using a suitable fungicide. Newer varieties offer greater resistance to the disease.

Bergamots can die out after a few years if they are not lifted and divided regularly (every two to three years).

'Croftway Pink'

'Scorpio'

Which variety?

M. didyma has been grown In Britain since the eighteenth century and the oldest variety, 'Cambridge Scarlet', is still valued for its bright red flowers. However, we have selected **'Libra'** (syn. 'Balance'). It has deep pink flowers with brownish bracts and is one of a series of newer varieties named after signs of the zodiac that are thought to have some mildew resistance.

The following are around 60–75cm (24–30in) high and 30–45cm (12–18in) spread unless otherwise stated. **'Adam'** a newer version of 'Cambridge Scarlet' with a better habit at only 45cm (18in) height and spread. **'Aquarius'** violet flowers. **'Pisces'** (syn. 'Fishes') pink flowers. **'Beauty of Cobham'** light pink flowers with dark purple bracts. **'Cambridge Scarlet'** an old variety with red flowers and dark purple bracts. **'Capricorn'** a tall variety that reaches over 90cm (36in), red-purple flowers. **'Croftway Pink'** rose-pink flowers. **'Mahogany'** red-purple flowers with very dark purple bracts. **'Prairie Night'** (syn. 'Prärienacht') a slow-growing variety with purple flowers. **'Sagittarius'** (syn. 'Bowman') dark lilac flowers, 60cm (24in) high. **'Snow White'** (syn. 'Schneewittchen') white flowers. **'Scorpio'** (syn 'Scorpion') a tall variety up to 1.5m (5ft) high with violet flowers.

M. fistulosa tolerates drier conditions than most monardas. It has lavender flowers and grows to 1.2m (4ft) high.

'Beauty of Cobham'

Morina
Morina longifolia

Shape and size

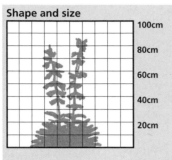

100cm
80cm
60cm
40cm
20cm

Position

Hardiness

Soil

MOIST

Uses

Features calendar

Jan	Feb	Mar	Apr	May	June
July	Aug	Sept	Oct	Nov	Dec

Buying tips *If you cannot find it in garden centres, it is widely sold by specialist herbaceous nurseries. Buy a young plant or try growing it from seed.*

Morina longifolia

Morina longifolia flower detail

Growing guide

This is a distinguished specimen – a bit like an elegant thistle – for late summer interest and winter flower arrangements.

The plant starts off with an evergreen basal rosette of prickly aromatic leaves, from this arise tall stems bearing whorls of hooded tubular flowers. The flowers are white at first, turning to pink, then to crimson. After the flowers, the dramatic outline of the stem is left. Cut down the stems in winter and in cold areas protect the roots with an insulating material over winter. The dried stems can be used in winter decorations.

A deep, moisture-retentive soil is essential for the long tap root. It prefers a sunny spot, but can cope with partial shade. Avoid exposed sites.

Good companions

It looks very effective rising out of carpets of hardy geraniums or catmint.

Propagation

Seed can be sown in early autumn or spring and kept in a coldframe. Prick out seedlings and grow on in a nursery bed for a year before planting out. Division is possible but difficult because of the tap roots.

Troubleshooting

Generally trouble-free, but can be killed in cold winters.

Which variety?

M. longifolia is the main species.

Nepeta
Nepeta 'Six Hills Giant'

Shape and size

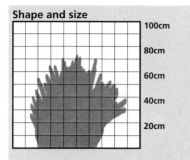

100cm
80cm
60cm
40cm
20cm

Position

Hardiness

Soil

WELL-DRAINED

Uses

Features calendar

Jan	Feb	Mar	Apr	May	June

July	Aug	Sept	Oct	Nov	Dec

Buying tips Buy as small plants in spring. Larger plants are often reduced in price after flowering when they look tatty but just need cutting back.

Nepeta 'Six Hills Giant'

Nepeta x faassenii

Growing guide

Catmint is the ideal flowering groundcover, offering flowers from June through until the autumn and evergreen foliage. Plant in drifts in medium or large borders where you want to reduce the maintenance. In smaller areas, position a clump near a favourite seat or path. As the foliage sprawls and gets trodden underfoot, it will release a pleasant aroma.

It attracts bees, butterflies and cats – a few sharp sticks or prickly twigs inserted in the middle of a clump might stop the latter flattening the plant.

A well-drained site in the sun is ideal but catmint can tolerate light shade. Clip back hard after the main flowering in June and plants will carry on intermittently until the beginning of October.

Good companions

Use it at the front of a large border beside a gravel path with *Alchemilla mollis* or as a mid-border plant with *Centranthus ruber*. Nepeta can also serve as an underplanting for roses.

Propagation

Division or basal cuttings in spring.

Troubleshooting

Sometimes the plants get powdery mildew. Pick off leaves with powdery white growth or yellow patches. Spray the remaining plant with a systemic fungicide. Prevent the soil drying out by mulching in spring and watering during dry spells. If the clump has become overcrowded, lift and divide in spring and fork in some well-rotted organic matter such as garden compost before replanting.

Which variety?

Two widely available catmints make good groundcover plants: **'Six Hills Giant'** at 90cm (36in) high and **N. x faassenii** at 45cm (18in) high. They both have similar uses but 'Six Hills Giant' is a better choice in cold, damp areas as it is hardier than *N.* x *faassenii*.

A surprisingly large number of other nepetas are available from specialists.

N. govaniana is an erect plant up to 90cm (36in) high with light yellow flowers. It needs cool, moist conditions. **N. nervosa** has a round, bushy habit 30–60cm (12–24in) high, spread 30cm (12in). **N. racemosa 'Snowflake'** is like *N.* x *faassenii*, but with white flowers. **N. sibirica** has lovely blue flowers that last all summer, height and spread 90x45cm (36x18in); the variety **'Souvenir d'André Chaudron'** (syn. 'Blue Beauty') is shorter at 45cm (18in) high. Both can be invasive.

Oenothera

Oenothera fruticosa 'Fireworks'

Shape and size

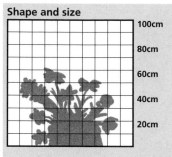

100cm
80cm
60cm
40cm
20cm

Position   Hardiness   Soil

WELL-DRAINED

Uses

Features calendar

Jan	Feb	Mar	Apr	May	June
					✿
✿	✿				
July	Aug	Sept	Oct	Nov	Dec

Buying tips *Some evening primroses such as 'Siskiyou' are promoted in garden centres when in flower – if you want them at other times of the year you might have to go to a specialist.*

'Fireworks'

Oenothera fruticosa 'Fireworks'

Growing guide

Evening primroses make neat plants with pretty flowers and can be used as fillers in most borders, gravel beds or herb gardens. They are excellent for attracting wildlife such as butterflies and bees without having to have wild areas as such.

All evening primroses need a sunny, well-drained spot to thrive. The flowers do not always open in the evening as their names suggests. Two night-flowering species, *O. biennis* and *O. stricta*, have a slight scent and are usually grown as biennials. *O. macrocarpa* flowers at night and through most of the next day.

Good companions

Sea hollies make an interesting contrast to evening primroses both in colour and flower form, and they like the same conditions.

Propagation

Division or seed (named varieties do not come true).

Troubleshooting

Generally trouble-free if the soil is well-drained – they can rot in wet soils. Some of the pink or white flowered varieties are short-lived.

Which variety?

Evening primroses differ in size and flower colour. It is worth looking out for ones with coloured foliage as this extends their period of interest.

O. fruticosa 'Fireworks' (syn. 'Fyrverkeri') has red buds, yellow flowers and purple foliage. A good free-flowering variety with a height of 60cm (24in). **O. glauca 'Erica Robin'** is a neat plant at 30cm (12in) with yellow flowers and apricot-coloured foliage. **O. macrocarpa** (syn. *O. missouriensis*) is a yellow-flowered, creeping one only 10–15cm (4–6in) high, but spreading to 45cm (18in). Use at the front of a border or in a rockery. Interesting seed pods. **O. speciosa 'Pink Petticoats'** and **'Siskiyou'** have pink flowers.

Omphalodes

Omphalodes cappadocica

Shape and size

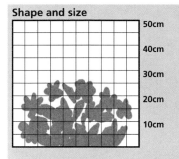

50cm
40cm
30cm
20cm
10cm

Position

Hardiness   Soil

MOIST

Uses

Features calendar

Jan	Feb	Mar	Apr	May	June
		✿	✿	✿	
July	Aug	Sept	Oct	Nov	Dec

Omphalodes verna

Omphalodes cappadocica 'Starry Eyes'

Growing guide

O. cappadocica can add spring interest to shady beds and borders. It is a bit like a forget-me-not with sprays of rich blue flowers that last for up to two months. In the right conditions, this is a long-lived plant.

It likes peaty, woodland conditions in shade or partial shade. If the soil is on the dry side, incorporate plenty of garden compost or leafmould. A sheltered site is ideal and winter protection may be necessary, although named varieties are thought to be tougher than the species. Plant in spring for the best results. Cut off faded flower stems to prolong flowering.

Good companions

Use drifts of navelwort under or between summer-flowering, shade-loving shrubs such as hydrangeas. Or use with other early perennials such as pulmonarias, along with bulbs, to make a herbaceous border attractive in spring.

Propagation

Division or seed.

Troubleshooting

Generally trouble-free.

Which variety?

O. cappadocica is a particularly beautiful perennial one. You may come across the following named varieties: **'Alba'** with white flowers; **'Anthea Bloom'** grey-green leaves and sky-blue flowers; **'Cherry Ingram'** large blue flowers; **'Starry Eyes'** has blue and white flowers.

O. verna (Blue-eyed Mary) is another perennial variety but less showy.

Ophiopogon
O. planiscapus 'Nigrescens'

Shape and size

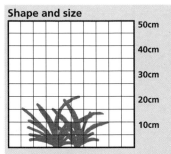

50cm
40cm
30cm
20cm
10cm

Position

Hardiness Soil

ANY

Uses

Features calendar

| Jan | Feb | Mar | Apr | May | June |
| July | Aug | Sept | Oct | Nov | Dec |

Buying tips

These plants can be quite expensive as they are slow-growing and tricky to divide. Buy a few and wait until they slowly seed themselves around.

Ophiopogon jaburan 'Vittatus'

Ophiopogon planiscapus 'Nigrescens'

Growing guide

This plant is grown for its unusual black grassy foliage that lasts all year. Although it looks like a grass, it is only related to the evergreen perennial *Liriope muscari*. It bears small pink flowers in summer, followed by clusters of black-purple berries, although these are not very noticeable among the leaves.

It is a very adaptable plant, growing in heavy clay or well-drained chalk, in shade or in sun. But it is at its best when given some shelter from cold winds. It can be used as foliage interest for autumn, winter or early spring containers when combined with spring-flowering bulbs or winter pansies.

Good companions

Use it as a colour contrast to other foliage plants. For example, grasses such as the blue *Festuca glauca* or a yellow grass like *Hakonechloa macra* 'Alboaurea' or the heart-shaped leaves and bronze tints of epimediums. Pink or plum-coloured hellebores would add flowering interest in early spring.

Propagation

Division or seed (sow when fresh).

Troubleshooting

Generally trouble-free, although it can be slow to establish as groundcover and can get damaged in severe winters.

Which variety?

O. planiscapus **'Nigrescens'** (syn. 'Black Dragon') is the best variety to choose and is widely available from garden centres. You may also come across *O. jaburan* **'Vittatus'** (syn. 'Variegatus') or *O. intermedius* **'Argenteomarginatus'** both of which have green- and silver-variegated leaves. They tend to be more expensive and not as hardy.

Origanum

Origanum vulgare 'Aureum'

Shape and size

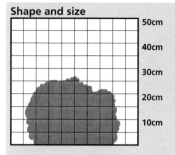

50cm
40cm
30cm
20cm
10cm

Position   Hardiness   Soil

WELL-DRAINED

Uses

Features calendar

Jan	Feb	Mar	Apr	May	June
July	Aug	Sept	Oct	Nov	Dec

Buying tips Most garden centres and seed companies will stock some marjorams along with other herbs but for the greatest choice visit a herb specialist.

Origanum laevigatum

Origanum vulgare 'Aureum'

Growing guide

Marjorams are valued in the kitchen, but they are also easy plants for the front of borders, in containers or for rockeries.

They are excellent for attracting bees and butterflies. Give them a well-drained soil in a warm, sheltered position. A sunny spot is best for most flowers or green-leaved types For unscorched foliage, grow the yellow forms in light shade. Keep plants well watered through the growing season. It is not necessary to feed plants grown as herbs but a weak well-balanced liquid feed can improve the appearance of the foliage on poor soils.

Good companions

Golden marjoram and purple sage are a classic combination. For flowering interest grow interplanted with *Viola tricolor*.

Propagation

Seed (most species will be variable from seed). Cuttings in August. Division in autumn.

Troubleshooting

Plants can become woody and straggly after about three years and need replacing. This process can be slowed down if you cut back established plants by two-thirds before the autumn.

Which variety?

We have chosen the golden marjoram **Origanum vulgare 'Aureum'** for its colourful yellow foliage and flavour. It is slower-growing and not as hardy as the species. There are plenty of others for cooking or as garden plants.

O. laevigatum is a hardy, clump-forming plant offering purple flowers in late summer. The foliage is not edible. Height 45cm (18in). **O. onites** (pot marjoram, sometimes wrongly called French marjoram) forms a bush 35cm (15in) high with edible green leaves and pale pink flowers. It is fairly hardy but may need winter protection in cold areas. **O. vulgare** (wild marjoram) is a native plant found on chalky grasslands in the south of England. A hardy plant with edible green leaves growing to 30–45cm (12–18in) with pink or purple flowers from July to October.

149

Paeonia
Paeonia mlokosewitschii

Shape and size

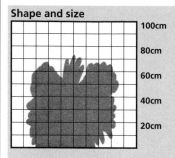

100cm
80cm
60cm
40cm
20cm

Position

Hardiness Soil

MOIST

Uses

Features calendar

Jan	Feb	Mar	Apr	May	June
July	Aug	Sept	Oct	Nov	Dec

Buying tips *You can pick up some lovely scented varieties, such as 'Duchesse de Nemours' or 'Sarah Bernhardt', at garden centres. Peony specialists offer the most choice but send your order in by September, that way you should be able to plant well before Christmas. Ordering late could mean you get bare-rooted plants that have started into growth in spring and these will not establish well.*

Paeonia officinalis 'Rubra Plena'

Growing guide

Peonies are well-known for their impressive blooms in late spring and early summer. Add to this the red-bronze foliage in early spring, scent and their longevity and it is clear they can earn their place in the garden.

Peonies needs shelter from wind but otherwise are tolerant of a wide range of growing conditions. Although they flower best in sun, they are worth trying in partial shade. In fact, they thrive where the rays of the early morning sun miss them, so that any buds that have been frosted overnight have a chance to thaw out slowly.

For the biggest, most free-flowering plants, you need to provide a soil that is moisture-retentive yet well drained and fertile. There are plenty of examples of peonies doing well on acid to alkaline soils, heavy and light soils but it pays to prepare a decent planting hole (60cm/24in wide, one spade's depth) and to improve the soil with well-rotted garden compost. When planting, the crown of the plant should be covered with 2.5–5cm (1–2in) of soil. Some plant supports will be needed in most locations.

Plants take a year or two to settle down. They need little attention. A top-dressing of fertiliser, an annual mulch and tidying up the leaves in autumn are the basic tasks.

Good companions

Peonies have bold flowers so combine them with plants that have masses of smaller flowers like frothy *Alchemilla mollis*, catmint or *Veronica gentianoides*. Peony foliage unfolds in spring and then fills out, playing a useful role in hiding the foliage of spring-flowering bulbs.

Propagation

Division in autumn or early winter.

Troubleshooting

Sometimes no flowers are produced which is very disappointing. This could be due to a number of reasons. With new plants, planting too deeply is usually the cause. Flower buds that form but then shrivel are a sign of lack of water or food. Sprinkle a general fertiliser such as growmore around the plants in spring.

Peony wilt causes buds to turn black, there will also be grey, fluffy mould on the plant. Cut out affected parts and spray the remaining plant with a suitable fungicide. Reapply if necessary. *P. lactiflora* varieties are prone to fungal diseases in cool, wet springs.

Paeonia mlokosewitschii

'Bowl of Beauty'

'Duchesse de Nemours'

Which variety?

We have picked an unusual peony – **P. mlokosewitschii** (syn. 'Molly the Witch'). We feel it is worth searching out for its all-round beauty. It is one of the earliest to flower and the single, pale yellow flowers complement the grey-green, downy foliage and purple stems. Height 75cm (30in).

You are more likely to come across a selection of the many **P. lactiflora** varieties. These bear big, beautiful flowers and are hardy and long-lived. However, they are prone to fungal diseases and those with double flowers cannot cope well with heavy rain. A good choice is the scented **'Bowl of Beauty'** which has pink flowers with a creamy centre in June, 90cm (36in) high. Other ones noted for their scent include: **'Albert Crousse'** (bright pink); **'Duchesse de Nemours'** (white); **'Inspecteur Lavergne'** (crimson); **'Sarah Bernhardt'** (pale pink) and **'White Wings'**.

P. officinalis varieties (cottage peonies) are long-lived and reliable. Most are 70–90cm (30–36in) high and flower in May.

Papaver

Papaver orientale 'Mrs Perry'

Shape and size

100cm
80cm
60cm
40cm
20cm

Position

Hardiness

Soil

MOIST

Uses

Features calendar

Jan	Feb	Mar	Apr	May	June
				✿	✿
July	Aug	Sept	Oct	Nov	Dec
✿					

Buying tips *You can easily grow oriental poppies from seed, but for named varieties you will need to buy container-grown plants. They are best bought and planted in autumn.*

'Picotée'

Papaver orientale 'Mrs Perry'

Growing guide

Poppies can add dramatic highlights to early summer with their spectacular blooms. The typical oriental poppy is a hardy perennial that produces scarlet flowers with a black blotch at the bottom of each petal. However, there are varieties in other colours, including pink, orange and white, and some with decorative frilly-edged petals too. For blue Himalayan ones, see *Meconopsis* on page 139.

Oriental poppies are easy to grow in a good moist soil in full sun. Most varieties need staking as the stems are floppy.

If you want them as cut flowers, cut them in bud the evening before you want them. After the impact of the flowers in early summer, the plants look tatty and are best cut down to prevent self-seeding.

Good companions

Oriental poppies need companions that will cover up the gap they leave behind. The fast-growing frothy flowers of *Gypsophila paniculata* would fit the bill so would penstemon or agapanthus. For plants that flower at the same time, consider tall delphiniums or lupins as partners.

Propagation

Division (best in autumn). Root cuttings can be taken in winter or early spring.

Troubleshooting

The roots can be difficult to get rid of once established, so choose a permanent place for them.

'Curlilocks'

'Black and White'

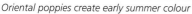

Oriental poppies create early summer colour

Which variety?

We picked **'Mrs Perry'** for its desirable salmon-pink blooms. The following are sold by a number of specialists. Most oriental poppies are 45–90cm (18–36in) high.

'Allegro' orange flowers, no blotch. **'Beauty of Livermere'** (syn. 'Goliath Group') a strong red with black blotch. **'Black and White'** large white poppies with a basal blotch of maroon-black. **'Cedric Morris'** pale pink with a maroon-black blotch. **'Curlilocks'** orange flowers with serrated petals, black blotch, **'Picotée'** pinkish-orange flowers with white base, frilled petals. **'Turkish Delight'** (syn. 'Türkenlouis') pale salmon-pink flowers with no blotch.

'Turkish Delight'

Penstemon
Penstemon hybrids

Shape and size

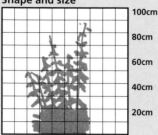

100cm
80cm
60cm
40cm
20cm

Position   Hardiness   Soil

WELL-DRAINED

Uses

Features calendar

Jan	Feb	Mar	Apr	May	June
					✽
✽		✽	✽	✽	
July	Aug	Sept	Oct	Nov	Dec

Buying tips *Garden centres sell hybrids in flower in large (2 litre) pots for instant summer colour. Nurseries will have a wider range of varieties in smaller pots earlier in the year.*

'White Bedder'

'Burgundy'

Growing guide

Penstemons produce elegant spires of foxglove-like flowers in a range of beautiful warm reds, pinks, purples and blues, and whites. They are ideal for adding colour to your border from June onwards. They have an unfair reputation for being tender, whereas in fact winter losses are usually due to winter wet.

Penstemons need full sun and a well-drained soil. In areas with heavy rainfall, cover the crown of the plants with a cloche over winter. On poor soils, add extra nutrients by watering with a high-potash liquid feed in June and again at the beginning of August, but do not feed beyond the end of August. Cut back in late March to 12cm (5in) from ground level to keep the plants bushy and prevent flopping.

Good companions

Penstemons fit into all styles of mixed border among dwarf shrubs and other perennials. They complement grey foliage plants and roses.

Propagation

Cuttings from leafy side shoots in autumn. Division and seed is possible with some types.

Troubleshooting

Winter losses are usually due to wet soil over winter or the crown rotting, rather than the plants being tender. Taking cuttings is a sensible precaution. The chrysanthemum eelworm can attack penstemons, causing plants to become stunted and discoloured with purple-black blotches on the leaves which then turn brown, wither and die. Dig up and destroy affected plants. Keep the area weed-free for at least three months before replanting.

Which variety?

Most hybrids start flowering between mid-June and early July. The main flush lasts six to eight weeks, followed by a lesser display of flowering side shoots. Most are 75–90cm (30–36in) high unless otherwise stated.

WHITES
'White Bedder' (syn. 'Snow Storm', 'Snowflake') is a widely available hybrid that opens to white from pink-flushed buds. For a smaller plant with lots of creamy-white flowers look for **P. hartwegii 'Alba'**. **'Thorn'** is white with pink tips.

PINKS
For the front of the border consider the soft pink **'Evelyn'** at 60cm (24in) high or the similar **'Pink Endurance'**. For a pink and white variety, go for **'Beech Park'** (syn. 'Barbara Barker') or the similar **'Apple Blossom'**. The tallest and most graceful pink-flowered one is **'Pennington Gem'**. **'Hewell's Pink Bedder'** is an old variety with shrimp-pink and white flowers, and contrasting purple stems. **P. digitalis 'Husker's Red'** has pink flowers from May to July and purple foliage on small plants 30x30cm (12x12in). **'Hidcote Pink'** has pink and red flowers.

REDS
'Rubicunda' has very large flared flowers in deep matt red with a white throat, **'King George V'** is similar, but does not flower for as long. The following have red flowers as described by their variety name: **'Burgundy'** (syn. 'Burford Purple'); **'Chester Scarlet'**; **'Firebird'** (syn. 'Schoenholzeri') bright red; **'Garnet'** (syn. 'Andenken an Friedrich Hahn') wine red; **P. hartwegii** red flowers; **'Rich Ruby'** has deep red flowers.

PURPLES
The palest pastel blue-lilac is **'Alice Hindley'**. **'Blackbird'** is a rich reddish-purple with deep purple flower stems, a tall variety at

'Thorn'

100cm (39in). **'Raven'** has the darkest purple flowers with white throats and stems of a contrasting light green. **'Hidcote Purple'** is similar. Two smaller species are **P. campanulatus** (syn. P. kunthii) and **P. heterophyllus**. The first is 45x30cm (18x12in) with long, narrow, tubular flowers the colour of port-wine. The other has mauve-blue flowers with a touch of pink on low mounds 38x90cm (15x36in). Several named forms are available. **'Catherine de la Mare'** has purplish blue flowers on mound-like plants 30x60cm (12x24in). The variety **'Sour Grapes'** has a metallic sheen to it which resembles the purple-green of grapes.

'Garnet'

155

Persicaria (was Polygonum)
Persicaria affinis 'Darjeeling Red'

Shape and size

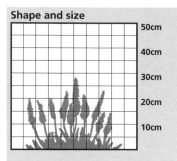

50cm
40cm
30cm
20cm
10cm

Position   Hardiness   Soil

MOIST

Uses

Features calendar

Jan	Feb	Mar	Apr	May	June
July	Aug	Sept	Oct	Nov	Dec

Persicaria affinis 'Darjeeling Red'

Buying tips *Many garden centres will have a reasonable selection either in the herbaceous section or with groundcover plants.*

Persicaria virginiana 'Painter's Palette'

Growing guide

Persicaria include many excellent garden plants – the best ones make compact groundcover or easy border plants for light shade. But there are some rampant thugs amongst them, too, so you need to choose carefully.

For groundcover, use varieties of *P. affinis* for long-lasting flower spikes and foliage that has autumn tints and remains attractive all winter. To cover the edge of a raised bed, consider the creeping *P. vacciniifolia*. Taller varieties are ideal for borders. Their striking flowers make them suitable for use as specimens in the border, but they can also be planted *en masse* in low-maintenance schemes.

All persicaria thrive in moist, semi-shade but many can cope with sunny positions so long as the soil does not dry out in summer.

Good companions

Silver-leaved *Lamium* likes the same conditions and gives a contrast of foliage shape and colour. Border persicaria also combine well with asters, together they offer rich colours for the late summer border.

Propagation
Division.

Troubleshooting

To keep the more vigorous herbaceous ones under control, divide them each spring. *P. virginiana* 'Painter's Palette' is best restricted in a container.

Persicaria bistorta 'Superba'

Persicaria amplexicaulis 'Firetail'

Persicaria amplexicaulis 'Alba'

Persicaria campanulata

Which variety?

For groundcover we recommend **P. affinis** and its varieties which are about 15cm (6in) high and spread to about 60cm (24in). The species has rosy-red flowers from August to September, named varieties often flower earlier, **'Darjeeling Red'** has pink/crimson flowers from July to September, **'Donald Lowndes'** has salmon-pink flowers from June to July, **'Superba'** has white/crimson flowers from June to September.

P. amplexicaulis and its varieties are useful border plants. Typically they reach 60–120cm (24–48in) high and 60–80cm (24–32in) wide with flowers from June to October, unless otherwise stated. **'Alba'** is a slow-growing form with white flowers. **'Atrosanguinea'** has dark crimson flowers from June to September. **'Firetail'** is a small variety at 90x60cm (36x24in) with bright crimson flowers from June to September. **'Pendula'** (syn. 'Arun Gem') is very small at 30x30cm (12x12in) with dark pink drooping flower spikes from June to September. Good for containers.

P. bistorta 'Superba' has beautiful pale pink poker flowers on elegant stems from May to June. It is ideal for a shady bog garden. Height 90cm (36in). **P. campanulata** is an attractive, veined foliage plant with fawn undersides for a moist border. It reaches 60–90cm (24–36in) high. **P. vacciniifolia** forms a tight evergreen carpet with showy pink flowers from September to October. Height and spread 15x90cm (6x36in).

P. virginiana 'Painter's Palette' boasts brilliantly variegated foliage of green, yellow and red brown. Height and spread 60cm (24in). Very invasive, so beware.

157

Phlox
Phlox maculata 'Alpha'

Shape and size

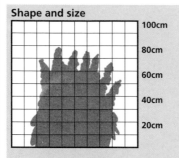

100cm
80cm
60cm
40cm
20cm

Position

Hardiness Soil

MOIST

Uses

Features calendar

Jan	Feb	Mar	Apr	May	June
✸	✸	✸			
July	Aug	Sept	Oct	Nov	Dec

Buying tips *Avoid buying unnamed varieties. Many plants on sale have phlox eelworm. Inspect carefully before buying and avoid any with thickened stems or distorted leaves.*

'Otley Choice'

Phlox maculata 'Alpha'

Growing guide

Border phlox are grown for their late summer display of white, pink, mauve or crimson flower heads which may have an appealing nutty fragrance.

For impressive flowering displays and healthy plants, give them a moist but not waterlogged soil that does not dry out in summer. They are suitable for sunny or partially shaded beds.

The flowers should not need staking except in windy gardens or after heavy summer showers. They are attractive to bees and butterflies and make impressive cut flowers.

Good companions

Use drifts of border phloxes in the middle of borders to provide intense pools of summer colour. Plant herbaceous potentillas, sidalceas or small asters in front to hide bare phlox stems. Phloxes are ideal follow-on plants for poppies.

Propagation

Division. Root cuttings (variegated varieties will not come true from root cuttings). Young basal cuttings in spring or stem cuttings in summer.

Troubleshooting

Phlox eelworm is a common and serious problem for *P. paniculata* varieties. The stems become thickened and stunted and may split. Plants may also have thin distorted leaves at the shoot tips and fail to flower. There is no chemical control, dig up and destroy affected plants. Do not replant with phlox or related plants for two years. If you have a favourite plant, you can try propagating from root cuttings.

Powdery mildew can be a problem especially in dry conditions. Try to keep the soil moist and spray plants with a suitable fungicide. If you do not want to use chemicals, thin out the weakest stems. *P. maculata* varieties have some resistance to mildew.

Which variety?

Phlox varieties are a mixed bag. Try to visit collections or displays in flower and take note of those which offer the size, scent and colour which appeal to you. All the following are 75–90cm (30–36in) high and flower from July to September unless otherwise stated.

P. maculata varieties have tall cylindrical flower heads and fragrant flowers. You are most likely to come across **'Alpha'** which has lilac-pink flowers or **'Omega'** which has white flowers with a pink eye.

P. paniculata varieties have pyramid-shaped flower heads and come in a wide range of colours.

WHITES
There are pure whites such as **'Fujiyama'** (syn. 'Mount Fujiyama') and the slightly taller **'White Admiral'**. And varieties with a contrasting coloured eye: **'Blue Ice'** with a blue-pink eye; **'Europa'** with a carmine eye; and **'Mother of Pearl'** white, slightly pink towards centre.

ORANGES
'Brigadier' is salmon-orange with a red eye. **'Prince of Orange'** is free flowering.

PINKS/REDS
'Bright Eyes' is bright pink with a crimson eye. **'Harlequin'** has pink flowers, red eye and variegated foliage. **'Otley Choice'** deep rose, only 60cm (24in) tall. **'Rijnstroon'** bears large flowers of rose-pink with white. **'Sandringham'** is pink with dark eye. **'Starfire'** is a vigorous variety with deep red flowers and dark foliage. **'Windsor'** carmine-rose with magenta eye.

LILACS
'Border Gem' violet purple. **'Eventide'** very branched habit. **'Franz Schubert'** pale lilac. **'Norah Leigh'** pale variegated foliage with pale purple flowers. **'Prospero'** and **'Skylight'**.

Phlox paniculata 'Norah Leigh'

'Blue Ice'

'Starfire'

Phygelius

Phygelius capensis

Shape and size

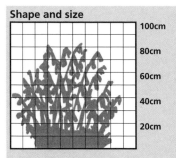

	100cm
	80cm
	60cm
	40cm
	20cm

Position · Hardiness · Soil

WELL-DRAINED

Uses

Features calendar

Jan	Feb	Mar	Apr	May	June
✿	✿	✿	✿		
July	Aug	Sept	Oct	Nov	Dec

Buying tips *You may find this on sale in flower at large garden centres and nurseries selling unusual plants. Otherwise order from mail-order specialists or buy seed.*

Phygelius x rectus 'Devil's Tears'

Phygelius capensis 'Coccineus'

Growing guide

These are unusual autumn-interest perennials. Although their nodding tubular flowers first appear in late July, they usually carry on well into October or November.

In mild areas against a warm wall, *Phygelius* are rather tender shrubby evergreens but, if cut back to the ground each autumn, they are hardy enough in most orders. They will thrive in a sunny, sheltered spot and on any soil that is reasonably well-drained.

Plant in April, no staking is needed if they are grown as border plants. *P. capensis* needs securing to trellis if grown as a wall shrub. Mulch over winter in colder areas or when young.

Good companions

Works well when planted with bronze-leaved cannas or other temporary plants like dahlias.

Older plants also develop into fine specimen plants in favourable areas.

Propagation

Division or seed.

Troubleshooting

Generally trouble-free.

Which variety?

There is not much to choose between the species and varieties available apart from the flower colour.

P. aequalis has a bushy habit with orange-buff flowers. You are most likely to come across the variety **'Yellow Trumpet'** (syn. 'Aureus', 'Creamy Trumpet') with creamy pale yellow flowers. Height 90cm (36in).

P. capensis has sparser branches, usually 90cm (36in) in borders. It can reach 1.8m (6ft) as a wall shrub in mild areas. The species has rust-red flowers, but there is a variety **'Coccineus'** with scarlet flowers.

P. x rectus is a hybrid with many named varieties. Height 60–90cm (24–36in). The dusky red **'African Queen'** is a popular variety, but you might also come across **'Devil's Tears'** (pinkish red), **'Moonraker'** (pale yellow) or **'Salmon Leap'** (orange).

Physalis

Physalis alkekengi 'Franchetii'

Shape and size

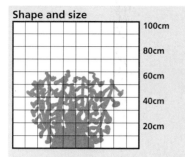

	100cm
	80cm
	60cm
	40cm
	20cm

Position

Hardiness

Soil

ANY

Uses

Features calendar

Jan	Feb	Mar	Apr	May	June
		🌼	🌼	🌼	
July	Aug	Sept	Oct	Nov	Dec

Buying tips *It is not always available at garden centres. However, as it spreads so readily, anyone who has it growing in the garden will maybe give you a bit of root which can be planted in spring.*

The attractive Chinese lanterns last into the autumn

Foliage and seedheads of Physalis alkekengi 'Franchetii'

Growing guide

Chinese lanterns, also known as winter cherries, are grown mainly for their unusual decorative orange-red seedheads which are lantern-shaped. These lanterns look attractive both in the garden and when cut and dried. The colourful inflated calyx forms the 'lantern' around the edible fruits.

To harvest them for indoor decoration, cut the fruiting stems as the calyces turn in colour and hang them upside down in an airing cupboard to dry.

The plants will thrive in any soil in sun or shade; in fact they can overrun neighbouring plants with their spreading roots. In summer there are insignificant white flowers, like those of the potato, and the foliage is undistinguished.

Good companions

Plant them in shady, dry areas under trees and shrubs where little else will grow rather than in borders with other plants. Try it with *Iris foetidissima* which has similar coloured berries.

Propagation

Division in spring, or seed.

Troubleshooting

They can be very invasive so choose the planting site with care. You can control it from spreading by severing the runners with a sharp spade and digging them out.

Which variety?

You are most likely to come across **P. alkekengi 'Franchetii'**. There are named varieties, but these are hard to obtain. **'Gigantea'** at 90cm (36in) has particularly prominent lanterns. **'Variegata'** has variegated foliage.

Physostegia

Physostegia virginiana 'Vivid'

Shape and size

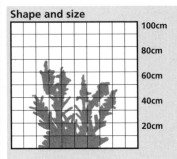

Position

Hardiness

Soil

Uses

Features calendar

Jan	Feb	Mar	Apr	May	June
July	Aug	Sept	Oct	Nov	Dec

Features: flowers Aug, Sept, Oct

Buying tips *Check that the compost is moist and that there are no signs that the plants have been allowed to dry out.*

'Summer Snow'

Physostegia virginiana 'Vivid'

Growing guide

The obedient plant, especially the rosy-crimson 'Vivid', is a bright and easy plant for autumn. It produces a dense mass of flowering stems that makes it ideal as a colourful border filler. The common name reflects the fact that the individual flowers can be pushed to one side and stay there.

Plant in a sunny or lightly shaded position. Any garden soil will do if it is well-drained in winter and moist in summer. Prevent the roots drying out in summer by watering or mulching well in spring. Tall varieties may need staking in rich soils.

Good companions

Combine 'Vivid' with other autumn flowering plants which are more airy in habit, such as Japanese anemones or *Chelone obliqua*.

Propagation

Division, or cuttings of young shoots in spring.

Troubleshooting

'Vivid' is generally trouble-free. However, other plants have spreading roots that dislike competition so they need their own space. Plants can disappear if not divided every couple of years to reinvigorate them.

Which variety?

Most cultivated obedient plants are varieties of *P. virginiana* with a typical height of 75–120cm (30–48in) and flowering from July to August, maybe into September. We have chosen **'Vivid'** a smaller variety at 60cm (24in) because it flowers from August to October and is easier to grow with other plants. It has deep rose-pink flower spikes.

Other varieties you may come across include the following: *P. speciosa* **'Bouquet Rose'** a tall one at 90–120cm (36–48in) with rather coarse leaves. Pale lilac-pink flowers from July to September. **'Variegata'** pink flowers from July to September, with the bonus of white-edged foliage, only 60cm (24in) high. **'Summer Snow'** (syn. 'Snow Queen') pure white flowers from July to August, height 45–75cm (18–30in). Look for a recent selection of this variety called **'Crown of Snow'** (syn. 'Schneekrone').

Platycodon

Platycodon grandiflorus

Shape and size

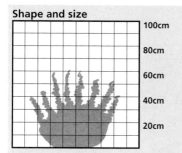

```
100cm
80cm
60cm
40cm
20cm
```

Position   Hardiness   Soil

Uses

Features calendar

Jan	Feb	Mar	Apr	May	June
✹	✹				
July	Aug	Sept	Oct	Nov	Dec

Buying tips *You should be able to find balloon plants in the alpine or herbaceous sections of a garden centre. Many seed catalogues promote varieties that they claim flower in their first year.*

Platycodon grandiflorus

'Mariesii'

Growing guide

This relative of the campanula adds pretty summer flowers to beds, borders or rock gardens. The name 'balloon flower' refers to the shape of the buds before they open into eye-catching saucer-shaped flowers. The taller varieties make superb cut flowers.

Plant in a sunny place in a fertile, well-drained garden soil. Choose its position carefully as the roots do not like to be disturbed – it is best left to grow in one place for many years. Keep cultivation around the roots to a minimum. If this is not possible, mark the position of the plant if you need to cultivate the ground in spring.

Good companions

The blue flowers and blue-green foliage combine well with *Achillea x* 'Moonshine' or use *Sedum* 'Ruby Glow' for follow-on colour in a mixed border.

Propagation

Division of established plants is possible but the plants may be slow to establish. It is easier to raise them from seed in spring, taking care with the roots.

Troubleshooting

Generally trouble-free.

Which variety?

P. grandiflorus is the only species. This in itself is garden-worthy, but there are several forms which vary in flower colour and height. **'Albus'** has white flowers. **'Fuji Pink'** has pink flowers. **'Hakone'** has double, purplish blue flowers on tall stems 60–75cm (24–30in) high. **'Mariesii'** has large blue flowers on smaller (30cm/12in) plants. **'Mother of Pearl'** has pale pink flowers.

Polemonium

P. caeruleum 'Brise d'Anjou'

Shape and size

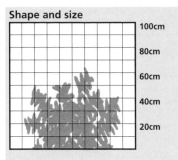

100cm
80cm
60cm
40cm
20cm

Position

Hardiness   Soil

MOIST

Uses

Features calendar

Jan	Feb	Mar	Apr	May	June
July	Aug	Sept	Oct	Nov	Dec

Buying tips Polemonium caeruleum *and* P. reptans *can be found in garden centres. The variegated Jacob's ladder is often promoted in spring. For others mentioned, try specialist herbaceous nurseries.*

Polemonium foliosissimum

Polemonium caeruleum 'Brise d'Anjou'

Growing guide

Jacob's ladder is an easy plant to grow and provides early summer flowers of blue or white. It gets its common name from the leaflets which are arranged in pairs on each midrib – making the stems look like a ladder. The new variegated variety makes an excellent foliage plant – you can cut off the flowers which add little to the mounds of handsome yellow-edged leaves.

Polemonium is a woodland edge and meadow plant, so when choosing a place for it in the garden look for a bed with moist to damp soil in sun or partial shade. After the first flowers have faded, cut back straight away for a second flush of flowers in high summer.

The plants are not long-lived, but they do produce plenty of seedlings.

Good companions

Use with other spring- and early summer-flowering plants such as aquilegia, geum and trollius in cottage garden plantings. The variegated Jacob's ladder makes a fine single subject in a container.

Propagation

Division, or lift the self-sown seedlings.

Troubleshooting

Generally trouble-free, but flowering will not be so prolific in poor soils.

Which variety?

The species **P. caeruleum** has been around for years. There is a highly valued white form **'Lacteum'** (syn. 'Album'). **'Brise d'Anjou'** is a new variety that produces masses of yellow-edged foliage which extends the season of interest and uses of the plant.

There are lots of other Polemonium species available from specialists. **P. carneum** is only moderately hardy but has attractive, pale pink, silky flowers on 10–40x20cm (4–6x8in) plants. **P. foliosissimum** is sought after for its lilac flowers and orange stamens but it is hard to obtain. Height 75cm (30in). **P. reptans** (creeping Jacob's ladder) is a spreading plant 30x45cm (12x18in). The form **'Blue Pearl'** is a good compact variety at 25cm (10in).

Polygonatum

Polygonatum x hybridum

Shape and size

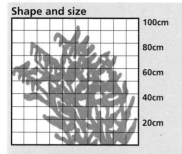

100cm
80cm
60cm
40cm
20cm

Position

Hardiness

Soil

MOIST

Uses

Features calendar

Jan	Feb	Mar	Apr	May	June
July	Aug	Sept	Oct	Nov	Dec

Buying tips *Buy at any time of year either as small plants in spring or large plants in summer or autumn, but check for sawfly damage.*

Polygonatum x hybridum growing with Smilacina and Ajuga reptans

Polygonatum x hybridum

Growing guide

Solomon's seal is an elegant plant for shady areas. It has gracefully arching stems bearing pairs of leaves and small clusters of creamy coloured flowers in June.

P. x hybridum will grow in most soils if the roots are kept cool and moist. Other species are best in soils enriched with plenty of leafmould in partial shade. Polygonatums are best left alone to form long-lived clumps, but a few stems can be cut for flower arranging. The plants can be cut down in late autumn.

Good companions

Ferns, hostas or lily-of-the-valley are the ideal partners to create a cool woodland planting.

Propagation

Division.

Troubleshooting

Solomon's seal and other polygonatums can be attacked by sawfly larvae in June. In July the larvae move to the soil where they overwinter. The adults emerge in May the following year and lay rows of eggs in the stems. A purple scar may develop. The plant usually recovers well and produces plenty of foliage the following year.

Which variety?

P. x hybridum (syn. *P. multiflorum*) is a useful and widely available plant for lighting up shady areas in spring. You may come across a variety **'Striatum'** (syn. 'Variegatum', *P. odoratum* 'Grace Barker') with striped cream leaves.

A few other species are sought after by collectors, but most offer the same features on larger or smaller plants. *P. biflorum* (syn. *P. canaliculatum*) a large version of *P. x hybridum*. *P. falcatum* and its variety **'Variegatum'** have pointed leaves and reddish stems. *P. odoratum* (syn. *P. officinale*) has scented flowers, height and spread 60x30cm (24x12in).

Potentilla

Potentilla 'Gibson's Scarlet'

Shape and size

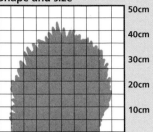

50cm
40cm
30cm
20cm
10cm

Position   Hardiness   Soil

WELL-DRAINED

Uses

Features calendar

Jan	Feb	Mar	Apr	May	June
					🌸

July	Aug	Sept	Oct	Nov	Dec
🌸	🌸				

Buying tips *You can purchase young plants in spring or early summer from garden centres. Alternatively, get some species as seed.*

'Miss Willmott'

Potentilla 'Gibson's Scarlet'

Growing guide

These are easy perennials for bright colour schemes from July until the first frosts. The leaves resemble those of strawberry plants which form the perfect backdrop to the superb flower sprays of single or double blooms in reds, oranges or yellows. Plants are usually 45–60cm (18–24in) in height and spread, but many flop and are best used supported by other plants at the front of a border.

Potentillas like to be in full sun and thrive in any reasonable garden soil, provided it drains well over winter and retains moisture in summer. A good mulch in spring will help plants on poor soils. Some species will die back naturally at the end of the season. Cut back any stems that remain to ground level in spring.

Good companions

Use with purple or copper-coloured foliage; they would be ideal for planting around a phormium or purple-leaved berberis. They are worth trying as container plants.

Propagation

Division or seed.

Troubleshooting

Some species are short-lived and do not divide easily, these are best raised from seed.

Which variety?

We have selected the widely sold variety **'Gibson's Scarlet'**, which bears red single flowers from June to August and makes a clump-forming plant. Height and spread 45x60cm (18x24in).

You might also find one or more of the following varieties: **'Blazeaway'** has orange-red flowers and greyish leaves. **'Etna'** maroon flowers and **'Flamenco'** scarlet blooms. **'William Rollison'** has semi-double orange flowers. **'Yellow Queen'** bears semi-double bright yellow flowers with grey foliage.

P. nepalensis is rather upright with deep green leaves. It bears lots of branched flower heads but plants are short-lived and are best cut back after flowering. Varieties you may come across include **'Miss Willmott'** with pink flowers, and **'Roxana'** which boasts flowers that are a coppery-pink with a red eye.

P. megalantha (syn. *P. fragiformis*) has yellow flowers with an orange centre and greyish foliage. It is short-lived. ***P. recta* 'Warrenii'** (syn. 'Macrantha') has bright yellow flowers and reaches 60cm (24in) high. ***P. x tonguei*** has small apricot flowers on mat-like plants 20x45cm (8x18in).

Primula

Primula japonica

Shape and size

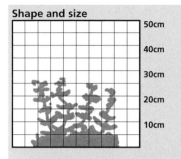

50cm
40cm
30cm
20cm
10cm

Position   Hardiness   Soil

   MOIST

Uses

Features calendar

Jan	Feb	Mar	Apr	May	June
				❀	❀
❀					
July	Aug	Sept	Oct	Nov	Dec

Buying tips *Primulas may be sold alongside bedding plants or in the alpine section of garden centres, or they can be obtained from alpine or bog-plant specialists.*

'Miller's Crimson'

Primula japonica en masse lights up a shady glade

Growing guide

Candelabra primroses are among the most striking flowering perennials for spring interest in moist ground. Their characteristic whorls of bright flowers are perfect for adding a splash of colour beneath shrubs and trees or at the front of borders. They are also useful container plants.

They prefer a moist, fertile soil that does not dry out. The easiest way to provide this is to add plenty of garden compost or leafmould. They are happy in full sun or partial shade. Space plants 23–30cm (9–12in) apart.

Primulas tend to be short-lived but a spring mulch, watering during summer dry spells and deadheading faded blooms will help keep them going.

Good companions

Candelabra primroses associate well with rhododendrons and *Meconopsis* where the soil is suitable for these plants. Otherwise, let the elegant flowers add colourful highlights to clumps of hostas.

Propagation

Division after flowering, or seed (named varieties do not come true).

Troubleshooting

The worst pest is vine weevil which is usually introduced via bought plants. Look amongst the compost for white grubs, remove and repot in fresh compost. Aphids can also be a problem, spray with a suitable insecticide. The roots can suffer from rots, and viruses can affect the leaves. In both cases dig up and remove infected plants.

Which variety?

We have selected *P. japonica* because it is reliable and offers the distinctive candelabra primrose blooms. Named single-coloured varieties are **'Miller's Crimson'** and **'Postford's White'**. Other types include: *P. pulverulenta* with crimson flowers in June and July. Height 60–90cm (24–36in). *P. bulleyana* has light orange flowers from June to July. Height 60–90cm (24–36in). *P. beesiana* lilac-purple flowers with a yellow eye in June and July. Height 60cm (24in).

Prunella

Prunella grandiflora 'Loveliness'

Shape and size

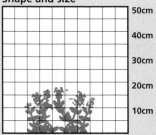

50cm
40cm
30cm
20cm
10cm

Position

Hardiness

Soil

MOIST

Uses

Features calendar

Jan	Feb	Mar	Apr	May	June
					❁
❁	❁	❁	❁		
July	Aug	Sept	Oct	Nov	Dec

Buying tips *This is not widely seen, you will probably have to visit or order from a specialist. Check the compost in the pots is moist.*

Prunella grandiflora 'Pink Loveliness'

Prunella grandiflora

Growing guide

As its common name suggests, selfheal (the native *P. vulgaris*) was used to heal wounds – as a gargle for mouth ulcers and sore throats.

For gardens, opt for *P. grandiflora* which makes an excellent groundcover for moist, shady areas. Plant 45cm (18in) apart. *P. grandiflora* can also cope with sun, but is best reserved for the trickier parts of the garden. It forms a weed-suppressing mat with small flower spikes from mid-summer onwards.

Plant in spring, mulch well and water in dry spells over the summer. Deadheading is needed if you want to prevent self-seeding with inferior seedlings.

Good companions

Grow in the shade of spring-flowering shrubs. Or use at the front of a border or in a large rockery.

Propagation

Division.

Troubleshooting

It can spread and compete with other plants, although dead heading can help control this.

Which variety?

P. grandiflora (syn. *P.* x *webbiana*) and its varieties are the ones to grow. The variety 'Loveliness' with pale violet flowers is highly regarded; there is also a pink form and a white form. 'Alba' is another white variety.

Pulmonaria

Pulmonaria saccharata 'Argentea'

Shape and size

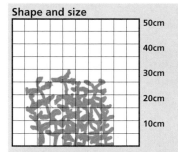

50cm
40cm
30cm
20cm
10cm

Position

Hardiness

Soil

MOIST

Uses

Features calendar

Jan	Feb	Mar	Apr	May	June
July	Aug	Sept	Oct	Nov	Dec

Buying tips *It is worth buying named varieties. Young plants can be bought in spring but you may find larger plants reduced in price in autumn. Buy these and divide them up.*

Pulmonaria rubra 'Redstart'

Pulmonaria saccharata 'Argentea'

Growing guide

Pulmonarias make excellent early-flowering perennials for shady areas. They are easy to grow and most have attractive foliage for much of the year.

For the best results, give them a moist soil in partial shade. Apart from *P. angustifolia*, which prefers an open position and fairly light soil, they can only be grown in full sun if the soil is kept moist over the summer.

Planting is best carried out in autumn. Dig in plenty of garden compost or well-rotted manure before planting. Plant most types 15–20cm (6–8in) apart, except *P. saccharata* (20–30cm/8–12in apart) and *P. officinalis* (30–40cm/12–16in apart).

Good companions

Use them as groundcover massed among shrubs. The white and red ones are lovely with hellebores or snowdrops while the blues work well with forsythia.

Propagation

Division or seed.

Troubleshooting

If the leaves get mildew in a dry spring, cut the plants right back, water and liquid feed – new leaves should appear and last throughout the year.

Which variety?

P. saccharata offers particularly handsome foliage – evergreen and heavily spotted with silver. Of the many named varieties the violet-flowered 'Argentea' is best.

Other worthwhile ones are as follows: ***P. angustifolia*** and varieties are noted for their bright blue flowers with plain green leaves. ***P. longifolia*** has tight heads of blue-mauve flowers on 20–30cm (8–12in) stems. Long, narrow leaves spotted with silver.

P. officinalis has heart-shaped leaves blotched with silver; **'Sissinghurst White'** is a popular variety.

P. rubra and its varieties are vigorous, **'Redstart'** is a good one for flowers. For foliage choose the variegated **'David Ward'**.

Ranunculus

R. aconitifolius 'Flore Pleno'

Shape and size

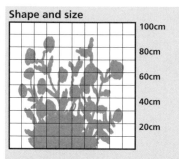

- 100cm
- 80cm
- 60cm
- 40cm
- 20cm

Position

Hardiness   Soil

MOIST

Uses

Features calendar

Jan	Feb	Mar	Apr	May	June
				✿	✿

July	Aug	Sept	Oct	Nov	Dec

'Brazen Hussy'

Ranunculus aconitifolius 'Flore Pleno'

Growing guide

Although best known as a lawn weed, the genus of buttercup (*Ranunculus*) includes many garden-worthy plants and some gems which merit seeking out. For instance, *Ranunculus aconitifolius* 'Flore Pleno' offers branching sprays of white flowers in late spring. Each flower looks like a neat button and contrasts well with dark green foliage. The blooms are good for cutting.

Plant 38cm (15in) apart in a fertile, moisture-retentive soil in light shade or sun.

Good companions

Grow in a shady spot with a carpet of *Lamium* such as 'White Nancy'. Or use as a cottage garden plant in sun. When its flowers are over, fill the gap with nigella.

Propagation

Division in autumn.

Troubleshooting

Generally trouble-free. On dry soils, dig in plenty of well-rotted organic matter.

Which variety?

R. aconitifolius **'Flore Pleno'** has double white button flowers; the species has single flowers and starts flowering earlier in April. *R. acris* **'Flore Pleno'** is taller at 90cm (36in) and has double, yellow flowers. The lesser celandine (*R. ficaria aurantiacus*) is a charming sign of spring, but it is invasive. **'Brazen Hussy'** is a named variety you are likely to come across. It has chocolate-coloured foliage which sets off the yellow flowers.

Rheum

R. palmatum 'Atrosanguineum'

Shape and size

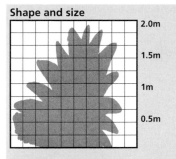

- 2.0m
- 1.5m
- 1m
- 0.5m

Position

Hardiness Soil Uses

  MOIST

Features calendar

Jan	Feb	Mar	Apr	May	June
July	Aug	Sept	Oct	Nov	Dec

Buying tips *You may find these in garden centres as specimen plants in 2 litre pots. Otherwise, try general specialists (many shrub nurseries also sell them).*

'Ace of Hearts'

Rheum palmatum 'Atrosanguineum'

Growing guide

This is a spectacular plant that makes a superb focal point. However, it needs plenty of space as the mature leaves can be 90cm (36in) long. The young leaves are bright purplish-red and the undersides stay red until flowering. The small vivid crimson flowers are formed on a dense spire 1.8m (6ft) high in early summer.

Ornamental rhubarbs need a sheltered site with a deep, moist soil in sun or partial shade. Extra watering may be needed during dry spells. Once the flowering spike has faded, cut back down to the base.

Good companions

Do not crowd *Rheum* with other plants, grow them as specimens beside ponds or place at the end of a bed or border. Remember, once the flower stem has been cut down, there will be a gap.

Propagation

Division or seed.

Troubleshooting

Generally trouble-free if given enough space and moisture.

Which variety?

Any form of *R. palmatum* is worth growing but **'Atrosanguineum'** (syn. 'Atropurpureum') merits seeking out for its colour and impact. Height and spread 1.8x1.8m (6x6ft).

R. alexandrae is less demanding on space at only 90x60cm (36x24in) high, but is harder to grow unless you live in a cool, wet area. The leaves are 15cm (6in) long, oval with deep veins, but it is the flower stems that provide interest. The flowers are hidden behind large creamy-yellow bracts, hanging down and overlapping. **'Ace of Hearts'** (syn. 'Ace of Spades') has red-purple, heart-shaped leaves and tall pale pink flower spikes from May to June. Height and spread 90x120cm (36x48in).

Rodgersia
Rodgersia aesculifolia

Shape and size

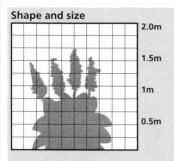

- 2.0m
- 1.5m
- 1m
- 0.5m

Position

Hardiness

Soil

MOIST

Uses

Features calendar

Jan	Feb	Mar	Apr	May	June
July	Aug	Sept	Oct	Nov	Dec

Buying tips *You may find these plants at garden centres but be prepared to order from a foliage or bog-plant specialist.*

Rodgersia pinnata 'Superba'

Rodgersia aesculifolia

Growing guide

Rodgersias offer beautiful foliage for the border and waterside, with a bonus of feathery plumes in shades from creamy white to pink in mid- to late summer. They have horse chestnut-shaped leaves that are often attractively tinted in spring as they unfurl.

To get the best from rodgersias, be prepared to leave them undisturbed, preferably in a damp, sheltered spot enriched with leafmould. They are happy in either sun or partial shade. Plant in spring with the crowns 2.5cm (1in) below the surface. Additional watering may be needed during dry spells for the first couple of seasons. Cut down flower spikes after flowering.

Good companions

They associate well with most woodland or bogside plants. Blue-leaved hostas would be ideal companions with the pink-flowered types. Another suitable partner for foliage contrast would be *Iris pseudacorus* 'Variegata'.

Propagation

Division or seed.

Troubleshooting

Generally trouble-free, but they take a couple of years to establish.

Which variety?

We have picked the taller **R. aesculifolia** for its broad, crinkled leaves that are attractively tinted with bronze. The flowers vary from creamy white to pale pink.

There are many other worthwhile species and varieties. All the following are 90x60cm (36x24in). **R. pinnata** is smaller and the variety **'Superba'** is prized for its good bronze spring foliage which ages to green and its bright pink flowers.

R. podophylla provides foliage that changes with the seasons, first bronze in spring then purplish in summer if given enough sun. There are whitish flowers, but these can be sparse. It is more tolerant of drier conditions than most rodgersias.

Roscoea

Roscoea cautleoides

Shape and size

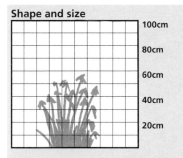

100cm
80cm
60cm
40cm
20cm

Position

Hardiness

Soil

MOIST

Uses

Features calendar

Jan	Feb	Mar	Apr	May	June
July	Aug	Sept	Oct	Nov	Dec

Buying tips *These plants can be hard to find, try seed catalogues or bulb specialists as well as unusual plant nurseries.*

Roscoea purpurea

Roscoea cautleoides 'Beesiana'

Growing guide

These plants bear exotic, orchid-like flowers during early summer. Some have attractive foliage too and make an unusual talking point at the front of a border or in a container. They originate from the mountain woodlands of sub-tropical China, but they are reasonably hardy here if given the right conditions.

Related to root ginger, they have a fleshy root a bit like a dahlia. Plant 10cm (4in) deep in spring in any reasonable garden soil that retains moisture over the summer without waterlogging in winter. Improve the ground before planting by adding plenty of well-rotted garden compost or leafmould. Protect over winter with an insulating layer of chipped bark. Roscoea can cope with sun or partial shade and flourish in a sheltered spot. Alternatively, they can be forced on in pots.

Good companions

Use at the front of borders to follow on from primulas or for summer interest in a spring-flowering rockery.

Propagation

Division in spring. Seed.

Troubleshooting

Choose the planting site carefully as these plants resent disturbance. New growth does not appear above ground until May, so take care when cultivating the border. *R. cautleoides* may self-seed.

Which variety?

R. cautleoides is the one you are most likely to come across. It has attractive yellow flowers with tall, upright foliage. The variety **'Beesiana'** is similar. *R. auriculata* offers interesting lance-shaped foliage, purple flowers that reach a height of 45cm (18in). *R. purpurea* has long leaves and flowers that vary from purple and mauve to white.

Cone flower

Rudbeckia
R. fulgida sullivantii 'Goldsturm'

Shape and size

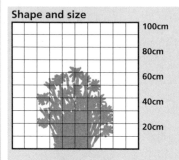

100cm
80cm
60cm
40cm
20cm

Position

Hardiness

Soil

MOIST

Uses

Features calendar

Jan	Feb	Mar	Apr	May	June
✹	✹	✹	✹		
July	Aug	Sept	Oct	Nov	Dec

Buying tips *'Goldsturm' and 'Goldquelle' are widely available as plants in most garden centres. For the others you might have to visit a specialist. It is worth trying them from seed too – many flower in their first year.*

'Goldsturm' is hard to beat for flower power in the late summer border

Growing guide

Rudbeckias are strong-growing plants that light up late summer and autumn with their showy, yellow daisy flowers. They are called coneflowers because their petals hang down making the dark, central cone very prominent.

Heights range from 60cm (24in) to over 180cm (72in) depending on the variety, so there is one to suit most border situations. They can even be grown in containers. The taller ones may need staking but apart from that they are very easy to grow. They will grow almost anywhere if given full sun and a reasonably fertile, moist soil. *R. fulgida* varieties can cope with partial shade.

The perennial rudbeckias make attractive cut flowers, too. A green-flowered variety called 'Green Wizard' can be dried.

Good companions

The smaller ones can be used in fiery late-summer displays with red-hot pokers or crocosmias in a border. As container plants they would add interest around a purple cordyline. Place the taller ones at the back of a border backed by wall-trained late-flowering clematis or roses such as *Rosa* 'Geranium'.

Propagation

Division or seed.

Troubleshooting

Generally trouble-free, although leaf-cutter bees can sometimes make a mess of *R. maxima* and new shoots of many types may attract the unwanted attention of slugs and snails.

'Deamii' grows to about 75cm (30in) and bears masses of 10cm (4in) daisies from July to September

Which variety?

R. fulgida sullivantii **'Goldsturm'** is one of the best varieties. At only 60–75x60cm (24–30x24in) it does not need staking and bears a succession of bright yellow, black-eyed daisies from July to October. You may also come across *R. fulgida* **'Deamii'** which is slightly taller and **'Speciosa'** which has narrower leaves. For a taller variety we would recommend **'Autumn Sun'** (syn. 'Herbstsonne'). It usually reaches 150–180cm (60–72in) or more, but the clumps only spread to about 75cm (30in).

Other varieties you may come across include **'Goldquelle'** which has double yellow flowers from August to October. Height and spread 90–120x60cm (36–48x24in).

R. laciniata has elegant, finely cut foliage and yellow flowers from August to September. **'Hortensia'** (syn. 'Golden Glow') is similar but is a double. Both these plants can be invasive in fertile soils. Height and spread 150–180x75cm (60–72x30in).

R. maxima has curiosity value as it looks more like a young cauliflower until the shuttlecock-shaped blooms appear. These are golden-yellow with long, black cones on stems up to 180cm (72in). It can tolerate drought. However, in cold, wet winters on heavy soil, it can be invasive. *R. subtomentosa* is also drought-tolerant. It has a tall, slim habit, grey-green, downy leaves and yellow flowers with dark brown centres. Height and spread 120–150x75–90cm (48–60x30–36in).

R. occidentalis **'Green Wizard'** has no petals, just a ring of bright green sepals around a black cone. When dried, the sepals lose their colour, but retain their unusual shape. Height and spread 120–150x75cm (48–60x30in).

'Goldquelle' is a double variety

Salvia

Salvia nemorosa 'East Friesland'

Shape and size

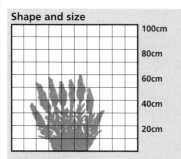

100cm
80cm
60cm
40cm
20cm

Position   Hardiness Soil

WELL-DRAINED

Uses

Features calendar

Jan	Feb	Mar	Apr	May	June
✿	✿				
July	Aug	Sept	Oct	Nov	Dec

Buying tips *You should find some of these salvias in garden centres in spring. If not, visit a herbaceous specialist. The more tender ones will be found among the patio plant displays in early summer.*

Salvia nemorosa 'East Friesland'

Growing guide

The intense flower colours of hardy salvias make them suitable for creating a focal point in borders or informal areas of the garden. Worth growing for their long flowering season, the blooms also attract bees and butterflies.

S. nemorosa varieties and *S.* x *superba* are the most reliable. They do well on all reasonable garden soils and will grow in light shade as well as sunny positions. You can encourage the salvias to keep blooming into September if you remove the flower spikes as soon as they fade. Even without deadheading, the colourful bracts still provide interest for at least a month after flowering.

Most other hardy perennial salvias need a sunny spot in a fertile, but well-drained soil. Mulch well in spring with well-rotted organic matter or old potting compost. Give them a balanced liquid feed several times during summer.

Good companions

The purple upright spikes of *S. nemorosa* 'East Friesland' contrast well with yellow flowers such as achilleas or *Anthemis tinctoria* 'E. C. Buxton'. Yellow flowers also complement blue-flowered salvias, as will silver foliage plants.

Propagation

Division (not *S. uliginosa*, take cuttings instead). Seed.

Troubleshooting

Generally trouble-free.

Salvia 'Lubecca'

Salvia x sylvestris 'May Night'

Which variety?

We choose **S. nemorosa** varieties as they are easiest to grow. **'East Friesland'** (syn 'Ostfriesland') and **'Lubecca'** are compact at 45–60cm (18–24in) height and spread. **S. x sylvestris** is similar but taller at over 70cm (28in). The variety **'May Night'** (syn. 'Mainacht') has large indigo-blue flowers.

Other hardy perennial salvias for borders are as follows:

S. pratensis 'Haematodes Group' starts by forming a rosette of long, deep-green leaves from which emerge tall sprays of lavender flowers from June to September. **S. forsskaolii** (syn. S. forskaohlei) produces large, hairy leaves and 90cm (36in) high spires of blue-purple flowers in June.

S. uliginosa is an unusual plant for the back of the border. It has clear, sky-blue flowers on wiry stems up to 150cm (60in). These start in September and last until the first frosts. It needs staking and a winter layer of bark or leaves is beneficial.

Salvia pratensis 'Haematodes Group'

Salvia uliginosa

Saponaria
Saponaria officinalis

Shape and size

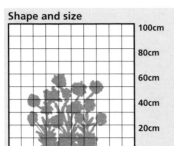

100cm
80cm
60cm
40cm
20cm

Position

Hardiness

Soil

WELL-DRAINED

Uses

Features calendar

Jan	Feb	Mar	Apr	May	June
✸	✸	✸			
July	Aug	Sept	Oct	Nov	Dec

Buying tips *You might find S. officinalis varieties and S. ocymoides in garden centres (try the alpine beds as well as the herbaceous plants). Alternatively, try a specialist.*

Saponaria ocymoides

Saponaria officinalis 'Rosea Plena'

Growing guide

Bouncing Bett has pretty, campion pink flowers in mid-summer. Height varies from 30–90cm (12–36in). The plant was once used as a soap substitute as its cut leaves release sap that lathers in water – hence the other common name, soapwort.

It has a spreading nature and has naturalised in many parts of Britain; it can even be found on shingle in coastal areas. It is worth considering for rock gardens or poor, stony areas that get a reasonable amount of sun. Deadheading will prolong flowering, then cut stems down to the ground in autumn.

Good companions

Grow in a wild garden or a cottage garden with perennial cornflower (*Centaurea dealbata*), feverfew or *Galega bicolor*.

Propagation
Division.

Troubleshooting

It has invasive roots and a lax habit which is very difficult to stake, so it is not ideal for a mixed border.

Which variety?

It is worth looking out for named varieties of **S. officinalis** such as the following: **'Alba Plena'**, which has double white flowers; **'Rosea Plena'** has double pink flowers; and **'Rubra Plena'** has double, crimson-purple flowers.

S. ocymoides is an easy, trailing alpine that could be considered for the front of a bed or border. Height and spread 15x60cm (6x24in). The variety **'Rubra Compacta'**, with a neat habit and dark red flowers, is very worthwhile growing.

Saxifraga
Saxifraga x urbium

Shape and size

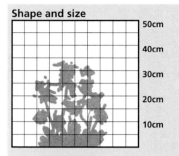

50cm
40cm
30cm
20cm
10cm

Position

Hardiness

Soil

ANY

Uses

Features calendar

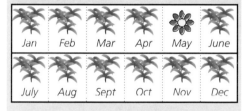

| Jan | Feb | Mar | Apr | May | June |
| July | Aug | Sept | Oct | Nov | Dec |

Buying tips *London pride is widely available in garden centres, but it may be in the alpine section or with shade-loving plants.*

Saxifraga fortunei

Saxifraga x urbium

Growing guide

London pride is an easy, flowering evergreen that is worth growing whatever the size of your garden. It is more vigorous than other saxifraga species and can be used at the front of borders or for groundcover. Plant 30cm (12in) apart for effective weed control.

London pride thrives in partial shade, but it is a tough plant that can cope with full shade or full sun and any type of soil.

Cut off the flower stems after flowering in May and you will be left with neat, green rosettes.

Good companions

Use London pride with pulmonarias to cover the ground between shrubs or, on a smaller scale, it can be used in a shady town garden with violas. Planted *en masse*, it makes a year-round edging to paths or drives.

Propagation

Division.

Troubleshooting

Generally trouble-free.

Which variety?

The plain green London pride may be found labelled **S. x urbium** or **S. umbrosa**. This species is perfectly serviceable for large areas. There is also a version called **S. 'Aureopunctata'** (syn. *S. umbrosa* 'Variegata') with leaves that are splashed with gold. There is a dwarf London pride (**S. umbrosa 'Primuloides'**) with deep pink flowers – worth searching out if you want something special for a small, shady corner.

S. fortunei has deciduous foliage that is green with red on the undersides. It has white flowers that bloom from October to November. Height 45cm (18in).

Scabiosa

Scabiosa caucasica 'Clive Greaves'

Shape and size

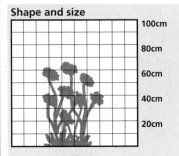

100cm
80cm
60cm
40cm
20cm

Position Hardiness Soil

WELL-DRAINED

Uses

Features calendar

Jan	Feb	Mar	Apr	May	June
					✿
✿	✿	✿	✿		
July	Aug	Sept	Oct	Nov	Dec

Buying tips *The varieties 'Pink Mist' and 'Butterfly Blue' are easy to find at garden centres when in flower. Other named varieties may have to be obtained from specialists.*

Scabiosa caucasica 'Butterfly Blue' and 'Pink Mist'

Scabiosa caucasica 'Clive Greaves'

Growing guide

Scabiosa can keep flowering from early summer until October or November. Although not many flowers are produced at any one time, they are particularly pretty with their 'pincushion' centres and are popular with butterflies and bees. They are valued for both fresh and dried flower arrangements.

Although they can be planted in any well-drained soil, they like chalky ground, and prefer a sunny spot. Plant in spring, putting down some slug pellets at the same time. The only aftercare needed is deadheading to prolong flowering. Cut down stems in late autumn.

Good companions

Grow with achilleas or sidalceas, which like the same conditions.

Propagation

Division in spring.

Troubleshooting

Generally trouble-free, but divide regularly (every three years) as young plants produce the best flowering display. They can suffer from root rot if soil conditions remain wet in winter.

Which variety?

Go for named varieties of the species, **S. caucasica**. We have chosen the lavender-blue **'Clive Greaves'**, but it is also worth trying the white-flowered **'Miss Willmott'**. You may come across other varieties, including dark blues at specialist nurseries.

There are two hybrids **'Butterfly Blue'** and **'Pink Mist'** which have become deservedly popular in recent years. They have larger flowers on smaller plants and are suitable for containers. Height and spread both 25cm (10in).

Schizostylis

Schizostylis coccinea 'Major'

Shape and size

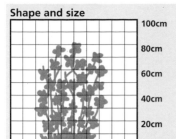

Position

Hardiness

Soil

Uses

Features calendar

Jan	Feb	Mar	Apr	May	June
July	Aug	Sept	Oct	Nov	Dec

Kaffir lily

Schizostylis coccinea 'Major'

Growing guide

Kaffir lilies are elegant autumn-flowering perennials for sunny, sheltered spots. They make good cut flowers, particularly the variety 'Major', as it has strong stems.

They are hardy in most areas but in colder regions cover them with a thick winter mulch or grow them in pots under glass. They need a soil that is well-drained in winter, but does not dry out in summer, so you may need to improve the soil with regular applications of garden compost or well-rotted manure.

Plant in spring with the rhizome 2.5–5cm (1–2in) deep. Several plants will be needed for impact and these should be only 23–30cm (9–12in) apart. A mulch will help retain moisture over the summer, though additional watering may be needed for the first couple of seasons.

Deadheading helps to prolong flowering. In winter, cut down the stems and protect the crowns with chipped bark.

Good companions

Asters make the ideal companion plants. Pink-flowered Kaffir lilies also complement silver foliage plants well.

Propagation

Division in spring.

Troubleshooting

In the right conditions the plants can spread and may need dividing every two to three years.

Which variety?

The **S. coccinea 'Major'** (syn. 'Grandiflora') bears large, deep red flowers and is widely available. Other varieties you may come across are as follows:

'Alba' has pure white flowers. **'Fenland Daybreak'** is a small variety at 45–60cm (18–24in) high, with pink flowers from August to November. **'Mrs Hegarty'** has clear pink flowers. **'Sunrise'** has salmon-pink flowers and **'Viscountess Byng'** is a vigorous schizostylis with pale pink flowers.

Buying tips *Dry rhizomes can be bought from February to April. If you cannot find them with the bulbs in garden centres, order from a bulb specialist. Pot-grown plants should be available with other herbaceous perennials from spring to September.*

'Sunrise'

Sedum

Sedum 'Autumn Joy'

Shape and size

100cm
80cm
60cm
40cm
20cm

Position

Hardiness

Soil

WELL-DRAINED

Uses

Features calendar

Jan	Feb	Mar	Apr	May	June
July	Aug	Sept	Oct	Nov	Dec

Buying tips Look for 'Autumn Joy' or S. spectabile 'Brilliant' *either as small plants in spring or as larger specimens in early summer.*

Sedum aizoon 'Euphorbioides'

Sedum 'Autumn Joy'

Growing guide

Sedums are the ideal plants to extend the seasonal interest in your garden. In spring and early summer they offer pale green, succulent foliage. Touch the leaves on a warm day and you will find them cold, hence the common name of iceplant. The flowers start to colour in late summer and put on a long-lasting show until well into autumn. Some varieties have seedheads that look good in winter, too.

S. spectabile and *S. telephium* varieties are popular with bees and butterflies, especially on warm September days. Hoverflies prefer the dark, mat-like *S. spurium*. Most sedums like a well-drained soil but they will grow in wetter soils, although they may suffer from stem rot in wet summers and flowering may be reduced. They are drought-tolerant and also make impressive container plants. The flowers can be picked for indoors too, but bear in mind that sedum can cause stomach upsets if ingested and the sap may irritate the skin.

Good companions

Create autumn interest by combining sedums with asters, or choose blue-flowered plants like *Ceratostigma willmottianum* or ornamental grasses.

Propagation

Division or cuttings.

Troubleshooting

Generally trouble-free, but after a couple of years the stems flop outwards leaving a bare centre – regular division will prevent this.

Iceplant

Sedum spectabile is noted for attracting bees and butterflies

'Bertram Anderson'

Sedums with Verbenia bonariensis

Which variety?

Gardening Which? has recently completed a two-year trial of 16 varieties at five sites throughout the UK. The longest flowering (in bloom for 5–10 weeks) were as follows: **'Autumn Joy'** (syn. 'Herbstfreude') which had flat heads of varying shades of salmon-pink to coppery-red from August to November. It provided a good clump of grey-green foliage and grew to a height of 60cm (24in).
S. spectabile 'Brilliant' had dark, rich pink flowers from August to November; height 25cm (10in).
S. spurium 'Variegatum', a ground-covering mat of 20cm (8in) stems, flowered from July until September. The leaves had a tiny cream edging around their margin.

Two other sedums worth considering are **S. telephium 'Munstead Dark Red'** rich red blooms for up to nine weeks from August or September and dark foliage. Height 45cm (18in). Other varieties of *S. telephium* looked untidy and unattractive in autumn and winter and are best cut down.
S. aizoon 'Euphorbioides' performed well in the north where its yellow flowers started in mid-summer and lasted up to 12 weeks. Its long stems are an advantage if you want to use them as cut flowers. Height 35–50cm (14–20in).

Other varieties tested include the following. **S. erythrostictum 'Mediovariegatum'** had creamy-yellow markings on the leaves, but it soon reverts to plain green unless such shoots are pulled out. Height 40cm (16in). The white-flowered **S. spectabile 'Stardust'** is a new, improved version of 'Iceberg' and grew to 60cm (24in). **'Bertram Anderson'** has rich pinkish-red flowers that reach to 25cm (10in). **'Ruby Glow'** flowered erratically for between three and eight weeks. **S. 'Vera Jameson'** had very erratic flowering lasting only 3 weeks in some areas. Height 25cm (10in).

Gardening Which? *trial of Sedums*

183

Senecio

Senecio smithii

Shape and size

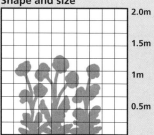

2.0m
1.5m
1m
0.5m

Position Hardiness Soil

MOIST

Uses

Features calendar

Jan	Feb	Mar	Apr	May	June
July	Aug	Sept	Oct	Nov	Dec

Buying tips *Nearly all the species mentioned here will have to be purchased from specialist nurseries, except the grey-leaved S. maritimus which is widely sold as a bedding plant.*

Senecio smithii flower detail

Senecio smithii

Growing guide

This is a remarkable plant for moist, sunny sites that combines familiar-looking flowers with unusual foliage.

It originates from the Falkland Islands and Southern Chile and can reach 1.2m (4ft) tall. The white daisies with yellow centres are produced in clusters on thick stems in the middle of summer. Fluffy seedheads follow. The leaves are dark green and puckered; they feel thick, almost rubbery. The spear-shaped foliage makes an impressive clump.

Grow it in a moist border or at the edge of a pond under a few centimetres of water.

Good companions

It combines well with many other bog plants such as *Ligularia* species.

Propagation

Division or seed.

Troubleshooting

Generally trouble-free, although the young leaves of **S. smithii** can scorch in direct sun.

Which variety?

We have chosen **S. smithii** as an unusual bog-side perennial. Only the species is available. You might come across some other species in specialist nurseries. All are very different from one another.

S. cineraria (syn. *S. maritimus*) is a well-known bedding plant, valued for its foliage and for its drought-tolerance. It is a perennial in mild coastal areas where it can reach 60cm (24in). The variety **'White Diamond'** is prized for its silvery white colour.

S. pulcher is interesting for its hairy leaves and magenta-coloured dandelions. It needs a well-drained but deep soil in a warm, sunny corner. Height 45cm (18in).

S. tanguticus (now correctly *Sinacalia tangutica*) is a tall, invasive plant with divided foliage and yellow daisies. The main feature is fluffy seedheads which make an excellent foil for berried shrubs. Height and spread 150x60cm (60x24in).

Sidalcea

Sidalcea 'Rose Queen'

Shape and size

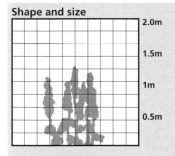

Position | Hardiness | Soil

Uses

Features calendar

Jan	Feb	Mar	Apr	May	June
✿	✿	✿			
July	Aug	Sept	Oct	Nov	Dec

Buying tips Most garden centres stock one pink variety. However, if you want a specific one you will need to go to a specialist.

'Elsie Heugh'

Sidalcea 'Rose Queen'

Growing guide

These are members of the mallow family and look like smaller versions of hollyhocks, but they are easier to grow. They are long flowering and will add a cottage-garden effect to the most modern setting.

Give sidalceas a sunny spot in any reasonable garden soil. As long as they are not baked dry or in full shade they are easy, reliable plants. Taller varieties may need staking. Cut down to 30cm (12in) above the ground soon after flowering – this will encourage lots of flowering side shoots.

Good companions

Sidalceas are ideal mid-border plants and will combine well with many old-fashioned varieties. The steely blue sea hollies make particularly striking partners.

Propagation

Division in spring.

Troubleshooting

Generally trouble-free.

Which variety?

There are several named varieties, mostly in shades of pink. Here is a selection of the ones you are most likely to come across. All flower from June to August and grow to 100–120cm (40–48in) unless otherwise stated.

'Elsie Heugh' is an old variety with fringed petals of light pink. **'Party Girl'** has bright pink flowers. **'Rose Queen'** has rose-pink flowers. **'Sussex Beauty'** has clear pink flowers. **'William Smith'** has warm salmon-pink flowers. It is slightly more compact at 100cm (40in) and flowers from July to September.

If you want white flowers, search for **S. candida** which has small white flowers on 90cm (36in) stems.

185

Silene

Silene schafta

Shape and size

	50cm
	40cm
	30cm
	20cm
	10cm

Position

Hardiness

Soil

WELL-DRAINED

Uses

Features calendar

Jan	Feb	Mar	Apr	May	June
✿	✿	✿	✿		
July	Aug	Sept	Oct	Nov	Dec

Buying tips *Look in the alpine sections of garden centres or order from alpine specialists. Many named varieties offer extra features like double flowers or variegated foliage.*

Sea campion (Silene maritima)

Silene schafta 'Abbotswood'

Growing guide

Perennial silenes are worth considering for their long flowering season and their ability to thrive in poor soils.

S. schafta is easy to grow, providing a carpet of summer flowers. It is usually grown as a rockery plant, but is worth considering at the front of borders or beds where the soil is sandy or chalky and low in nutrients. A sunny or partially shaded position is preferred.

Good companions

Combine with other rockery or front-of-the-border plants such as veronicas which provide colour in late spring.

Propagation

Seed for *S. schafta*. Basal cuttings of *S. maritima* in late spring.

Troubleshooting

Generally trouble-free but the plants do not thrive if their roots are disturbed, so avoid lifting and dividing.

Which variety?

S. schafta flowers profusely. Look out for named varieties like **'Abbotswood'** (correctly known as *Lychnis x walkeri* 'Abbotswood Rose') and **'Shell Pink'** (syn. 'Ralph Haywood') which has pale pink flowers.

Most silenes, like **S. schafta**, are carpeting plants, including native species like the moss campion (**S. acaulis**) and sea campion (**S. uniflora**, **S. maritima**). The moss campion has pink flowers from May to June. The sea campion bears white flowers from July to September. 'Flore Pleno' is an attractive double form. A few, such as **S. asterias** with crimson flowers, are taller at 30cm (12in).

Sisyrinchium

Sisyrinchium striatum

Shape and size

	100cm
	80cm
	60cm
	40cm
	20cm

Position   Hardiness   Soil

Uses

Features calendar

Jan	Feb	Mar	Apr	May	June
					✺

July	Aug	Sept	Oct	Nov	Dec
✺					

Buying tips *Look for plants with lots of healthy green leaf fans. Alternatively, anyone who already has an established plant in their garden should be able to spare some self-sown seedlings or a division or two.*

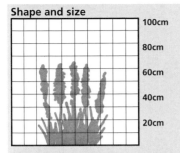

Sisyrinchium striatum

Sisyrinchium striatum 'Aunt May'

Growing guide

Drifts of sisyrinchiums make effective specimens as their foliage and flowers combine to make an interesting vertical shape. The leaves are semi-evergreen and form flat fans like an iris. In early summer, spikes of straw-coloured flowers are borne above the foliage.

Grow in any well-drained soil, in a sunny location. It is important to lift and divide the plant every year or so to ensure flowers are produced in future. Flowering causes the death of each individual fan, but the plant seeds itself freely.

The variegated form 'Aunt May' is not as hardy, so give it a sheltered, sunny position. It is worth potting up some of the divisions and keeping them under glass over the winter.

Good companions

S. striatum makes an effective specimen in gravel gardens and courtyards. It can be grown in borders where the vertical shape adds structure to soft mounds of plants like *Stachys lanata* or catmint (*Nepeta*). The yellow-variegated 'Aunt May' superbly sets off blue foliage plants such as rue.

Propagation

Division or seed.

Troubleshooting

Although the plant is semi-evergreen, the leaves often turn black or even die during winter.

Which variety?

S. striatum (syn. *Phaiophleps nigricans*) is widely available and the best choice in colder areas. The variety **'Aunt May'** (syn. 'Variegatum') has more to offer with its creamy-yellow vertical stripes on each leaf, though it is not as hardy. Most other sisyrinchiums are smaller and are grown in rock gardens.

Smilacina
Smilacina racemosa

Shape and size

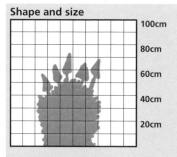

	100cm
	80cm
	60cm
	40cm
	20cm

Position

Hardiness Soil

MOIST

Uses

Features calendar

Jan	Feb	Mar	Apr	May	June
				✿	✿
July	Aug	Sept	Oct	Nov	Dec

Buying tips *Try nurseries that specialise in shade or woodland plants. Bulb specialists are also worth trying for dormant rhizomes.*

Smilacina stellata

Smilacina racemosa

Growing guide

This plant is related to Solomon's seal (*Polygonatum* x *hybridum*) and is similar in appearance. It bears elegant arching sprays of light green leaves. At the end of each leaf spray is a dense spike of creamy white flowers in spring. The flowers are scented and are sometimes followed by red berries.

This is a woodland plant best suited to a moist soil in partial shade or shade. You can improve the soil by adding leafmould or well-rotted garden compost when planting and by mulching each spring. The plant has rhizomatous roots which take a while to establish and then spread slowly. Plant 45cm (18in) apart and be prepared to leave them in place for several years.

Good companions

As a woodland plant smilacina could add interest to a shrub border. Underplant with spring-flowering bulbs and plants such as *Corydalis* species.

Propagation

Division in autumn (old plants only). Seed.

Troubleshooting

Generally trouble-free if you can provide the right conditions – it dislikes limy soils.

Which variety?

The only one you are likely to come across is **Smilacina racemosa**. This is better than the rarer **S. stellata** which is smaller and can be invasive.

Solidago

Solidago 'Queenie'

Shape and size

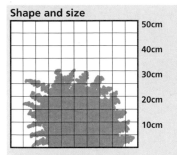

50cm
40cm
30cm
20cm
10cm

Position

Hardiness

Soil

ANY

Uses

Features calendar

Jan	Feb	Mar	Apr	May	June
					✿
✿	✿				
July	Aug	Sept	Oct	Nov	Dec

Buying tips *It is worth paying extra for a named variety. Inspect plants carefully for signs of powdery mildew.*

Solidago 'Goldenmosa'

Solidago 'Queenie'

Growing guide

Golden rod is an excellent border plant for creating a bold splash of yellow. It is an easy plant to grow in any soil in sun or in partial shade. It offers a long period of interest, bearing yellow flowers from July to August or August to September, depending on the variety. As well as being reliable front- or mid-border plants, solidago make good cut flowers. Although it has a reputation for being weedy and invasive, good named varieties have a better behaved habit than those varieties in wasteland areas.

Good companions

Coppery-bronze or orange heleniums are attractive as partners. Red crocosmias would also provide a contrast of colour and form.

Propagation

Division or seed.

Troubleshooting

Powdery mildew can be a problem. Tall varieties need staking.

Which variety?

Some golden rods are more garden-worthy than others, so the choice is important. The best ones for the garden are the dwarf named varieties such as **'Queenie'** (syn. 'Golden Thumb') a neat habit at only 30cm (12in) tall. Other dwarf ones to consider include **'Cloth of Gold'** with a loose, open habit at 45–50cm (18–20in) and **'Crown of Rays'** which has a stiff, upright habit and is 70cm (28in). These are all golden-yellow, do not need staking and are not invasive. **'Goldenmosa'**, with mimosa-like pale yellow flowers on 80cm (34in) stems, is prized for flower arranging.

x *Solidaster luteus*

(syn. x *S. hybridus*) is a cross between solidago and an aster. The result is a small plant with daisy-like yellow flowers – useful as a border plant and for cuttings. The variety **'Lemore'** has large, bright yellow flowers and grows up to 80cm (32in) high.

Stachys

Stachys byzantina 'Silver Carpet'

Shape and size

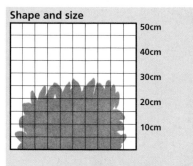

50cm
40cm
30cm
20cm
10cm

Position

Hardiness

Soil

WELL-DRAINED

Uses

Features calendar

Jan	Feb	Mar	Apr	May	June
July	Aug	Sept	Oct	Nov	Dec

Buying tips *S. byzantina is widely available, so is 'Silver Carpet'. Others may have to be obtained from specialists.*

Stachys byzantina foliage is covered in downy hairs

Stachys byzantina 'Silver Carpet'

Growing guide

Lambs' ears provides a silver carpet of foliage for most of the year and children love to stroke the soft, furry leaves. It is an easy and useful plant, tolerates drought and is a good choice for windy gardens.

Full sun is needed by *S. byzantina*, but *S. macrantha* can cope with shade. Both will grow in any soil that is well-drained. Plant 30cm (12in) apart for effective groundcover. These species usually flower profusely in summer, throwing up silvery spikes bearing small, purple flowers. This can spoil the carpet effect, and if the flowers are allowed to set seed, the rosettes tend to die out.

Good companions

An easy, reliable groundcover for sunny, well-drained banks. Use it to underplant roses or tall alliums, or combine it with other drought-tolerant plants such as sedums and ornamental grasses in a gravel garden. Small divisions can be planted up in containers.

Propagation

Division or seed.

Troubleshooting

Generally trouble-free. The leaves sometimes become spotted with fungal infection. Pick off and destroy affected leaves.

Which variety?

The basic species, which is now called **Stachys byzantina**, may still be sold as *S. olympica* or *S. lanata*. It is worth searching out non-flowering named varieties, as these make excellent groundcover plants. In *Gardening Which?* trials, we found **'Silver Carpet'** to be the best. It offers the best silver foliage groundcover plants with brightly coloured foliage and no flowers. **'Big Ears'** is also worth considering – it has large, broad leaves which are less furry than the species and are a grey-green. It produces a few flowers, which are best removed.

'Cotton Boll' (syn. 'Sheila McQueen') has sterile flowers that look like bobbles on the stems. Height and spread 60x90cm (24x36in). The new growth of **'Primrose Heron'** is yellow in spring then becomes green over the summer. **'Striped Phantom'** has yellow markings that get bolder in autumn; this mottled appearance is not to every gardener's taste.

S. macrantha (syn. *S. grandiflora*) is not evergreen but has more flowering interest, with purple flowers from May to July above dark green leaves. Height and spread 50x35cm (20x14in). It is worth looking for named varieties.

Stokesia

Stokesia laevis 'Blue Star'

Shape and size

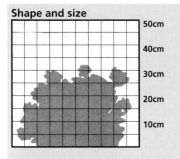

Position Hardiness Soil

Uses

Features calendar

Jan	Feb	Mar	Apr	May	June
					❋
July	Aug	Sept	Oct	Nov	Dec
❋	❋				

Buying tips *Not widely available, try unusual plant specialists. Best bought in spring or early summer.*

'Wyoming'

Stokesia laevis 'Blue Star'

Growing guide

Stokes' aster is easy to grow and provides long-lasting, large flowers on small plants. It is ideal for small gardens in raised beds or for narrow borders. The blooms look like a cross between an aster and a cornflower. Each flower is about 8cm (3in) across on plants that are only 30–45cm (12–18in) high.

The plant is evergreen, but dislikes damp and extreme cold, so it needs a warm, sunny position. Any reasonably fertile garden soil will do, so long as it is not cold and wet in winter.

Plant in spring. You may need to stake with twiggy sticks. Remove the dead flower heads in late autumn. Plants can be lifted in the autumn and brought into a greenhouse or conservatory where they can continue to flower.

Good companions

An invaluable plant for the front of small borders, Stokes' aster can be used to add flowering interest between foliage plants such as phormiums or *Stachys byzantina*.

Propagation

Division in spring or seed.

Troubleshooting

Generally trouble-free, though self-sown seedlings may be different in colour. If you have a named variety, you might want to deadhead plants before they set seed.

Which variety?

Stokesia laevis is the only species and this can have flowers in white, blue or pink. There are several named varieties: **'Blue Star'** is one of the best and is the one you are most likely to come across. **'Wyoming'** has purple-blue flowers, and **'Alba'** is white.

Symphytum
Symphytum 'Goldsmith'

Shape and size

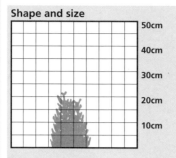

50cm
40cm
30cm
20cm
10cm

Position

Hardiness

Soil

MOIST

Uses

Features calendar

Jan	Feb	Mar	Apr	May	June
July	Aug	Sept	Oct	Nov	Dec

Buying tips *You are unlikely to come across Symphytum 'Goldsmith' at garden centres. Try nurseries that specialise in unusual foliage, shade-loving or unusual plants instead.*

Symphytum caucasicum

Symphytum 'Goldsmith'

Growing guide

This is a superb evergreen plant with large, vigorous leaves that will cover the ground and suppress weeds. The leaves are light green with broad cream margins. By cutting back after flowering you can encourage a neat habit and young foliage.

Grow symphytum in a partially shaded or shady position. It prefers a moist soil but is worth trying in drier areas. Plant 60cm (24in) apart.

Good companions

Grow it in a semi-wild part of the garden with clumps of bluebells and foxgloves. Ferns such as *Matteuccia struthiopteris* (shuttlecock fern) would add a foliage contrast.

Propagation

Division of the fleshy roots can be done in spring or autumn. Root cuttings.

Troubleshooting

The plants spread by stems that root at their tips. If they need to be removed they are easy to pull out.

Which variety?

***Symphytum* 'Goldsmith'** (syn. *S. ibericum* 'Variegatum', *S. grandiflorum* 'Variegatum') is recommended for its compact habit and the cream markings that can brighten shady corners. Do not confuse it with Russian comfrey (*S.* x *uplandicum* 'Variegatum'), a much bigger plant at 90x60cm (36x24in) which is also likely to lose its variegation.

For an interesting spring-flowering plant for shade, consider ***S. caucasicum.*** This produces a neat clump with clusters of blue flowers from April to June. Height and spread 60x60cm (24x24in).

Tanacetum

T. coccineum 'Eileen May Robinson'

Shape and size

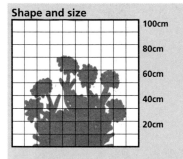

	100cm
	80cm
	60cm
	40cm
	20cm

Position　Hardiness　Soil

WELL-DRAINED

Uses

Features calendar

Jan	Feb	Mar	Apr	May ✿	June ✿
July	Aug	Sept	Oct	Nov	Dec

Buying tips *You may come across* T. coccineum *varieties in garden centres in the herbaceous section in late spring or early summer.* T. parthenium *varieties are often sold in strips or packs with bedding plants.*

Tanacetum parthenium 'Golden Ball'

Tanacetum coccineum 'Eileen May Robinson'

Growing guide

Better known under their old name pyrethrum, these hardy flowering plants are useful for beds, borders or for cutting.

The large daisy-like flowers, which are borne on long stalks above mounds of neat foliage, are the main feature of this plant. The flowers may need supports and these should be put in place in spring. The single-flowered varieties have a prominent yellow centre, but there are also double-flowered types too.

Give them a sunny spot in a fertile but well-drained soil. To prevent the soil drying out over the late spring and summer, mulch in spring and irrigate if needed. These plants cannot stand their roots being in wet soil during winter, so add soil improvers or grow on a slightly raised bed. Remove the flowering stems once the blooms fade to encourage more flowers to form.

Good companions

In the border, place in the middle with delphiniums or lupins behind. If you want them as cut flowers, grow in rows on the vegetable plot.

Propagation

Division in spring, July or August.

Troubleshooting

T. coccineum varieties are prone to winter damage if disturbed in the autumn so move in spring.

Which variety?

A dozen or so varieties of ***Tanacetum coccineum*** (syn. *Chrysanthemum coccineum*, *Pyrethrum coccineum*) are available. **'Eileen May Robinson'** is an old, established variety with single, clear pink flowers. They are all 75cm (30in) tall and flower from May to June: **'Aphrodite'** double white; **'Brenda'** vivid magenta; **'Robinson's Pink'** dark pink; **'Robinson's Red'** red; **'Salmon Beauty'** clear pink; **'Snow Cloud'** white; and **'Vanessa'** double, rosy-carmine with a flush of orange.

T. haradjanii needs sun and a poor, well-drained soil. It forms a mound of silvery, fern-like leaves and bears small yellow daisies in summer – remove these if you are growing it as a foliage plant. Height and spread 25x35cm (10x14in).
T. parthenium (feverfew) is a hardy but short-lived perennial. It is often grown as an annual, or it self-seeds. It is useful for adding flowering interest to herb gardens and it has small, white daisy-like flowers from July to September and aromatic foliage. Named varieties include **'Aureum'**, with greenish-gold foliage and white flowers, height 45cm (18in). **'Golden Ball'** is compact at 25cm (10in) with golden-yellow, ball-like flowers. **'White Bonnet'** has double, pure white flowers, 75cm (30in).

Tellima
Tellima grandiflora

Shape and size

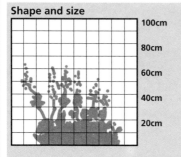

100cm
80cm
60cm
40cm
20cm

Position

Hardiness

Soil

ANY

Uses

Features calendar

| Jan | Feb | Mar | Apr | May | June |
| July | Aug | Sept | Oct | Nov | Dec |

Buying tips *Try groundcover, foliage or shade plant specialists. If you want a lot of plants for groundcover, buy large ones and divide them up before planting.*

Tellima grandiflora 'Rubra Group'

Tellima grandiflora

Growing guide

A useful semi-evergreen that can cope with dry shade. The leaves are similar to those of heuchera and are close to the ground. The plants provide excellent groundcover when planted 45cm (18in) apart. Flower spikes emerge above the foliage to give a display of green-yellow bells from April to June. Deadhead after flowering.

Plant in autumn or spring in any soil. It makes sense to keep them for shade or partially shaded areas where little else will grow, though they can cope with sun.

Good companions

Toad lilies (*Tricyrtis*) and *Thalictrum* would add late-season flowering interest to shady areas when *Tellima grandiflora* has finished flowering.

Propagation

Division or seed (purple-leaved forms do not come true from seed).

Troubleshooting

Generally trouble-free. The centre of the clumps can lift out of the ground with age, but regular mulching and division will overcome this.

Which variety?

Tellima grandiflora is the only species and is 40–80cm (16–32in). There are bronze-purple foliage forms such as **'Rubra Group'** (syn. 'Purpurea') and **'Purpurteppich'**, which often deepen in colour over winter.

Thalictrum

Thalictrum aquilegifolium

Shape and size

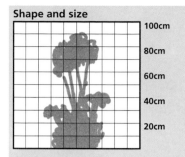

100cm
80cm
60cm
40cm
20cm

Position

Hardiness

Soil

MOIST

Uses

Features calendar

Jan	Feb	Mar	Apr	May	June
July	Aug	Sept	Oct	Nov	Dec

Buying tips *You should be able to get seed-raised ones fairly easily and cheaply from garden centres or specialists. 'Hewitt's Double' is more expensive as it is hard to propagate.*

Thalictrum delavayi

Thalictrum aquilegifolium

Growing guide

This is a showy plant with attractive summer flowers for the back of the border. Its graceful foliage looks like a maidenhair fern. Both the flowers and leaves are used for flower arranging.

Most species need a fertile, moisture-retentive soil, so add soil improvers before planting if the soil needs them. Follow this up with generous mulching each spring. Thalictrums thrive in sun or in partial shade. The stems need supporting with bamboo canes and should be cut down once flowering is over.

Good companions

The angel's fishing rod (*Dierama pulcherrimum*), foxgloves, delphiniums and hollyhocks would all combine well with thalictrums.

Propagation

Division (in spring) or seed. Both methods can be slow.

Troubleshooting

Generally trouble-free but *T. delavayi* needs a sheltered site, deep planting (23cm/9in deep) and firm staking.

Which variety?

A number of thalictrum species and varieties are available, but not all are worth growing. The following are recommended: *T. aquilegifolium* has pale grey-green foliage a bit like a columbine. It is the first variety to flower from June to July, then it produces good seedheads. The flowers are pale mauve. The named varieties like **'Album'** have white flowers; **'Thundercloud'** (**'Purple Cloud'**) has purple flowers.

T. delavayi (syn. *T. dipterocarpum*) has tall sprays of lilac flowers reaching 120cm (48in). Flowering lasts from July to September. The variety **'Hewitt's Double'** is very sought after; it has fully double, mauve flowers from July to August and is 90cm (36in) high. *T. flavum* **'Glaucum'** (syn. *T. speciosissimum*) is prized for its lovely blue-green foliage and lemon-yellow flowers from June to September. Height 150cm (60in). *T. isopyroides* is a smaller thalictrum at 60–75cm (24–30in) high. It has blue-green foliage and small yellow-green flowers with carmine stamens.

Tiarella

Tiarella cordifolia

Shape and size

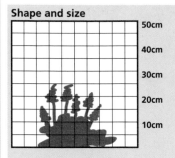

50cm
40cm
30cm
20cm
10cm

Position Hardiness Soil

MOIST

Uses

Features calendar

Jan	Feb	Mar	Apr	May	June

July	Aug	Sept	Oct	Nov	Dec

Tiarella cordifolia

Buying tips *You may come across T. cordifolia in garden centres either in the herbaceous section or with groundcover plants. Check the compost is moist before you buy.*

Tiarella wherryi

Growing guide

These evergreen perennials turn a reddish-bronze in winter, adding interest to the border at an otherwise dull time. They make good groundcover plants and another bonus is their ability to thrive in light shade. In early summer spikes of small creamy-white flowers appear, hence the common name, foam flower.

All tiarellas need a moist, ideally acidic, soil, in partial shade. Dig in plenty of leafmould when planting and mulch each spring. Plant *T. cordifolia* 30–45cm (12–18in) apart for quick foliage groundcover.

Good companions

Use at the front of a border, between and under shrubs or as groundcover. Grow with other woodland plants like pulmonarias.

Propagation

Division or seed.

Troubleshooting

Generally trouble-free so long as the soil does not dry out.

Which variety?

Tiarella cordifolia is the best choice for groundcover as it forms a dense carpet 10cm (4in) high. When in flower, it has a height of 20–25cm (8–10in).

T. polyphylla is taller and has more of a clump-forming habit. In flower it reaches 30–60cm (12–24in).

T. wherryi (syn. *T. cordifolia* '*Collina*') is a neat plant at 30x30cm (12x12in), with prettily marked, ivy-shaped leaves. It bears lots of creamy-white flowers from June to September.

Tradescantia

Tradescantia x andersoniana

Shape and size

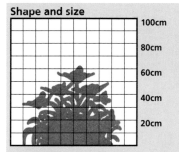

	100cm
	80cm
	60cm
	40cm
	20cm

Position

Hardiness

Soil

MOIST

Uses

Features calendar

Jan	Feb	Mar	Apr	May	June
					✿
July	Aug	Sept	Oct	Nov	Dec
✿	✿	✿			

Buying tips *The variety 'Osprey' is fairly easy to find. Avoid plants growing in dry compost and with brown, wilted or tatty foliage.*

'Osprey'

Tradescantia x andersoniana

Growing guide

These long-lived perennials are easy to grow. Their three-petalled flowers appear among a clump of strap-like foliage. Flowering lasts from early summer to autumn. The hardy varieties are suitable for growing in borders.

The plants are fairly tough but, as they originate from the wetlands of North America, a moist soil is best. During prolonged dry spells the leaves can die back. They are suitable for sun or partial shade. Stake with twiggy sticks and cut down plants in late autumn.

Good companions

The dense clumps of tradescantia make an effective shape from a distance so place at the front of a border, with a very floriferous backdrop such as *Campanula lactiflora*.

Propagation

Cuttings, or division in spring.

Troubleshooting

Generally trouble-free, but watch out for slugs. Remove spent flower stems and seedlings with wishy-washy, lilac-blue flowers as they may take over named varieties.

Which variety?

Tradescantia x *andersoniana* (syn. *T. virginiana*) is the main species. Around 20 named varieties are available, offering a wide range of colours including blue, pink, white and various shades of purple. The ones you are most likely to come across are as follows (most are 45–60cm/18–24in high and flower from June to September): **'Innocence'** has pure white flowers. **'Iris Prichard'** is white with blue markings. **'Isis'** has large, deep blue flowers. **'J. C. Weguelin'** has light blue flowers and **'Carmine Glow'** (syn. 'Karminglut') red flowers. **'Osprey'** bears white flowers, each with a blue centre. **'Pauline'** has lilac-pink flowers. **'Purple Dome'** has rich purple flowers and **'Zwanenberg Blue'** large blue blooms.

Varieties with golden-yellow leaves are a new development: **'Blue 'n' Gold'** has blue flowers and intense yellow foliage, but there is also **'Chedglow'** with mauve-pink flowers. These sound promising as the plants have more impact but we do not yet know if they are as easy to grow.

Tricyrtis

Tricyrtis formosana

Shape and size

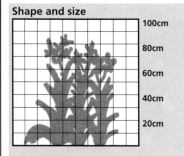

100cm
80cm
60cm
40cm
20cm

Position

Hardiness

Soil
Uses

MOIST

Features calendar

Jan	Feb	Mar	Apr	May	June
	✿	✿	✿		
July	Aug	Sept	Oct	Nov	Dec

Buying tips *Toad lilies can be hard to find in garden centres, so try nurseries specialising in rare or unusual plants. Buy and plant in spring, if possible.*

Tricyrtis hirta

Tricyrtis formosana

Growing guide

Toad lilies offer unusual flowers at the end of the growing season. Brown buds open into blooms of white or purple, each spotted with darker markings. As well as prettily marked petals, the centre of each flower is raised, giving an exotic touch.

All toad lilies thrive in an acidic soil in woodland conditions but they can cope with sunnier positions if the soil is fertile and retains moisture. In northern areas, they will need a sunny spot in order to flower. Plant 45–60cm (18–24in) apart in spring somewhere sheltered.

Good companions

Despite their height, these plants work well at the front of the border near paths or patios where their flowers can be seen at close quarters. The most suitable companions are shade-loving foliage plants such as ferns or hostas.

Propagation

Division in spring.

Troubleshooting

Slugs and snails can be a problem, so put down slug pellets regularly and replenish after rain.

Which variety?

Tricyrtis formosana (syn. *T. stolonifera*) is the one you are most likely to come across. This has glossy, dark green leaves and mauve flowers with dark purple spots. It reaches up to 90cm (36in).

T. hirta is a clump-forming species with hairy leaves. It grows to about 60cm (24in) and the flowers are white or mauve with darker spots. There are named varieties such as **'Alba'** which has no spots.

Trollius

Trollius x cultorum hybrids

Shape and size

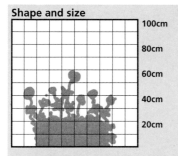

- 100cm
- 80cm
- 60cm
- 40cm
- 20cm

Position

Hardiness

Soil

MOIST

Uses

Features calendar

Jan	Feb	Mar	Apr	May ✹	June ✷
July	Aug	Sept	Oct	Nov	Dec

Buying tips *They may be sold in flower in late spring, but early autumn is the ideal time to plant them.*

Trollius x cultorum 'Superbus'

'Earliest of All'

Growing guide

Globe flowers brighten up mixed borders in early summer with their cheerful yellow flowers.

They like a moisture-retentive soil and will thrive in ground that has plenty of organic matter dug in. A sunny or partially shaded spot is suitable.

Plant in early autumn, preferably in positions where they can be left to establish into mature clumps.

Good companions

Their flowers follow on after tulips, so they are useful for extending the period of interest in a border. Or they can be grown beside a pond or in a bog garden. If you have the soil for rhododendrons and azaleas, they would be ideal for underplanting.

Propagation

Division.

Troubleshooting

Generally trouble-free.

Which variety?

A number of *Trollius* hybrids are now available as a result of breeding work with *T.* x *cultorum*. Most are 50–60cm (20–24in) high. **'Alabaster'** has creamy-white flowers, but is not a strong grower. **'Baudirektor Linne'** is an intense orange, and a strong grower that reaches 70cm (28in). **'Earliest of All'** is the first into flower in May with pale yellow blooms. **'Fireglobe'** (syn. 'Feuertroll') has dark orange flowers. **'Lemon Queen'** has lemon-yellow flowers. **'Orange Princess'** bears yellow-orange flowers and **'Superbus'** has lemon-yellow flowers.

T. chinensis **'Golden Queen'** has large, bowl-shaped, orange flowers and reaches 90cm (36in).

T. pumilus is much smaller 30x23cm (12x9in) with yellow flowers from May to June. Grow in alpine container or rock garden.

Veratrum
Veratrum nigrum

Shape and size

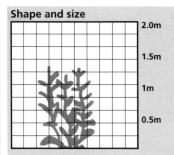

2.0m
1.5m
1m
0.5m

Position

Hardiness

Soil

MOIST

Uses

Features calendar

Jan	Feb	Mar	Apr	May	June
July	Aug	Sept	Oct	Nov	Dec

Buying tips *These plants are very hard to get hold of from garden centres. Try nurseries specialising in rare or unusual plants instead.*

WARNING
All parts of this plant are poisonous.

Veratrum album

Veratrum nigrum

Growing guide

These are impressive perennials with large leaves and long flower spikes crowded with small maroon or green flowers. They are an interesting curiosity if you have the right conditions.

Choose the planting position with care as they are long-lived plants. The ideal place would be a shady or partially shaded place where the soil is deep and fertile. A border that has been well-cultivated, with lots of well-rotted organic matter such as garden compost dug into it. Mulch each spring and add a top-dressing of growmore if the soil is low in nutrients.

The plants are poisonous and were once used to make insecticides. The flowers smell of rotten fruit and attract flies.

Good companions
They are best grown on their own as a specimen plant, but they could be combined with summer-flowering bulbs such as agapanthus or lilies.

Propagation
Division in autumn. Seed is possible, but takes a long time.

Troubleshooting
Generally trouble-free.

Which variety?

Veratrum are not widely sold, but the one you are most likely to come across is **Veratrum nigrum** which has maroon flowers and can top 1.2m (4ft). **V. album** (false hellebore) is similar, but the flowers are pale greenish-white and appear in late summer. **V. viride** has green flowers on 1.8m (6ft) spikes.

Verbascum

Verbascum chaixii

Shape and size

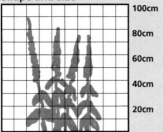

100cm
80cm
60cm
40cm
20cm

Position   Hardiness   Soil

WELL-DRAINED

Uses

Features calendar

Jan	Feb	Mar	Apr	May	June
✳	✳				
July	Aug	Sept	Oct	Nov	Dec

Buying tips

Short-lived, seed-raised species such as V. phoeniceum are cheap and are easily obtained from garden centres or seed catalogues. Others, such as 'Helen Johnson', are propagated by root cuttings and cost more.

'Cotswold Queen'

Verbascum chaixii 'Album'

Growing guide

Verbascums will add impact to planting schemes with their unmissable flower spikes reaching up to 1.5m (5ft). All are either biennial or short-lived perennials, so they flower in the first or second summer after sowing. They then usually die, but they self-seed readily.

All verbascums are drought-tolerant and thrive in the sun on well-drained soils which are low in nutrients. In a more fertile soil, they tend to grow taller which means they are more likely to need staking and any tendency to being short-lived is increased. Remove faded flower spikes.

Good companions

They make impressive specimens in gravel gardens. Those with yellow flowers and grey foliage can be partnered with lower-growing blue-flowered plants such as sea hollies or the shrubby *Ceratostigma willmottianum*.

Propagation

Seed or root cuttings.

Troubleshooting

Watch out for mildew, especially on *V. thapsus*. You can treat plants with a suitable fungicide, or try to prevent mildew by growing them in an open position. Verbascums can be devastated by mullein moth caterpillars; pick them off the plant as soon as they are seen in early June.

Which variety?

Given enough sun, **Verbascum chaixii** is one of the most reliable perennial verbascums. It has bold spikes 90cm (36in) high of yellow flowers from July to August. The following named varieties are worth looking for – they flower from May to August unless otherwise stated: **'Album'** has white flowers. **'Cotswold Queen'** has yellow flowers with a terracotta centre, and **'Pink Domino'** has pink flowers. **'Gainsborough'** bears pale yellow flowers, while **'Royal Highland'** boasts yellow and apricot flowers from July to August and is 120–150cm (48–60in).

'Helen Johnson' is a recent addition, with coppery-orange flowers and grey, felty foliage.

Perennial mulleins that die after about three years are still worth considering. For example, **V. phoeniceum** – with its pink or purple spires 90cm (36in) tall – is easier than most as it thrives in light shade as well as sun and is not fussy about soil type.

Verbena
Verbena 'Homestead Purple'

Shape and size

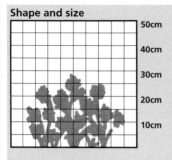

50cm
40cm
30cm
20cm
10cm

Position

Hardiness Soil

WELL-DRAINED

Uses

Features calendar

Jan	Feb	Mar	Apr	May	June
					✿
July	Aug	Sept	Oct	Nov	Dec
✿	✿	✿	✿		

Buying tips *'Homestead Purple' is widely promoted in garden centres when in flower. V. bonariensis may be found in large garden centres or at specialists, but it can be grown from seed.*

Verbena bonariensis is easy to raise from seed

Verbena 'Homestead Purple' and 'Silver Anne'

Growing guide

Most verbenas are tender perennials, but some are frost-hardy. *Verbena* 'Homestead Purple' was introduced into Britain in 1994 from Georgia, USA. It has proved to be hardy on a well-drained soil. The plant is very free-flowering with intense purple flowers from June until October. It has a low-growing habit, making it suitable for covering soil between specimen plants in the border, or as a container plant. It performs well in sun or partial shade.

Good companions

This plant can be used at the front of borders with silver foliage plants or with yellow daisy flowers. It is also an excellent single subject for hanging baskets.

Propagation

Seed (*V. bonariensis*). Cuttings (*V.* 'Homestead Purple').

Troubleshooting

Generally trouble-free in mild areas.

Which variety?

'Homestead Purple' is worth trying for its flowering impact and hardiness. Height and spread 30x45cm (12x18in).

Another excellent one is *V. bonariensis* (syn. *V. patagonica*). This is a tall plant that can reach 1.5–1.8m (5–6ft) and becomes more branched as the summer progresses. It has an 'airy' appearance because its long, slender stems and small leaves allow you to look through it to plants beyond. Try it at the front or at the end of borders, or use it as a specimen. It has soft, lavender-blue flowers that start in June and continue until the frosts.

It is a short-lived perennial, not hardy in all areas, but in warmer, southern regions it will set seed.

Veronica

Shape and size

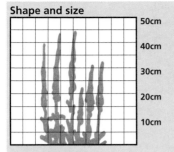

50cm
40cm
30cm
20cm
10cm

Position   Hardiness   Soil

WELL-DRAINED

Uses

Features calendar

Jan	Feb	Mar	Apr	May	June
				✿	✿
July	Aug	Sept	Oct	Nov	Dec

Buying tips *Most garden centres should have the smaller border veronicas such as* V. gentianoides. *For named varieties or the taller ones you might need a specialist.*

Veronica spicata incana

Veronica gentianoides

Growing guide

Veronicas provide easy flowering plants for small areas in early summer. Some have attractive foliage and all are popular with bees and butterflies.

Give them a sunny, well-drained site – they thrive on chalky soils. Plant in spring or autumn 25cm (10in) apart for the smaller border types, 30–45cm (12–18in) for the tall ones. Cut back flowering stems after flowering.

Good companions

Most of the border types are best as frontal plants. They do not like to be crowded by other plants but, by combining them with later-flowering frontal plants such as *Silene schafta*, you can extend the seasonal interest of the border.

Propagation

Division or seed.

Troubleshooting

Generally trouble-free.

Which variety?

The hardy, taller ones suitable for beds and borders include the following: ***V. gentianoides*** with its pale blue flowers in May and June is the one you are most likely to come across. Height and spread 45x45cm (18x18in). The variety **'Variegata'** has cream markings on the leaves.

V. peduncularis **'Georgia Blue'** bears rich blue flowers from April to June on a carpet of bronze-purple foliage. Height and spread 15x30cm (6x12in)

Named varieties of ***V. spicata*** are worth looking for. **'Heidekind'** has rose-pink flowers and **'Icicle'** has white flowers. Both are 15x23cm (6x9in) and flower from June to August.

V. spicata incana (syn. *V. incana*) has blue flowers from June to August. It also has the bonus of silver-grey foliage that is almost evergreen. Look out for named varieties like **'Silver Carpet'** which has larger leaves. Height and spread 30x30cm (12x12in).

Taller veronicas include ***V. exaltata*** with light blue flowers in late summer. This reaches 120x30cm (48x12in), but does not need staking. ***V. longifolia*** usually needs some support but a number of good named varieties are available. Height and spread 90x30cm (36x12in).

Viola

Viola odorata

Shape and size

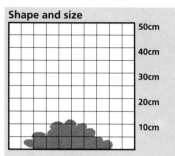

Position

Hardiness   Soil

MOIST

Uses

Features calendar

Jan	Feb	Mar	Apr	May	June
	✽	✽	✽		
July	Aug	Sept	Oct	Nov	Dec

Buying tips *Spring-flowering violets are not widely available but you should find V. riviniana 'Purpurea' and V. sororia in garden centres – try the alpine sections. Most of the other varieties will have to be ordered from specialist nurseries.*

'Duchesse de Parme'

Viola odorata

Growing guide

Sweet violets and other spring-flowering violas offer flowers from February to April, a time when most borders are still dormant. The sweet violets have the bonus of scented flowers – to appreciate them try a few as cut flowers.

Violets can be grown in any part of the garden, provided they receive some protection from midday sun. Their vigorous, fibrous roots need a soil that is well cultivated with plenty of organic matter. Plant the crowns at ground level, about 30cm (12in) apart and firm the soil around the roots. Scatter around slug pellets after planting. Regular watering may be needed during dry spells to reduce the risk of attack by spider mite.

Good companions

Grow sweet violets under deciduous shrubs – this way they will still get the spring sunshine to encourage the flower buds to form.

Other hardy violets can be allowed to self-seed in paving cracks. *V. cucullata* (syn. *V. obliqua*) makes a pretty underplanting for roses.

Propagation

Division of mature crowns. Named varieties are easy to propagate from rooted runners. Seed is the best method for *V. cucullata* and *V. sororia*. With sweet violets the seedlings can be variable.

Troubleshooting

Plants can be attacked by spider mites. Spray with a suitable insecticide at the first sign of attack – look for yellowing foliage and white flecking on the leaves.

Well-established sweet violets will spread by runners and this is an easy way to propagate them. However, to get the best flowering performance, remove the runners as they appear. If flowering and vigour become poor, lift and divide the clumps. Then replant into fresh soil with added organic matter.

Viola riviniana 'Purpurea'

Which variety?

The sweet violets (**V. odorata**) are the ones to go for if you want hardy, fragrant plants. Named varieties are not widely available, though you might come across the following. All are about 10–15cm (4–6in) high.

'Mrs R. Barton' has white flowers with a purple fleck. **'Norah Church'** has violet-mauve flowers.

'Princesse de Galles' (syn. 'Princess of Wales') boasts violet-blue flowers with long stems, one of the best for cutting.

Parma violets need cloche or coldframe protection during the winter months. They have fragrant flowers from April onwards. Worthwhile varieties are the pale lavender **'Comte de Brazza'** and **'Duchesse de Parme'**, or the darker mauve **'Marie Louise'**.

Other hardy violets include the following, none of which is scented: **V. cucullata** (syn. *V. obliqua*) is very free-flowering. Flowers are produced from May to June in blue, white or pink. Height and spread 30x30cm (12x12in). **V. riviniana 'Purpurea'** (syn. *V. labradorica*, *V. labradorica* 'Purpurea') has attractive purplish foliage and light blue flowers from April to June. It can be vigorous and self-seeds readily. Height and spread 10–15cmx30cm (4–6inx12in). **V. sororia 'Freckles'** is similar in habit to *V. cucullata*, but the petals are speckled with a mass of minute violet-blue dots.

Viola cucullata

Viola sororia 'Freckles'

Viola odorata

Waldsteinia
Waldsteinia ternata

Shape and size

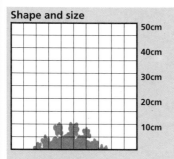

50cm
40cm
30cm
20cm
10cm

Position   Hardiness   Soil

ANY

Uses

Features calendar

Jan	Feb	Mar	Apr	May	June
			✿	✿	✿
July	Aug	Sept	Oct	Nov	Dec

Buying tips *Look for it in the groundcover section of garden centres or order from a groundcover or herbaceous plant specialist.*

Waldsteinia ternata makes ideal ground cover

Waldsteinia ternata

Growing guide

Waldsteinia ternata is a useful flowering groundcover plant with evergreen foliage. The leaves resemble those of a strawberry and are a fresh green. The flowers are bright yellow and are borne en masse from April to June.

Being a woodland plant, Waldsteinia ternata is an ideal choice for lighting up the dappled shade of late spring or early summer under trees or deciduous shrubs. It is also a useful addition to the front of a herbaceous border where it forms a neat, colourful edging.

Use this plant in any soil; a partially shaded site is preferred. But it can tolerate a sunny position provided the soil does not dry out too much. Plant 30cm (12in) apart. It spreads by runners.

Good companions

Since it flowers early in the year, from April to June, use it to brighten up the front of summer-flowering borders. Or use with other low-growing, shade-tolerant perennials such as pulmonarias, or *Tiarella cordifolia*.

Propagation
Division.

Troubleshooting
Generally trouble-free. Flowering can decline after several years, lifting and dividing plants can help.

Which variety?

Waldsteinia ternata
(syn. *W. trifolia*) is the only widely available species. It is a semi-evergreen, spreading groundcover plant with bright green foliage and clear yellow flowers.

Zantedeschia

Zantedeschia aethiopica 'Crowborough'

Shape and size

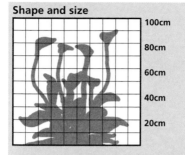

100cm
80cm
60cm
40cm
20cm

Position   Hardiness   Soil

MOIST

Uses

Features calendar

Jan	Feb	Mar	Apr	May	June
		✿	✿	✿	✿

July	Aug	Sept	Oct	Nov	Dec
🌿	🌿	🌿			

Buying tips Dry rhizomes can be bought pre-packed from garden centres or from bulb specialists in early spring. Later, pot-grown plants should be available from late spring to early summer. Aquatic or foliage plant specialists are worth trying, too.

Zantedeschia 'Green Goddess'

Zantedeschia aethiopica 'Crowborough'

Growing guide

The arum lily can grow to form an impressive specimen plant. Although the white 'flowers' (correctly called spathes) with their yellow central spike are the primary attraction during early summer, arum lilies also make valuable foliage plants at other times of the year. The leaves are shaped like large spears and create a lush green effect on mature plants. Both spathes and foliage are sought after by flower arrangers.

Most Zantedeschias are only half-hardy or are tender and need to be grown in greenhouses in pots. However, varieties of Z. aethiopica can be grown outdoors in favourable areas. The hardiest is 'Crowborough', which is hardy once established, but it needs winter protection for the first two years and a thick mulch in subsequent years.

Grow in a sunny border or bed in a well-cultivated soil that does not dry out in summer. If growing in water, plant in a pot at least 20cm (8in), covered with 30-60cm (12-24in) of water for best protection. If this is not possible a minimum depth of 15cm (6in) will do.

Good companions

Grow in a pond as a contrast of form to water irises. Alternatively, grow as a mid-border specimen, planting 10cm (4in) deep. It makes a fine container specimen too – try it in a half barrel along with small hostas.

Propagation

Division, root cuttings or seed.

Troubleshooting

Generally trouble-free if grown in the right area and given protection.

Which variety?

'Crowborough' has the most to offer as it is the hardiest. Height and spread 90x60cm (36x24in). There are other named varieties such as 'Green Goddess' which has very large green spathes with cream markings and dwarf varieties like 'Little Gem' which is about half the size of 'Crowborough'.

Carex

Carex hachijoensis 'Evergold'

Shape and size

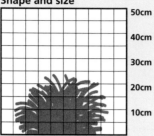

50cm
40cm
30cm
20cm
10cm

Position   Hardiness   Soil

MOIST

Uses

Features calendar

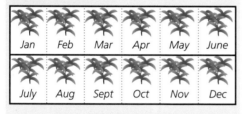

| Jan | Feb | Mar | Apr | May | June |
| July | Aug | Sept | Oct | Nov | Dec |

Buying tips *You should be able to find* C. *hachijoensis 'Evergold' at most garden centres with an ornamental grasses section. Look for a good leaf colour and healthy, yellowy-brown roots.*

Carex with gazania and tagetes

Carex hachijoensis 'Evergold'

Growing guide

Carex is a large genus of grassy perennials. The best, such as *C. hachijoensis* 'Evergold' (syn. C. morrowii), form clumps with a neat, well-behaved habit and foliage that contributes colour all year round.

The ideal position for the best foliage is in partial shade in a soil that does not dry out, but the plants are tolerant of other sites. The bronze-coloured forms often look more attractive in sunlight.

Good companions

Use the evergreen golden foliage forms to brighten up conifers or heathers. Or grow as a single subject in a container for the patio. Carex also looks effective beside a pond.

Propagation

Division.

Troubleshooting

Trouble-free.

Which variety?

Carex hachijoensis 'Evergold' stands out as the best variety for its bright, year-round foliage and neat habit. As its name suggests, it has evergreen foliage with a vertical gold stripe down the leaves. Small brown flowers in June. Height and spread 25x45cm (10x18in).

Others you may come across include the following:
C. buchananii is not reliably hardy except in mild areas, where it is worth insulating during winter. Its clumps are made up of masses of buff-coloured stems, which look attractive where the light catches them. Height and spread 70x20cm (28x8in). **C. comans 'Bronze Form'** has bronze foliage and a height and spread of 40x40cm (16x24in). **'Frosted Curls'** is similar, but with a creamy-white frosted effect on the leaves. **C. elata 'Aurea'** (syn. C. stricta 'Bowles Golden') is a deciduous sedge with bright golden foliage and small brown flowers in June. Height and spread 60x45cm (24x18in). It likes a moist soil in the sun. **C. testacea** is similar to C. comans, but with yellow-green foliage in summer and bronze-green in winter.

One to avoid is C. riparia 'Variegata' an invasive species with white-striped foliage.

Cortaderia

Cortaderia selloana 'Pumila'

Shape and size

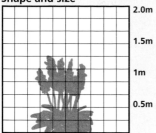

2.0m
1.5m
1m
0.5m

Position   Hardiness   Soil   Uses

WELL-DRAINED

Features calendar

Jan	Feb	Mar	Apr	May	June
July	Aug	Sept ✿	Oct ✿	Nov ✿	Dec

Buying tips *Buy and plant in spring. Be wary of advertisements for bright pink plumed pampas grass – these are misleading. Buy named varieties such as 'Rendatleri' or 'Pink Feather'.*

Cortaderia selloana 'Aureolineata'

Cortaderia selloana 'Pumila'

Growing guide

Pampas grass is the first ornamental grass most people think of. A spectacular specimen which has plumes that are excellent for drying, it is best reserved for large gardens.

It is evergreen in mild areas, but dies back to the ground in most regions. Plant in spring in a position that gets full sun, with some shelter if possible. Any well-drained, fertile soil is suitable.

Dead pampas leaves should be left standing over winter and chopped back or carefully burnt off in February. A very hot fire could damage the new growth.

It has sharp-edged leaves so do not plant it near where children play and wear gloves when handling it.

Good companions

Pampas grass is best grown as a specimen on its own. It is often seen in lawns but is equally effective surrounded by gravel or pebbles.

Propagation

Division in spring but only if necessary as it does not like to be disturbed.

Troubleshooting

Seed-raised plants may not flower if they are from a poor strain. To encourage flowering, feed in spring with 50g (2oz) of sulphate of potash. If there are no flowers by the next season, replace with a named variety.

Which variety?

Cortaderia selloana (syn. *C. argentea*) is the main species. Named varieties may vary in their height, foliage and hardiness. Height varies from 1.2–3m (4–10ft), allow for spread of 0.9–1.8m (3–6ft). We have chosen the variety **'Pumila'** which is the smallest and hardiest. It reaches about 1.8x1.2m (5x4ft) when in flower. Two other varieties are worth looking out for, but they need more sheltered positions. **'Aureolineata'** ('Gold Band') a variegated one that reaches 2.1m (7ft). **'Sunningdale Silver'** has lots of large, creamy-white plumes but grows to 3x2.4m (10x8ft).

Fargesia

Fargesia murieliae

Shape and size

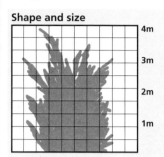

4m
3m
2m
1m

Position

Hardiness

Soil

MOIST

Uses

Features calendar

Jan	Feb	Mar	Apr	May	June
July	Aug	Sept	Oct	Nov	Dec

Buying tips *You might find* F. murieliae *and* F. nitida *at garden centres in 5–7.5 litre pots. Or visit a bamboo specialist for smaller or larger sizes. Avoid pots crowded with old stems as these may not get established.*

Fargesia murieliae 'Simba'

Fargesia murieliae

Growing guide

This is a medium-sized bamboo that would be ideal as an evergreen screening plant or garden divider. It is dense, compact and hardy and would create much less shade than a tree of equivalent height.

For a gap-free hedge in five years, plant 60–90cm (24–36in) apart. To keep it dense with plenty of leaf cover, cut to ground level all stems older than four or five years.

Like most bamboos, fargesia prefers a moist soil or compost in a sunny or partially shaded position. Apply a granular fertiliser such as growmore each spring.

Good companions

These bamboos make good single subjects. The smaller *F. murieliae* 'Simba' could be planted among paving, beside any water feature or in a container.

Propagation

Division.

Troubleshooting

Generally trouble-free; the ones we have mentioned here are not invasive.

Which variety?

There are two main species you are likely to come across. **Fargesia murieliae** has small green leaves and a height and spread of 4x1m (15x3ft). **F. nitida** is similar, but has purple-brown canes and the new stems do not produce leaves until their second year.

For a smaller one, look out for **F. murieliae 'Simba'** which reaches 1.8–2.4m (6–8ft).

Festuca

Festuca glauca

Shape and size

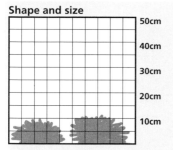

Position **Hardiness** **Soil**

WELL-DRAINED

Uses

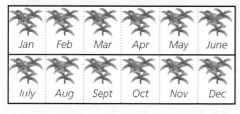

Features calendar

Jan	Feb	Mar	Apr	May	June
July	Aug	Sept	Oct	Nov	Dec

Buying tips *F. glauca is widely available, but named varieties may have to be bought from a specialist. Avoid plants with any signs of rot or die-back in the middle and overwet compost.*

Festuca 'Elijah Blue'

Festuca glauca

Growing guide

This is a bluish evergreen grass, small enough for any garden. It forms neat tussocks of foliage and although flower spikes are produced in summer, these are often cut off to enhance the foliage.

Grow them on a light, well-drained soil, as on wet ground they can rot. They are ideal for chalky soil and need plenty of sun to develop a noticeable blue colour. Plant 15–25cm (6–10in) apart.

Good companions

Blue fescue makes an ideal frontal or edging plant in a border. Interplant with *Ophiopogon planiscapus* 'Nigrescens' and pink bedding plants. Alternatively grow them on a sunny bank with heathers.

Propagation

Division in spring, or seed.

Troubleshooting

Generally trouble-free, though foliage colour deteriorates if plants are not lifted and divided regularly. It is best to divide them every year or every other year.

Which variety?

The species is widely available, but an increasing number of named varieties are now on sale. These offer improvements such as a more intense blue colour or fewer flowers.

The ones you are most likely to come across are as follows (all have a height and spread of 15x23cm (6x10in) unless otherwise stated).

'Blue Fox' (syn. 'Blaufuchs') has silver-blue foliage, while **'Blue Glow'** (syn. 'Blaugut') has silver-blue leaves and showy flowers. **'Elijah Blue'** has silver-blue foliage that lasts well into the winter. **'Harz'** has dark blue-green foliage. **'Seven Seas'** (syn *F. glaucantha* 'Silbersee', 'Silver Sea') has very low clumps 5cm (2in) high. ***F. eskia*** has soft green foliage, height 15cm (6in).

Hakonechloa

Hakonechloa macra 'Alboaurea'

Shape and size

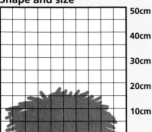

Position

Hardiness Soil

MOIST

Uses

Features calendar

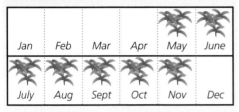

Jan	Feb	Mar	Apr	May	June
July	Aug	Sept	Oct	Nov	Dec

Buying tips *You will probably have to order from a specialist – try those that stock unusual plants or foliage plants as well as those that sell only ornamental grasses.*

Hakonechloa macra 'Aureola'

Hakonechloa macra 'Alboaurea'

Growing guide

This plant looks like a miniature bamboo and is valued for its outstanding foliage colour and the shape of the plant. The leaves are quite broad and they arch gently to form a spread of green and gold. Fluffy brown flowers are borne in summer. Although it is deciduous, there is some late-season interest from reddish-brown tints in autumn.

It will do best in a sheltered site in partial shade and can be used to brighten up a dull area of the border. The soil should be fertile and well-cultivated, with plenty of well-rotted organic matter so that it can retain moisture over the summer.

Good companions

Grow it as a single subject in a large pot and move it around the garden as a feature. It is an ideal plant for a raised bed as the leaves will appear to tumble over the edge. It also makes an impressive partner for large clumps of other foliage plants such as hostas or purple-leaved sage. In time, it will produce an attractive dense, spreading groundcover, if planted 45cm (18in) apart.

Propagation

Division.

Troubleshooting

It is not reliably hardy in very cold areas, so you may be restricted to growing it in a pot and keeping it in a cold greenhouse over winter.

Which variety?

Hakonechloa macra is the only species sold. You will probably come across one of two similar varieties. **'Alboaurea'** (syn. 'Variegata') and **'Aureola'** both have stripes of green and yellow.

Miscanthus

Miscanthus sinensis 'Variegatus'

Shape and size

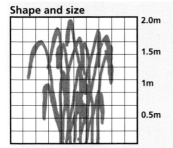

- 2.0m
- 1.5m
- 1m
- 0.5m

Position

Hardiness

Soil

MOIST

Uses

Features calendar

Jan	Feb	Mar	Apr	May	June
July	Aug	Sept	Oct	Nov	Dec

Buying tips *You should be able to get M. sinensis 'Variegatus' or 'Zebrinus' from garden centres. Look among the aquatic plants as well as in the ornamental grasses sections.*

Miscanthus sinensis 'Zebrinus'

Miscanthus sinensis 'Variegatus'

Growing guide

Miscanthus are quick growers that form impressive specimens. They have arching, reed-like foliage. Some produce brown flowers in autumn, but for others, the growing season is not long enough.

They do well on a fertile soil, that is moist but not boggy. They will grow in sun or partial shade. Being deciduous, the plants turn yellow in winter and may shed their leaves which can blow about the garden. Cut the stems down in autumn or early spring.

Good companions

They are best grown as isolated specimens for the most impact. However, they can be grown as part of a pondside bed – not in the boggy area next to the water but further back. They can also provide a dramatic backdrop to a traditional border.

Propagation

Division.

Troubleshooting

Generally trouble-free, though some like *M. floridulus* may need winter protection.

Which variety?

Miscanthus sinensis is the main species, but there are many named varieties. These vary greatly in their height, whether they flower, their foliage colours and their hardiness, so check you have a suitable one before buying. We have chosen **'Variegatus',** one of the many variegated varieties. This has leaves striped with white, it does not flower and is less vigorous than **'Zebrinus'**. Height and spread 180x60cm (72x24in).

Other varieties you might come across: **'Gracillimus'** is an upright grower to nearly 1.8m (6ft) with very narrow leaves. It flowers only in warm summers. A new selection is **'Graziella'** which has an open habit and flowers early. **'Purpurascens'** is shorter than most varieties at 90cm (36in) and has foliage that turns reddish-brown in summer. It sometimes produces brown flowers in October and has good autumn colour. **'Silver Feather'** (syn. 'Silberfeder') is hardier than the species and flowers regularly in September, bearing large feathery plumes of pale browny-pink on 2.1m (7ft) stems. The leaves of **'Zebrinus'** (zebra grass) have distinctive yellow bands. Stems are 1.5m (5ft) and droop attractively.

M. floridulus is among the tallest at over 2.1m (7ft), so is often used for screening. It seldom flowers and loses its leaves in winter. **M. sacchariflorus** makes a fine specimen; grow it on its own to show off the fountain effect to full advantage.

Molinia

Molinia caerulea 'Variegata'

Shape and size

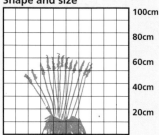

100cm
80cm
60cm
40cm
20cm

Position   Hardiness   Soil

MOIST

Uses

Features calendar

Jan	Feb	Mar	Apr	May	June
July	Aug	Sept	Oct	Nov	Dec

Buying tips *You should find* M. caerulea *'Variegata' in most garden centres that have an ornamental grasses section. Avoid plants with unhealthy foliage and dry compost.*

Molinia caerulea 'Moorhexe'

Molinia caerulea 'Variegata'

Growing guide

This is a deciduous grass valued for its colourful foliage and purplish autumn flowers. Its foliage forms dense but neat tufts, with each leaf variegated green and cream. The foliage turns beige in winter.

Grow in moist soil in full sun. If the soil is on the dry side, improve it by digging in well-rotted organic matter to enhance water retention. Mulching and watering in dry spells will also help this plant to thrive.

Good companions

As this grass has a well-behaved habit it could easily be accommodated in a border at the front or in the middle. When in flower, it would contrast with the daisy-like flowers of autumn such as asters and rudbeckias. As a foliage plant it would contrast with the rounded leaves of hostas, bergenias or *Alchemilla mollis*. In winter, the moor grass foliage lightens – a

backdrop of dark evergreens would show this off well.

Propagation

Division.

Troubleshooting

Generally trouble-free.

Which variety?

Molinia caerulea **'Variegata'** is the variety you are most likely to come across and it is one of the best variegated grasses. Height and spread 60x60cm (24x24in).

There are other named varieties, but they are not widely available. For example, **'Moorhexe'** which is shorter at 40x40cm (16x16in) with green leaves and purplish flowers. **'Heidebraut'** has good autumn flowers and seedheads.

M. caerulea **'Arundinacea'** (syn. *M. altissima, M litoralis*), a more vigorous grass reaching 1.5–1.8m (5–6ft), is worth growing for autumn colour. **'Fontane'** has pendulous flower heads. **'Windspiel'** has smaller golden-brown flower heads in autumn.

Phalaris

Phalaris arundinacea 'Picta'

Shape and size

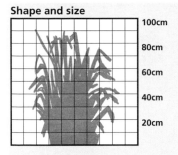

Position

Hardiness

Soil

ANY

Uses

Features calendar

Jan	Feb	Mar	Apr	May	June
July	Aug	Sept	Oct	Nov	Dec

Buying tips *Buy from a large garden centre with an ornamental grasses section or ask a friend who has it for a division.*

Phalaris arundinacea 'Picta'

Phalaris arundinacea 'Picta'

Growing guide

Gardener's garters is a deciduous grass, well-known for its bright foliage which can be used in flower arrangements. The green and white-striped leaves are pink when young.

It will establish itself in any reasonable garden soil or compost in a sunny or partially shaded position. Be careful when introducing into the garden as it is invasive.

Good companions

This grass is best grown as a single subject in a container. It can be used as groundcover – plant 60cm (24in) apart. Avoid planting it in small or medium-sized borders.

Propagation

Division.

Troubleshooting

This grass spreads rapidly as it has creeping roots. Grow it only where its roots can be confined; in a container, for example. The alternative is to lift and replant every few years, but this is hard work.

Which variety?

***Phalaris arundinacea* 'Picta'** is the one you are most likely to come across. It is a variegated grass of cream and green. Creamy flowers appear in June or July, but are less of a feature than the plant's foliage. Height and spread 90x60cm (36x24in).

Pleioblastus

Pleioblastus variegatus

Shape and size

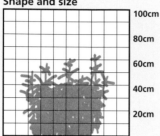

100cm
80cm
60cm
40cm
20cm

Position

Hardiness Soil

MOIST

Uses

Features calendar

Jan | Feb | Mar | Apr | May | June

July | Aug | Sept | Oct | Nov | Dec

Buying tips *Larger garden centres may sell both these variegated bamboos in 5–7.5 litre pots – avoid pots crowded with old stems. At a specialist, you may have the choice of small plants or larger specimens.*

Pleioblastus auricomus

Pleioblastus variegatus

Growing guide

This small bamboo is worth growing for its foliage. It would make a colourful addition to the front of a sunny or partially shaded bed so long as the soil was moist and fertile. However, it forms large clumps, so you would need to take its spreading habit into account.

If growing it as a container plant, choose a pot at least 45cm (18in) in diameter. Line the sides of terracotta pots with polythene before planting, but do not cover the bottom drainage holes. This will prevent drying out without water-logging.

To encourage brighter foliage, cut back the canes in spring before new shoots appear. Sprinkle on a balanced granular feed such as growmore.

Good companions

This plant makes a fine single subject in a border or a container. Try it alongside bergenias.

Propagation

Division.

Troubleshooting

P. variegatus is moderately invasive which might be useful if you want it for groundcover, but otherwise consider growing it in a container.

Which variety?

Pleioblastus variegatus (syn. *P. fortunei*) with its green and white striped leaves is widely available and is a useful size at 30–90x75cm (12–36x30in). *P. auricomus* (syn. *P. viridistriatus*) has a purple tint to its canes and green-and-yellow leaves. Height and spread 120–150x75cm (48–60x30in).

Stipa

Stipa gigantea

Shape and size

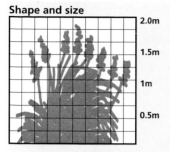

- 2.0m
- 1.5m
- 1m
- 0.5m

Position   Hardiness   Soil

Uses

Features calendar

Jan	Feb	Mar	Apr	May	June
				🌿	✳
July	Aug	Sept	Oct	Nov	Dec
✳	✳	✳	✳		

Buying tips *You may find this on sale in garden centres that have an ornamental grasses section. For other species of feather grass you will probably need a grass or foliage specialist.*

Stipa arundinacea

Stipa gigantea

Growing guide

This is a clump-forming grass with semi-evergreen foliage which is grown for its excellent flowers. These hang down like giant oats, they start off silvery-purple turning to gold and last throughout the summer. They can be cut and dried in summer for winter floral arrangements.

This grass will grow well in any well-drained but fertile garden soil. Full sun is essential.

Good companions

Planted at the back of the border, the soft haze of the flower heads makes a suitable backdrop. Or use it to add height and interest to drought-tolerant plantings such as lavender, santolina or phormiums.

Propagation

Division.

Troubleshooting

Generally trouble-free; a good alternative to pampas grass.

Which variety?

Stipa gigantea is widely available and makes a fine specimen plant. It offers flowers that last from June to October and beyond. Height and spread 1.8–2.1x 0.6m (6–7x2ft).

You may also come across **S. arundinacea** which is a much smaller grass at 45x60cm (18x24in). It makes a compact clump of bronze-green stems and bears brownish flowers in summer. The foliage takes on colourful tints in winter.

S. tenuifolia makes a small but graceful clump that is the ideal size for mid-border plantings. Height and spread 60x45cm (24x18in).

Plant selector

Red valerian (Centranthus) *is at home on sea cliffs, and is very wind-tolerant*

Seaside gardens

The following perennials can tolerate salt-laden winds. In mild coastal areas, you may be able to grow the more tender perennials.

Achillea	Kniphofia
Agapanthus	Ligularia
Anaphalis	Limonium
Anemone	Lychnis
Aquilegia	Nepeta
Aruncus	Oenothera
Aster	Physalis
Astrantia	Polygonatum
Bergenia	Persicaria
Campanula	Potentilla
Centaurea	Primula
Centranthus	Pulmonaria
Crocosmia	Pyrethrum
Doronicum	Salvia
Erigeron	Sedum
Gaillardia	Sidalcea
Geum	Tradescantia
Hemerocallis	Verbascum
Heuchera	

Achillea filipendula *'Gold Plate' stands up to salt-laden winds*

Crocosmia *'Mars', a brilliant choice for seaside gardens*

Heucheras have delicate flowers but stand up well to wind. This is Heuchera 'Palace Purple'

Geranium 'Johnson's Blue' – a good choice in a windy garden

Lamiums create a carpet of green and silver leaves all winter

Windy gardens

The following plants are all suitable for exposed gardens as they can withstand wind without needing to be staked.

Alchemilla	Hemerocallis
Anaphalis	Heuchera
Anemone	Hosta
Aquilegia	Kniphofia
Armeria	Ligularia
Aster (some)	Lychis
Astilbe	Oenothera
Astrantia	Persicaria
Bergenia	Polygonatum
Campanula	Potentilla
(some)	Primula
Centranthus	Pulmonaria
Convallaria	Salvia
Crocosmia	Sedum
Doronicum	Stachys
Erigeron	
Euphorbia	
Geranium	
Geum	
Helleborus	

Rich purple bergenias contrast well with variegated evergreens in winter

Evergreen perennials

As these evergreen perennials retain their foliage throughout the year, they help to cover the bare earth in borders.

Ajuga
Artemisia
Asarum
Bergenia
Carex
Dianthus
Dierama
Epimedium (some)
Euphorbia (some)
Fargesia
Festuca
Geranium (some)
Helleborus
Heuchera
Iris
Kniphofia
Lamium
Limonium
Liriope
Morina
Pleioblastus
Pulmonaria
Saxifraga
Sisyrinchium
Stachys
Tellima
Tiarella

The modern garden pink, 'Doris', has sturdy stems and a fine scent

Ligularia dentata 'Desdemona' a dramatic contrast of gold and bronze

Lush hostas are easy to grow

Big leaves

Nothing beats bold foliage for creating an impact in the garden. Most large-leaved plants require a moist soil so take this into account when choosing a planting site.

Bergenia
Gunnera
Hosta
Ligularia
Macleaya
Rheum
Rodgersia

Butterfly plants

Butterflies prefer single flowers, often the more natural species rather than the highly bred double flowers.

Achillea	Knautia
Ajuga	Liatris
Anchusa	Ligularia
Armeria	Linaria
Aster	Lysimachia
Centranthus	Melissa
Coreopsis	Nepeta
Delphinium	Origanum
Echinacea	Phlox
Echinops	Scabiosa
Erigeron	Sedum
Eryngium	Solidago
Helenium	

Small tortoiseshell butterflies love Sedum spectabile

Spectacular Gunnera manicata has the biggest leaves of all. It needs wet soil and winter protection

Globe thistles (Echinops) attract bees and butterflies

Stately Acanthus spinosus *flowers from June to September*

Long flowering

Many perennials will flower most of the summer and on into the autumn. Regular deadheading will help prolong flowering. The following plants can be expected to flower for 3 to 4 months.

Acanthus
Achillea
Anemone
Anthemis
Aster (some)
Centranthus
Coreopsis
Dicentra
Erisymum
Geranium
Geum
Linaria

Lythrum
Malva
Nepeta
Oenothera
Persicaria
Phygelius
Prunella
Rudbeckia
Scabiosa
Sedum
Viola

Drought-resistant

In a long, hot summer these plants should do better than most as they are very tolerant of drought. Remember that they still need watering until their roots have established.

Armeria
Artemisia
Bergenia
Campanula (some)
Coreopsis
Echinacea
Eryngium
Gaillardia
Geranium
Heliopsis
Liatris
Sedum
Verbascum
Waldsteinia

Delicate dicentras flower in spring and early summer

Pink echinaceas are a valuable drought-tolerant border plant

Coreopsis 'May Field Giant' tolerates dry conditions well

Rudbeckia 'Goldsturm' brings long-lasting colour to the late-summer border

Deep-rooting verbascums cope well with drought

Cheerful Caltha palustris *loves wet and boggy spots*

Stately astilbes do best on deep moist soils

Blue-green hostas and variegated iris contrast in a shady, dry bed

Silver-spotted pulmonarias brighten shady, dry spots

Foxgloves lend an informal touch to a mixed border

Mixed primulas create a hedgerow effect

Boggy soils

Perennials in general are very adaptable as far as soil is concerned. However, the combination of cold, wet soil over winter can cause losses. If you have a boggy area either plant in spring so that you get a full growing season for the roots to establish before winter or choose plants that are naturally adapted to boggy conditions. The following plants can cope with this kind of soil.

Aruncus
Astilbe
Caltha
Cimicifuga
Filipendula
Gunnera
Iris (some)
Ligularia
Primula
Rodgersia
Trollius

Dry shade

While many woodland plants can be grown in moist, shady spots, dry shade is very difficult to plant successfully. Prepare the ground well by adding soil improvers before planting.

Ajuga
Euphorbia
Geranium
Hemerocallis
Hosta
Lamium
Iris (some)
Polygonatum
Pulmonaria
Tiarella

Natural planting

Using perennials to create more natural-looking beds, rather than simply using them in formal borders, is becoming increasingly popular. Here are some suitable plants with which to experiment.

Achillea
Anthemis
Aquilegia
Aruncus
Aster
Caltha
Campanula
Centaurea
Digitalis
Doronicum
Eupatorium
Filipendula
Geranium
Hemerocallis
Inula
Knautia
Lysimachia
Lychnis
Malva
Penstemon
Polemonium
Primula
Ranunculus
Rudbeckia
Silene
Smilacina
Solidago
Trollius
Viola

A plain container shows off a graceful agapanthus

Perennials from seed

Raising your own perennials from seed is quick and easy if you choose the right species. There are hundreds to choose from but we have found all these flower in their first year from a spring sowing.

Achillea
Aquilegia
Catananche
Coreopsis
Digitalis
Gaillardia
Geum
Helenium
Knautia
Liatris
Lobelia
Lupinus
Lychnis
Malva
Polemonium
Viola

Containers

Specimens

Acanthus spinosus
Agapanthus
Aquilegia
Dendranthema
Dicentra spectabilis
Euphorbia characias 'Wulfenii'
Geranium
Hakonechloa macra 'Aureola'
Hellebores
Hemerocallis
Hostas
Scabiosa 'Butterfly Blue'
Sedum spectabile
Zantedeschia aethiopica 'Crowborough'

Others

Ajuga reptans
Alchemilla mollis
Bergenia
Carex
Campanula carpatica
Dianthus
Euphorbia myrsinites
Festuca glauca
Lamium maculatum
Ophiopogon planiscapus 'Nigrescens'
Primula

Invasive plants for containers

Convallaria majalis
Houttuynia cordata 'Chamaeleon'
Persicaria virginiana 'Painter's Palette'
Phalaris arundinacea 'Picta'
Physalis franchetii

Hostas in containers suffer less from slug damage

Garden varieties such as Penstemon 'Garnet' look natural when planted informally

Index of Plants

ACKNOWLEDGEMENTS

Front cover (Inset): Photos Horticultural

A–Z Botanical Collection
176, 177

Photographers:
Mrs Ailsa M. Allaby; 216
Chris Martin Bahr; 33
Ron Bonser; 70
J. Brunsden Rapkins; 149
Michael R. Chandler; 85, 89
Robert J. Erwin; 188
Neil Joy; 214
Sam Ke Tran; 61
Maurice Nimmo ; 138, 186
Sheila Orme; 194
David Roach; 140
Paul Shoesmith; 149
Daryl Sweetland; 176
H. Thomson; 59
A. Young; 124

Pat Brindley
115

Eric Crichton Photos
88

Liz Dobbs Photography
100, 114

Garden Picture Library
Photographers:
Kim Blaxland; 121, 205
Philippe Bonduel; 37, 41, 103
Clive Boursnell; 30
Linda Burgess; 81, 113, 173
Chris Burrows; 35
Bob Challinor; 55, 67
Kathy Charlton; 139
Brian Carter; 35, 44, 45, 73, 90, 108, 113, 130, 132, 150, 158, 175, 193, 205
Henk Dijkman; 28
David England; 119
Ron Evans; 82, 145, 177
Christopher Fairweather; 64, 91
Vaughan Fleming; 26, 143
John Glover; 23, 31, 34, 45, 46, 51, 66, 67, 71, 76, 77, 78, 80, 85, 91, 107, 111, 120, 121, 142,143, 154, 164, 169, 177, 191, 199, 202, 204, 205, 211

Sunniva Harte; 24, 70, 71, 72, 75, 155, 157, 170
Marijke Heuff; 104, 162, 194
Neil Holmes; 45, 74, 84, 93, 101, 121, 146, 150, 151, 153, 164, 181, 187, 199
Michael Howes; 105
Jacqui Hurst; 203
Lamontagne; 106, 144, 152, 177
Jane Legate; 71, 84
Mayer/Le Scanff; 57
Clive Nichols; 90
Jerry Pavia; 39, 57, 83, 87, 92, 163, 193
Howard Rice; 35, 42, 73, 77, 87, 91, 92, 99, 103, 118, 121, 127, 130, 142, 143, 146, 147, 151, 157, 175, 178, 181, 196, 198, 201
Gary Rogers; 28, 109
David Russel; 60
J.S. Sira; 34, 44, 112, 133, 138, 141, 157, 162, 185, 189, 207, 210
Brigitte Thomas; 129
Juliette Wade; 141
Mel Watson; 74, 144, 200

Didier Willery; 50, 77, 86, 93, 126, 151, 153, 157
Steven Wooster; 41, 201

Harry Smith Collection
108, 125

Photos Horticultural
25, 33, 39, 40, 47, 54, 59, 61, 67, 69, 71, 72–73, 79, 97, 98, 113, 125, 128, 129, 131, 148, 154, 156, 168, 171, 173, 180, 182, 184, 185, 206, 210, 215

S. & O. Mathews Photography
48, 81, 110, 170

Gardening Which?
All remaining photographs were provided by *Gardening Which?* Picture Library, with special thanks to Lynne Mack.